FR ~~DATE DUE~~

Dear Customer,

~~MAY 2 3 2018~~

Thank you for your purchase f ~~JUL 1 2018~~ ...onor and privilege that you have purchased our product and w... your satisfaction.

As a way of showing our appreciation and to help us better serve you, we have developed a Study Skills DVD that we would like to give you for <u>FREE</u>. **This DVD covers our "best practices" for studying for your exam, from using our study materials to preparing for the day of the test.**

All that we ask is that you email us your feedback that would describe your experience so far with our product. Good, bad or indifferent, we want to know what you think!

To get your **FREE Study Skills DVD**, email <u>freedvd@mometrix.com</u> with "FREE STUDY SKILLS DVD" in the subject line and the following information in the body of the email:

    a.   The name of the product you purchased.

    b.   Your product rating on a scale of 1–5, with 5 being the highest rating.

    c.   Your feedback. It can be long, short, or anything in-between, just your impressions and experience so far with our product. Good feedback might include how our study material met your needs and will highlight features of the product that you found helpful.

    d.   Your full name and shipping address where you would like us to send your free DVD.

If you have any questions or concerns, please don't hesitate to contact me directly.

Thanks again!

Sincerely,

Jay Willis
Vice President
<u>jay.willis@mometrix.com</u>
1-800-673-8175

M⊘metrix
T E S T   P R E P A R A T I O N
The World's #1 Test Preparation Company

ACT® Exam
SECRETS

Study Guide
Your Key to Exam Success

ACT Test Review for the
ACT Test

Published by
Mometrix Test Preparation
ACT Exam Secrets Test Prep Team

Written and edited by the ACT Exam Secrets Test Prep Staff

Printed in the United States of America

This paper meets the requirements of ANSI/NISO Z39.48-1992 (Permanence of Paper).

Mometrix offers volume discount pricing to institutions. For more information or a price quote, please contact our sales department at sales@mometrix.com or 888-248-1219.

ACT® is the registered trademark of ACT, Inc. Mometrix Test Preparation has no affiliation with ACT, Inc., and ACT Exam Secrets is not approved or endorsed by ACT, Inc.

ISBN 13: 978-1-5167-0740-9
ISBN 10: 1-5167-0740-0

Dear Future Exam Success Story:

Congratulations on your purchase of our study guide. Our goal in writing our study guide was to cover the content on the test, as well as provide insight into typical test taking mistakes and how to overcome them.

Standardized tests are a key component of being successful, which only increases the importance of doing well in the high-pressure high-stakes environment of test day. How well you do on this test will have a significant impact on your future- and we have the research and practical advice to help you execute on test day.

The product you're reading now is designed to exploit weaknesses in the test itself, and help you avoid the most common errors test takers frequently make.

How to use this study guide

We don't want to waste your time. Our study guide is fast-paced and fluff-free. We suggest going through it a number of times, as repetition is an important part of learning new information and concepts.

First, read through the study guide completely to get a feel for the content and organization. Read the general success strategies first, and then proceed to the content sections. Each tip has been carefully selected for its effectiveness.

Second, read through the study guide again, and take notes in the margins and highlight those sections where you may have a particular weakness.

Finally, bring the manual with you on test day and study it before the exam begins.

Your success is our success

We would be delighted to hear about your success. Send us an email and tell us your story. Thanks for your business and we wish you continued success-

Sincerely,

Mometrix Test Preparation Team

Need more help? Check out our flashcards at: http://MometrixFlashcards.com/ACT

ACT® is the registered trademark of ACT, Inc. Mometrix Media LLC has no affiliation with ACT, Inc., and ACT Exam Secrets is not approved or endorsed by ACT, Inc.

TABLE OF CONTENTS

Top 20 Test Taking Tips

1. Carefully follow all the test registration procedures
2. Know the test directions, duration, topics, question types, how many questions
3. Setup a flexible study schedule at least 3-4 weeks before test day
4. Study during the time of day you are most alert, relaxed, and stress free
5. Maximize your learning style; visual learner use visual study aids, auditory learner use auditory study aids
6. Focus on your weakest knowledge base
7. Find a study partner to review with and help clarify questions
8. Practice, practice, practice
9. Get a good night's sleep; don't try to cram the night before the test
10. Eat a well balanced meal
11. Know the exact physical location of the testing site; drive the route to the site prior to test day
12. Bring a set of ear plugs; the testing center could be noisy
13. Wear comfortable, loose fitting, layered clothing to the testing center; prepare for it to be either cold or hot during the test
14. Bring at least 2 current forms of ID to the testing center
15. Arrive to the test early; be prepared to wait and be patient
16. Eliminate the obviously wrong answer choices, then guess the first remaining choice
17. Pace yourself; don't rush, but keep working and move on if you get stuck
18. Maintain a positive attitude even if the test is going poorly
19. Keep your first answer unless you are positive it is wrong
20. Check your work, don't make a careless mistake

The English Test

Overview

The English portion of the ACT will have questions about underlined portions of text, with possible replacements as answer choices. Read the text four times, each time replacing the underlined portion with one of the choices. While reading the choices, read the sentence before, the sentence containing, and the sentence after the underlined portion. Sometimes an answer may make sense until you read the following sentence and see how the two sentences flow together. Transitional words should create smooth, logical transitions and maintain a constant flow of text.

Some questions will be concerning sentence insertions. In those cases, do not look for the ones that simply restate what was in the previous sentence. New sentences should contain new information and new insights into the subject of the text. If asked for the paragraph to which a sentence would most naturally be added, find a key noun or word in that new sentence. Then find the paragraph containing that exact word, or another word closely related to that key noun or word. That is the paragraph that should include the new sentence.

Some questions will ask what purpose a phrase fulfilled in a particular text. It depends upon the subject of the text. If the text is dramatic, then the phrase was probably used to show tension. If the text is comedic, then the phrase may have been there to relieve tension.

In related cases, you may be asked to provide a sentence that summarizes the text. Simple sentences, without wordy phrases, are usually best. If asked for a succinct answer, then the shorter the answer, the more likely it is correct.

Topic Development

Understanding the Assignment

For your exam, you will be given a prompt (i.e., a writing assignment) that needs your response within the time limit. However you feel about the prompt, you need to give an answer that addresses the entire prompt. Your response needs to be creative and informed. In other words, you need to keep the attention and interest of your audience. Most importantly, you need to show your readers that you know what you are talking about in your essay. As you consider the prompt, you may want to ask these questions to understand the assignment:

1. What specifically is the assignment asking you to do?
2. What information or knowledge is necessary to fulfill the assignment?
3. Are there other requirements for the assignment?
4. What is the purpose of the assignment?
5. Who is the intended audience?
6. What is the length of the assignment?

After you read the prompt, you need to determine what you know about the topic. You may think that you have very few ideas when you first read the prompt. However, you can use some strategies to think of ideas. These strategies include brainstorming, free writing, looping, and questioning.

Purposes of Writing

Before you begin writing your essay, you need to ask: *What is the main purpose of the proposed piece?* This may be focused or unclear. You should be clear about the purpose of your writing. Generally, purposes may be divided into three groups:

1. To educate or inform
2. To entertain
3. To persuade or convince

For your essay, you will be asked to persuade or inform; however, an assignment could ask for both. When you identify the major purpose of your prompt, you should consider if there are any secondary purposes. For example, the major purpose of a prompt may be to persuade your audience, and the secondary purpose would be to educate your audience.

A speaker's argument and claims need to be evaluated for their soundness and relevance. While it is tempting to believe everything that an excellent speaker tells you, it is because of that excellence that a listener should be critical of everything that is being said. While listening, critique what the person is saying. Determine if there is a clear delineation between evidence and theory. Make sure to determine whether the speaker's arguments are logical or emotional, and make sure there is sufficient reasoning to support any claims.

Precise Language

When writing informational or explanatory texts it is of utmost importance to use precise language and domain-specific vocabulary to explain your main idea and supporting details. Generalized vocabulary will not help the audience grasp the points that you are attempting to make because they will not accurately reflect your main idea and supporting details. Domain-specific vocabulary is important to use because it will accurately describe or explain the ideas or processes that are central to your text. When you research a subject, make sure to familiarize yourself with any vocabulary that is involved in its explanation. Use context clues, dictionaries, or, if necessary, a technical dictionary to decode any words that you are not familiar with. Also include definitions of domain-specific vocabulary in your text to enlighten readers.

Read the excerpt and analyze the language.

> At dawn, in a stuffy and smoky second-class car in which five people had already spent the night, a bulky woman in deep mourning was hoisted in—almost like a shapeless bundle. Behind her, puffing and moaning, followed her husband—a tiny man, thin and weakly, his face death-white, his eyes small and bright and looking shy and uneasy.

The language selected by the author is filled with fresh and precise words that describe and color the two passengers as well as the setting of the excerpt. The author describes the car as "stuffy and smoky," "second-class," and "in which five people had already spent the night." All this conjures up a dreary train car. The author describes the woman as "a shapeless bundle." Her husband is "tiny," "thin," and "weakly" with a "death-white" face. These words not only lend freshness to the writing, they also clearly depict what the people look like for the reader. This is the way that a writer can color his story and the characters in it.

Organization, Unity, and Cohesion

Practice Makes Prepared Writers

Writing is a skill that continues to need development throughout a person's life. For some people, writing seems to be a natural gift. They rarely struggle with writer's block. When you read their papers, they have persuasive ideas. For others, writing is an intimidating task that they endure. As you practice, you can improve your skills and be better prepared for writing a time-sensitive essay.

A traditional and reliable way to prepare for the writing section is to read. When you read newspapers, magazines, and books, you learn about new ideas. You can read newspapers and magazines to become informed about issues that affect many people. As you think about those issues and ideas, you can take a position and form opinions. Try to develop these ideas and your opinions by sharing them with friends. After you develop your opinions, try writing them down as if you were going to spread your ideas beyond your friends.

Remember that you are practicing for more than an exam. Two of the most valuable things in the workplace are the abilities to read critically and to write clearly. When you work on evaluating the arguments of a passage and explain your thoughts well, you are developing skills that you will use for a lifetime. In the following pages, you will find strategies and tools that will prepare you to write better essays.

> ➢ **Review Video: <u>Writing Strategies</u>**
> *Visit **mometrix.com/academy** and enter **Code: 396837***

Point of View

Point of view is the perspective from which writing occurs. There are several possibilities:
- *First person* is written so that the *I* of the story is a participant or observer.
- *Second person* is a device to draw the reader in more closely. It is really a variation or refinement of the first-person narrative.
- *Third person*, the most traditional form of point of view, is the omniscient narrator, in which the narrative voice, presumed to be the writer's, is presumed to know everything about the characters, plot, and action. Most novels use this point of view.

> ➢ **Review Video: <u>Points of View</u>**
> *Visit **mometrix.com/academy** and enter **Code: 383336***

Brainstorming
Brainstorming is a technique that is used to find a creative approach to a subject. You can accomplish this by simple free-association with a topic. For example, with paper and pen, you write every thought that you have about the topic in a word or phrase. This is done without critical thinking. Everything that comes to your mind about the topic, you should put on your scratch paper. Then, you need to read the list over a few times. Next, you look for patterns, repetitions, and clusters of ideas. This allows a variety of fresh ideas to come as you think about the topic.

<u>Free Writing</u>

Free writing is a form of brainstorming, but the method occurs in a structured way. The method involves a limited amount of time (e.g., 2 to 3 minutes) and writing everything that comes to mind about the topic in complete sentences. When time expires, you need to review everything that has been written down. Many of your sentences may make little or no sense, but the insights and observations that can come from free writing make this method a valuable approach. Usually, free writing results in a fuller expression of ideas than brainstorming because thoughts and associations are written in complete sentences. However, both techniques can be used to complement the other.

Revisions

A writer's choice of words is a signature of their style. Careful thought about the use of words can improve a piece of writing. A passage can be an exciting piece to read when attention is given to the use of specific nouns rather than general ones.
Example:
General: His kindness will never be forgotten.

Specific: His thoughtful gifts and bear hugs will never be forgotten.

Attention should also be given to the kind of verbs that are used in sentences. Active verbs (e.g., run, swim) should be about an action. Whenever possible, an active verb should replace a linking verb to provide clear examples for arguments and to strengthen a passage overall.
Example:
Passive: The winners were called to the stage by the judges.

Active: The judges called the winners to the stage.

Revising sentences is done to make writing more effective. Editing sentences is done to correct any errors. Sentences are the building blocks of writing, and they can be changed by paying attention to sentence length, sentence structure, and sentence openings.

You should add variety to sentence length, structure, and openings so that the essay does not seem boring or repetitive. A careful analysis of a piece of writing will expose these stylistic problems, and they can be corrected before you finish your essay. Changing up your sentence structure and sentence length can make your essay more inviting and appealing to readers.

> ➤ **Review Video: <u>Making Sentences More Distinct</u>**
> *Visit **mometrix.com/academy** and enter **Code: 538557***

> ➤ **Review Video: <u>Editing Sentences to Read Better</u>**
> *Visit **mometrix.com/academy** and enter **Code: 239392***

Recursive Writing Process

However you approach writing, you may find comfort in knowing that the revision process can occur in any order. The recursive writing process is not as difficult as the phrase appears to you. Simply put, the recursive writing process means that the steps in the writing process occur in no particular order. For example, planning, drafting, and revising (all a part of the writing process) take place at about the same time and you may not notice that all three happen so close together. Truly, the writing process is a series of moving back and forth between planning, drafting, and revising. Then, more planning, more drafting, and more revising until the writing is complete.

> **Review Video: Recursive Writing Process**
> *Visit mometrix.com/academy and enter Code:* **951611**

Introduction

An introduction announces the main point of the passage. Normally, the introduction ranges from 50 to 70 words (i.e., 3 or 4 sentences). The purpose of the introduction is to gain the reader's attention and conclude with the essay's main point. An introduction can begin with an interesting quote, question, or strong opinion that grabs the reader's attention. Your introduction should include a restatement of the prompt, a summary of the main points of your essay, and your position on the prompt (i.e., the thesis sentence/statement). Depending on the amount of available time, you may want to give more or less information on the main points of your essay. The important thing is to impress the audience with your thesis statement (i.e., your reason for writing the essay).

> **Review Video: Introduction I**
> *Visit mometrix.com/academy and enter Code:* **961328**

> **Review Video: Introduction II**
> *Visit mometrix.com/academy and enter Code:* **254411**

Thesis Statement
A thesis gives the main idea of the essay. A temporary thesis should be established early in the writing process because it will serve to keep the writer focused as ideas develop. This temporary thesis is subject to change as you continue to write.

The temporary thesis has two parts: a topic (i.e., the focus of your paper based on the prompt) and a comment. The comment makes an important point about the topic. A temporary thesis should be interesting and specific. Also, you need to limit the topic to a manageable scope. These three criteria are useful tools to measure the effectiveness of any temporary thesis:
   1. Does the focus of my essay have enough interest to hold an audience?
   2. Is the focus of my essay specific enough to generate interest?
   3. Is the focus of my essay manageable for the time limit? Too broad? Too narrow?

The thesis should be a generalization rather than a fact because the thesis prepares readers for facts and details that support the thesis. The process of bringing the thesis into sharp focus may help in outlining major sections of the work. Once the thesis and introduction are complete, you can address the body of the work.

> ➢ **Review Video: <u>Thesis Statements</u>**
> *Visit **mometrix.com/academy** and enter **Code: 691033***

<u>Supporting the Thesis</u>
Throughout your essay, the thesis should be explained clearly and supported adequately by additional arguments. The thesis sentence needs to contain a clear statement of the purpose of your essay and a comment about the thesis. With the thesis statement, you have an opportunity to state what is noteworthy of this particular treatment of the prompt. Each sentence and paragraph should build on and support the thesis.

When you respond to the prompt, use parts of the passage to support your argument or defend your position. With supporting evidence from the passage, you strengthen your argument because readers can see your attention to the entire passage and your response to the details and facts within the passage. You can use facts, details, statistics, and direct quotations from the passage to uphold your position. Be sure to point out which information comes from the original passage and base your argument around that evidence.

> ➢ **Review Video: <u>Drafting a Thesis Statement</u>**
> *Visit **mometrix.com/academy** and enter **Code: 515327***

> ➢ **Review Video: <u>Writing a Response to the Text</u>**
> *Visit **mometrix.com/academy** and enter **Code: 185093***

Paragraphs

Following the introduction, you will begin with body paragraphs. A paragraph should be unified around a main point. Normally, a good topic sentence summarizes the paragraph's main point. A topic sentence is a general sentence that gives an introduction to the paragraph. The sentences that follow are a support to the topic sentence. You may use the topic sentence as the final sentence to the paragraph if the earlier sentences give a clear explanation of the topic sentence. Overall, you need to stay true to the main point. This means that you need to remove unnecessary sentences that do not advance the main point.

The main point of a paragraph requires adequate development (i.e., a substantial paragraph that covers the main point). A paragraph of two or three sentences does not cover a main point. This is true when the main point of the paragraph gives strong support to the argument of the thesis. An occasional short paragraph is fine as a transitional device. However, you should aim to have six to seven sentences for each paragraph.

> ➢ **Review Video: <u>Drafting Body Paragraphs</u>**
> *Visit **mometrix.com/academy** and enter **Code: 724590***

Methods of Developing Paragraphs

A common method of development in your essay can be done with **examples**. These examples are the supporting details to the main idea of a paragraph or passage. When you write about something that your audience may not understand, you can provide an example to show your point. When you write about something that is not easily accepted, you can give examples to prove your point.

Illustrations are extended examples that require several sentences. Well selected illustrations can be a great way to develop a point that may not be familiar to your audience. With a time limit, you may have enough time to use one illustration. So, be sure that you use one that connects well with your main argument.

Analogies make comparisons between items that appear to have nothing in common. Analogies are employed by writers to provoke fresh thoughts about a subject. They may be used to explain the unfamiliar, to clarify an abstract point, or to argue a point. Although analogies are effective literary devices, they should be used carefully in arguments. Two things may be alike in some respects but completely different in others.

Cause and effect is an excellent device used when the cause and effect are accepted as true. One way of using cause and effect is to state the effect in the topic sentence of a paragraph and add the causes in the body of the paragraph. With this method, your paragraphs can have structure which always strengthens writing.

> ➤ **Review Video: <u>Cause and Effect</u>**
> *Visit mometrix.com/academy and enter Code:* **428037**

Types of Paragraphs

A **paragraph of narration** tells a story or a part of a story. Normally, the sentences are arranged in chronological order (i.e., the order that the events happened). However, you can include flashbacks (i.e., beginning the story at an earlier time).

> ➤ **Review Video: <u>Rhetorical Strategy of Narration</u>**
> *Visit mometrix.com/academy and enter Code:* **827871**

A **descriptive paragraph** makes a verbal portrait of a person, place, or thing. When you use specific details that appeal to one or more of the senses (i.e., sight, sound, smell, taste, and touch), you give your readers a sense of being present in the moment.

A **process paragraph** is related to time order (i.e., First, you open the bottle. Second, you pour the liquid, etc.). Usually, this describes a process or teaches readers how to perform a process.

Comparing two things draws attention to their similarities and indicates a number of differences. When you contrast, you focus only on differences. Both comparisons and contrasts may be used point-by-point or in following paragraphs.

Reasons for starting a new paragraph include:
1. To mark off the introduction and concluding paragraphs
2. To signal a shift to a new idea or topic
3. To indicate an important shift in time or place
4. To explain a point in additional detail
5. To highlight a comparison, contrast, or cause and effect relationship

Conclusion

A good conclusion should leave readers satisfied and provide a sense of completeness. Many conclusions state the thesis in different words and give a summary of the ideas in the body paragraphs. Some writers find ways to conclude in a dramatic fashion. They may conclude with a vivid image or a warning and remind readers of the main point. The conclusion can be a few sentences because the body of the text has made the case for the thesis. A conclusion can summarize the main points and offer advice or ask a question. You should never introduce new ideas or arguments in a conclusion. Also, you need to avoid vague and aimless endings. Instead, close with a clear and specific paragraph.

> ➤ **Review Video: <u>Drafting Conclusions</u>**
> *Visit **mometrix.com/academy** and enter **Code:** **209408***

Paragraph Length

Most readers find that their comfort level for a paragraph is between 100 and 200 words. Shorter paragraphs cause too much starting and stopping, and give a choppy effect. Paragraphs that are too long often test the attention span of readers. Two notable exceptions to this rule exist. In scientific or scholarly papers, longer paragraphs suggest seriousness and depth. In journalistic writing, constraints are placed on paragraph size by the narrow columns in a newspaper format.

The first and last paragraphs of a text will usually be the introduction and conclusion. These special-purpose paragraphs are likely to be shorter than paragraphs in the body of the work. Paragraphs in the body of the essay follow the subject's outline; one paragraph per point in short essays and a group of paragraphs per point in longer works. Some ideas require more development than others, so it is good for a writer to remain flexible. A paragraph of excessive length may be divided, and shorter ones may be combined.

Coherent Paragraphs

A smooth flow of sentences and paragraphs without gaps, shifts, or bumps will lead to paragraph coherence. Ties between old and new information can be smoothed by several methods:
- Linking ideas clearly, from the topic sentence to the body of the paragraph, is essential for a smooth transition. The topic sentence states the main point, and this should be followed by specific details, examples, and illustrations that support the topic sentence. The support may be direct or indirect. In indirect support, the illustrations and examples may support a sentence that in turn supports the topic directly.
- The repetition of key words adds coherence to a paragraph. To avoid dull language, variations of the key words may be used.

- Parallel structures are often used within sentences to emphasize the similarity of ideas and connect sentences giving similar information.
- Maintaining a consistent verb tense throughout the paragraph helps. Shifting tenses affects the smooth flow of words and can disrupt the coherence of the paragraph.

> ➤ **Review Video: Coherence in Writing**
> *Visit mometrix.com/academy and enter Code:* **592378**

Transitions

Transitions are bridges between what has been read and what is about to be read. Transitions smooth the reader's path between sentences and inform the reader of major connections to new ideas forthcoming in the text. Transitional phrases should be used with care, selecting the appropriate phrase for a transition. Tone is another important consideration in using transitional phrases, varying the tone for different audiences. For example, in a scholarly essay, *in summary* would be preferable to the more informal *in short.*

When working with transitional words and phrases, writers usually find a natural flow that indicates when a transition is needed. In reading a draft of the text, it should become apparent where the flow is uneven or rough. At this point, the writer can add transitional elements during the revision process. Revising can also afford an opportunity to delete transitional devices that seem heavy handed or unnecessary.

> ➤ **Review Video: Connecting Sentences**
> *Visit mometrix.com/academy and enter Code:* **948325**

Transitional words and phrases are used to transition between paragraphs and also to transition within a single paragraph. Transitions assist the flow of ideas and help to unify an essay. A writer can use certain words to indicate that an example or summary is being presented. The following phrases, among others, can be used as this type of transition: *as a result, as I have said, for example, for instance, in any case, in any event, in brief, in conclusion, in fact, in other words, in short, on the whole,* and *to sum it up.*

> ➤ **Review Video: Transitions**
> *Visit mometrix.com/academy and enter Code:* **707563**

Transitional Words

Link Similar Ideas
When a writer links ideas that are similar in nature, there are a variety of words and phrases he or she can choose, including but not limited to: *also, and, another, besides, equally important, further, furthermore, in addition, likewise, too, similarly, nor, of course,* and *for instance.*

Link Dissimilar or Contradictory Ideas
Writers can link contradictory ideas in an essay by using, among others, the following words and phrases: *although, and yet, even if, conversely, but, however, otherwise, still, yet, instead, in spite of, nevertheless, on the contrary,* and *on the other hand.*

Indicate Cause, Purpose, or Result

Writers may need to indicate that one thing is the cause, purpose, or result of another thing. To show this relationship, writers can use, among others, the following linking words and phrases: *as, as a result, because, consequently, hence, for, for this reason, since, so, then, thus,* and *therefore.*

Indicate Time or Position

Certain words can be used to indicate the time and position of one thing in relation to another. Writers can use, for example, the following terms to create a timeline of events in an essay: *above, across, afterward, before, beyond, eventually, meanwhile, next, presently, around, at once, at the present time, finally, first, here, second, thereafter,* and *upon.* These words can show the order or placement of items or ideas in an essay.

Knowledge of Language

Context Clues

Learning new words is an important part of comprehending and integrating unfamiliar information. When a reader encounters a new word, he can stop and find it in the dictionary or the glossary of terms but sometimes those reference tools aren't readily available or using them at the moment is impractical (e.g., during a test). Furthermore, most readers are usually not willing to take the time.

Another way to determine the meaning of a word is by considering the context in which it is being used. These indirect learning hints are called context clues. They include definitions, descriptions, examples, and restatements. Because most words are learned by listening to conversations, people use this tool all the time even if they do it unconsciously. But to be effective in written text, context clues must be used judiciously because the unfamiliar word may have several subtle variations, and therefore the context clues could be misinterpreted.

> **Review Video: <u>Prefixes, Suffixes, and Root Words</u>**
> Visit *mometrix.com/academy* and enter *Code:* **896380**

> **Review Video: <u>Textual Support for Interpretations</u>**
> Visit *mometrix.com/academy* and enter *Code:* **192438**

Context refers to how a word is used in a sentence. Identifying context can help determine the definition of unknown words. There are different contextual clues such as definition, description, example, comparison, and contrast. The following are examples:

- Definition: the unknown word is clearly defined by the previous words. – "When he was painting, his instrument was a __." (paintbrush)
- Description: the unknown word is described by the previous words. – "I was hot, tired, and thirsty; I was __." (dehydrated)
- Example: the unknown word is part of a series of examples. – "Water, soda, and __ were the offered beverages." (coffee)
- Comparison: the unknown word is compared to another word. – "Barney is agreeable and happy like his __ parents." (positive)
- Contrast: the unknown word is contrasted with another word. – "I prefer cold weather to __ conditions." (hot)

> **Review Video: <u>Context</u>**
> Visit *mometrix.com/academy* and enter *Code:* **613660**

Synonyms and Antonyms

When you understand how words relate to each other, you will discover more in a passage. This is explained by understanding **synonyms** (e.g., words that mean the same thing) and **antonyms** (e.g., words that mean the opposite of one another). As an example, *dry* and *arid* are synonyms, and *dry* and *wet* are antonyms.

There are many pairs of words in English that can be considered synonyms, despite having slightly different definitions. For instance, the words *friendly* and *collegial* can both be used to describe a warm interpersonal relationship, and one would be correct to call them synonyms. However, *collegial* (kin to *colleague*) is often used in reference to professional or academic relationships, and *friendly* has no such connotation.

If the difference between the two words is too great, then they should not be called synonyms. *Hot* and *warm* are not synonyms because their meanings are too distinct. A good way to determine whether two words are synonyms is to substitute one word for the other word and verify that the meaning of the sentence has not changed. Substituting *warm* for *hot* in a sentence would convey a different meaning. Although warm and hot may seem close in meaning, warm generally means that the temperature is moderate, and hot generally means that the temperature is excessively high.

Antonyms are words with opposite meanings. *Light* and *dark*, *up* and *down*, *right* and *left*, *good* and *bad*: these are all sets of antonyms. Be careful to distinguish between antonyms and pairs of words that are simply different. *Black* and *gray*, for instance, are not antonyms because gray is not the opposite of black. *Black* and *white*, on the other hand, are antonyms. Not every word has an antonym. For instance, many nouns do not: What would be the antonym of chair? During your exam, the questions related to antonyms are more likely to concern adjectives. You will recall that adjectives are words that describe a noun. Some common adjectives include *purple*, *fast*, *skinny*, and *sweet*. From those four adjectives, *purple* is the item that lacks a group of obvious antonyms.

> **Review Video: Synonyms and Antonyms**
> *Visit mometrix.com/academy and enter Code:* **105612**

Description

Occasionally, you will be able to define an unfamiliar word by looking at the descriptive words in the context. Consider the following sentence: *Fred dragged the recalcitrant boy kicking and screaming up the stairs.* The words *dragged*, *kicking*, and *screaming* all suggest that the boy does not want to go up the stairs. The reader may assume that *recalcitrant* means something like unwilling or protesting. In this example, an unfamiliar adjective was identified.

Additionally, using description to define an unfamiliar noun is a common practice compared to unfamiliar adjectives, as in this sentence: *Don's wrinkled frown and constantly shaking fist identified him as a curmudgeon of the first order.* Don is described as having a *wrinkled frown and constantly shaking fist* suggesting that a *curmudgeon* must be a grumpy man. Contrasts do not always provide detailed information about the unfamiliar word, but they at least give the reader some clues.

> **Review Video: Multiple Meaning Words**
> *Visit mometrix.com/academy and enter Code:* **407801**

When a word has more than one meaning, readers can have difficulty with determining how the word is being used in a given sentence. For instance, the verb *cleave*, can mean either *join* or *separate*. When readers come upon this word, they will have to select the definition that makes the most sense. Consider the following sentence: *Hermione's knife cleaved the bread cleanly.* Since, a knife cannot join bread together, the word must indicate separation.

A slightly more difficult example would be the sentence: *The birds cleaved together as they flew from the oak tree.* Immediately, the presence of the word *together* should suggest that in this sentence *cleave* is being used to mean *join*. Discovering the intent of a word with multiple meanings requires the same tricks as defining an unknown word: look for contextual clues and evaluate the substituted words.

> **Review Video:** <u>Determining Word Meanings</u>
> Visit *mometrix.com/academy* and enter *Code:* **894894**

Level of Formality

The relationship between writer and reader is important in choosing a level of formality as most writing requires some degree of formality. Formal writing is for addressing a superior in a school or work environment. Business letters, textbooks, and newspapers use a moderate to high level of formality. Informal writing is appropriate for private letters, personal e-mails, and business correspondence between close associates.

For your exam, you will want to be aware of informal and formal writing. One way that this can be accomplished is to watch for shifts in point of view in the essay. For example, unless writers are using a personal example, they will rarely refer to themselves (e.g., "*I* think that *my* point is very clear.") to avoid being informal when they need to be formal. Also, be mindful of an author who addresses his or her audience directly in their writing (e.g., "Readers, *like you*, will understand this argument.") as this can be a sign of informal writing. Good writers understand the need to be consistent with their level of formality. Shifts in levels of formality or point of view can confuse readers and discount the message of an author's writing.

Clichés
Clichés are phrases that have been overused to the point that the phrase has no importance or has lost the original meaning. The phrases have no originality and add very little to a passage. Therefore, most writers will avoid the use of clichés. Another option is to make changes to a cliché so that it is not predictable and empty of meaning.

Examples
When life gives you lemons, make lemonade.
Every cloud has a silver lining.

Jargon
Jargon is a specialized vocabulary that is used among members of a trade or profession. Since jargon is understood by a small audience, writers tend to leave them to passages where certain readers will understand the vocabulary. Jargon includes exaggerated language that tries to impress rather than inform. Sentences filled with jargon are not precise and difficult to understand.

Examples
"He is going to *toenail* these frames for us." (Toenail is construction jargon for nailing at an angle.)
"They brought in a *kip* of material today." (Kip refers to 1000 pounds in architecture and engineering.)

Slang
Slang is an informal and sometimes private language that is understood by some individuals. Slang has some usefulness, but the language can have a small audience. So, most formal writing will not include this kind of language.

Examples
"Yes, the event was a blast!" (In this sentence, *blast* means that the event was a great experience.)
"That attempt was an epic fail." (By *epic fail*, the speaker means that his or her attempt was not a success.)

<u>Colloquialism</u>
A colloquialism is a word or phrase that is found in informal writing. Unlike slang, colloquial language will be familiar to a greater range of people. Colloquial language can include some slang, but these are limited to contractions for the most part.

Examples
"Can *y'all* come back another time?" (Y'all is a contraction of "you all" which has become a colloquialism.)
"Will you stop him from building this *castle in the air*?" (A "castle in the air" is an improbable or unlikely event.)

Conventions of Standard English

The Eight Parts of Speech

Nouns

When you talk about a person, place, thing, or idea, you are talking about nouns. The two main types of nouns are common and proper nouns. Also, nouns can be abstract (i.e., general) or concrete (i.e., specific).

Common nouns are the class or group of people, places, and things (Note: Do not capitalize common nouns). Examples of common nouns:
People: boy, girl, worker, manager
Places: school, bank, library, home
Things: dog, cat, truck, car

Proper nouns are the names of a specific person, place, or thing (Note: Capitalize all proper nouns). Examples of proper nouns:
People: Abraham Lincoln, George Washington, Martin Luther King, Jr.
Places: Los Angeles, New York, Asia
Things: Statue of Liberty, Earth*, Lincoln Memorial

*Note: When you talk about the planet that we live on, you capitalize *Earth*. When you mean the dirt, rocks, or land, you lowercase *earth*.

General nouns are the names of conditions or ideas. **Specific nouns** name people, places, and things that are understood by using your senses.

General nouns:
Condition: beauty, strength
Idea: truth, peace

Specific nouns:
People: baby, friend, father
Places: town, park, city hall
Things: rainbow, cough, apple, silk, gasoline

Collective nouns are the names for a person, place, or thing that may act as a whole. The following are examples of collective nouns: *class, company, dozen, group, herd, team,* and *public.*

> ➢ **Review Video: Nouns In Different Roles**
> *Visit **mometrix.com/academy** and enter **Code: 653909***

Pronouns

Pronouns are words that are used to stand in for a noun. A pronoun may be grouped as personal, intensive, relative, interrogative, demonstrative, indefinite, and reciprocal.

Personal: Nominative is the case for nouns and pronouns that are the subject of a sentence. Objective is the case for nouns and pronouns that are an object in a sentence. Possessive is the case for nouns and pronouns that show possession or ownership.

Singular

	Nominative	Objective	Possessive
First Person	I	me	my, mine
Second Person	you	you	your, yours
Third Person	he, she, it	him, her, it	his, her, hers, its

Plural

	Nominative	Objective	Possessive
First Person	we	us	our, ours
Second Person	you	you	your, yours
Third Person	they	them	their, theirs

Intensive: I myself, you yourself, he himself, she herself, the (thing) itself, we ourselves, you yourselves, they themselves

Relative: which, who, whom, whose

Interrogative: what, which, who, whom, whose

Demonstrative: this, that, these, those

Indefinite: all, any, each, everyone, either/neither, one, some, several

Reciprocal: each other, one another

> ➢ **Review Video: <u>Nouns and Pronouns</u>**
> *Visit **mometrix.com/academy** and enter **Code: 312073***

Verbs

If you want to write a sentence, then you need a verb in your sentence. Without a verb, you have no sentence. The verb of a sentence explains action or being. In other words, the verb shows the subject's movement or the movement that has been done to the subject.

Transitive and Intransitive Verbs

A transitive verb is a verb whose action (e.g., drive, run, jump) points to a receiver (e.g., car, dog, kangaroo). Intransitive verbs do not point to a receiver of an action. In other words, the action of the verb does not point to a subject or object.

Transitive: He plays the piano. | The piano was played by him.

Intransitive: He plays. | John writes well.

A dictionary will let you know whether a verb is transitive or intransitive. Some verbs can be transitive and intransitive.

Action Verbs and Linking Verbs
An action verb is a verb that shows what the subject is doing in a sentence. In other words, an action verb shows action. A sentence can be complete with one word: an action verb. Linking verbs are intransitive verbs that show a condition (i.e., the subject is described but does no action).

Linking verbs link the subject of a sentence to a noun or pronoun, or they link a subject with an adjective. You always need a verb if you want a complete sentence. However, linking verbs are not able to complete a sentence.

Common linking verbs include *appear, be, become, feel, grow, look, seem, smell, sound,* and *taste*. However, any verb that shows a condition and has a noun, pronoun, or adjective that describes the subject of a sentence is a linking verb.

Action: He sings. | Run! | Go! | I talk with him every day. | She reads.

Linking:
Incorrect: I feel.
Correct: I am John. | I smell roses. | I feel tired.

Note: Some verbs are followed by words that look like prepositions, but they are a part of the verb and a part of the verb's meaning. These are known as phrasal verbs and examples include *call off, look up,* and *drop off*.

> ➤ **Review Video: <u>Action Verbs and Linking Verbs</u>**
> Visit ***mometrix.com/academy*** *and enter* ***Code*: 743142**

Voice
Transitive verbs come in active or passive voice. If the subject does an action or receives the action of the verb, then you will know whether a verb is active or passive. When the subject of the sentence is doing the action, the verb is active voice. When the subject receives the action, the verb is passive voice.

Active: Jon drew the picture. (The subject *Jon* is doing the action of *drawing a picture*.)

Passive: The picture is drawn by Jon. (The subject *picture* is receiving the action from Jon.)

Verb Tenses
A verb tense shows the different form of a verb to point to the time of an action. The present and past tense are shown by changing the verb's form. An action in the present *I talk* can change form for the past: *I talked*. However, for the other tenses, an auxiliary (i.e., helping) verb is needed to show the change in form. These helping verbs include *am, are, is* | *have, has, had* | *was, were, will* (or *shall*).

Present: I talk   Present perfect: I have talked
Past: I talked   Past perfect: I had talked
Future: I will talk   Future perfect: I will have talked

Present: The action happens at the current time.
Example: He *walks* to the store every morning.
To show that something is happening right now, use the progressive present tense: I *am walking*.

Past: The action happened in the past.
Example: He *walked* to the store an hour ago.

Future: The action is going to happen later.
Example: I *will walk* to the store tomorrow.

Present perfect: The action started in the past and continues into the present.
Example: I *have walked* to the store three times today.

Past perfect: The second action happened in the past. The first action came before the second.
Example: Before I walked to the store (Action 2), I *had walked* to the library (Action 1).

Future perfect: An action that uses the past and the future. In other words, the action is complete before a future moment.
Example: When she comes for the supplies (future moment), I *will have walked* to the store (action completed in the past).

> ➤ **Review Video: <u>Verb Tenses</u>**
> Visit *mometrix.com/academy* and enter *Code:* **809578**

> ➤ **Review Video: <u>Present Perfect, Past Perfect, and Future Perfect Verb Tenses</u>**
> Visit *mometrix.com/academy* and enter *Code:* **269472**

Conjugating Verbs
When you need to change the form of a verb, you are conjugating a verb. The key parts of a verb are first person singular, present tense (dream); first person singular, past tense (dreamed); and the past participle (dreamed). Note: the past participle needs a helping verb to make a verb tense. For example, I *have dreamed* of this day. | I *am dreaming* of this day.

Present Tense: Active Voice

	Singular	**Plural**
First Person	I dream	We dream
Second Person	You dream	You dream
Third Person	He, she, it dreams	They dream

Mood
There are three moods in English: the indicative, the imperative, and the subjunctive.

The **indicative mood** is used for facts, opinions, and questions.
Fact: You can do this.
Opinion: I think that you can do this.
Question: Do you know that you can do this?

The **imperative** is used for orders or requests.
Order: You are going to do this!
Request: Will you do this for me?

The **subjunctive mood** is for wishes and statements that go against fact.
Wish: I wish that I were going to do this.
Statement against fact: If I were you, I would do this. (This goes against fact because I am not you. You have the chance to do this, and I do not have the chance.)

The mood that causes trouble for most people is the subjunctive mood. If you have trouble with any of the moods, then be sure to practice.

Adjectives
An adjective is a word that is used to modify a noun or pronoun. An adjective answers a question: *Which one?*, *What kind of?*, or *How many?* . Usually, adjectives come before the words that they modify.

> ➢ **Review Video: <u>What is an Adjective?</u>**
> *Visit **mometrix.com/academy** and enter **Code: 407154***

> ➢ **Review Video: <u>Choosing the Correct Adjective</u>**
> *Visit **mometrix.com/academy** and enter **Code: 899043***

Which one? The *third* suit is my favorite.
What kind? The *navy blue* suit is my favorite.
How many? Can I look over the *four* neckties for the suit?

> ➢ **Review Video: <u>Adjectives in a Series</u>**
> *Visit **mometrix.com/academy** and enter **Code: 899314***

Articles
Articles are adjectives that are used to mark nouns. There are only three: the definite (i.e., limited or fixed amount) article *the*, and the indefinite (i.e., no limit or fixed amount) articles *a* and *an*. Note: *An* comes before words that start with a vowel sound (i.e., vowels include *a, e, i, o, u*, and *y*). For example, Are you going to get an **u**mbrella?

Definite: I lost *the* bottle that belongs to me.
Indefinite: Does anyone have *a* bottle to share?

Comparison with Adjectives
Some adjectives are relative and other adjectives are absolute. Adjectives that are relative can show the comparison between things. Adjectives that are absolute can show comparison. However, they show comparison in a different way. Let's say that you are reading two books. You think that one book is perfect, and the other book is not exactly perfect. It is <u>not</u> possible for the book to be more perfect than the other. Either you think that the book is perfect, or you think that the book is not perfect.

The adjectives that are relative will show the different degrees of something or someone to something else or someone else. The three degrees of adjectives include positive, comparative, and superlative.

The positive degree is the normal form of an adjective.
Example: This work is *difficult*. | She is *smart*.

The comparative degree compares one person or thing to another person or thing.
Example: This work is *more difficult* than your work. | She is *smarter* than me.

The superlative degree compares more than two people or things.
Example: This is the *most difficult* work of my life. | She is the *smartest* lady in school.

> ➤ **Review Video: Degrees of Comparison**
> *Visit mometrix.com/academy and enter Code:* **853658**

> ➤ **Review Video: Unequal Comparison Adjectives**
> *Visit mometrix.com/academy and enter Code:* **751059**

Adverbs
An adverb is a word that is used to modify a verb, adjective, or another adverb. Usually, adverbs answer one of these questions: *When?, Where?, How?,* and *Why?* . The negatives *not* and *never* are known as adverbs. Adverbs that modify adjectives or other adverbs strengthen or weaken the words that they modify.

Examples:
He walks quickly through the crowd.
The water flows smoothly on the rocks.

Note: While many adverbs end in *-ly*, you need to remember that not all adverbs end in *-ly*. Also, some words that end in *-ly* are adjectives, not adverbs. Some examples include: *early, friendly, holy, lonely, silly,* and *ugly*. To know if a word that ends in *-ly* is an adjective or adverb, you can check whether it answers one of the adjective questions or one of the adverb questions.

Examples:
He is *never* angry.
You talk *too* loud.

> ➤ **Review Video: Adverbs**
> *Visit mometrix.com/academy and enter Code:* **713951**

Comparison with Adverbs
The rules for comparing adverbs are the same as the rules for adjectives.

The positive degree is the standard form of an adverb.
Example: He arrives soon. | She speaks softly to her friends.

- 22 -

The comparative degree compares one person or thing to another person or thing.
Example: He arrives sooner than Sarah. | She speaks more softly than him.

The superlative degree compares more than two people or things.
Example: He arrives soonest of the group. | She speaks most softly of any of her friends.

> ➤ **Review Video: <u>Unequal Comparison Adverbs</u>**
> *Visit mometrix.com/academy and enter Code: 315825*

Prepositions
A preposition is a word placed before a noun or pronoun that shows the relationship between an object and another word in the sentence.

Common Prepositions:

about	before	during	on	under
after	beneath	for	over	until
against	between	from	past	up
among	beyond	in	through	with
around	by	of	to	within
at	down	off	toward	without

Examples:
The napkin is *in* the drawer.
The Earth rotates *around* the Sun.
The needle is *beneath* the haystack.
Can you find me *among* the words?

> ➤ **Review Video: <u>What is a Preposition?</u>**
> *Visit mometrix.com/academy and enter Code: 946763*

> ➤ **Review Video: <u>Preposition Overload</u>**
> *Visit mometrix.com/academy and enter Code: 498026*

Conjunctions
Conjunctions join words, phrases, or clauses, and they show the connection between the joined pieces. There are coordinating conjunctions that connect equal parts of sentences. Correlative conjunctions show the connection between pairs. Subordinating conjunctions join subordinate (i.e., dependent) clauses with independent clauses.

Coordinating Conjunctions
The coordinating conjunctions include: *and, but, yet, or, nor, for,* and *so*
Examples:
The rock was small, but it was heavy.
She drove in the night, and he drove in the day.

Correlative Conjunctions

The correlative conjunctions are: *either...or* | *neither...nor* | *not only... but also*

Examples:

Either you are coming, *or* you are staying. | He ran *not only* three miles, *but also* swam 200 yards.

> **Review Video: <u>Coordinating and Correlative Conjunctions</u>**
> *Visit **mometrix.com/academy** and enter **Code: 390329***

Subordinating Conjunctions

Common subordinating conjunctions include:

after	since	whenever
although	so that	where
because	unless	wherever
before	until	whether
in order that	when	while

Examples:

I am hungry *because* I did not eat breakfast.

He went home *when* everyone left.

> **Review Video: <u>Subordinating Conjunctions</u>**
> *Visit **mometrix.com/academy** and enter **Code: 958913***

<u>Interjections</u>

An interjection is a word for exclamation (i.e., great amount of feeling) that is used alone or as a piece to a sentence. Often, they are used at the beginning of a sentence for an introduction. Sometimes, they can be used in the middle of a sentence to show a change in thought or attitude.

Common Interjections: Hey! | Oh,... | Ouch! | Please! | Wow!

Punctuation

End Punctuation

Periods
Use a period to end all sentences except direct questions, exclamations, and questions.

Declarative Sentence
A declarative sentence gives information or makes a statement.
Examples: I can fly a kite. | The plane left two hours ago.

Imperative Sentence
An imperative sentence gives an order or command.
Examples: You are coming with me. | Bring me that note.

Question Marks
Question marks should be used following a direct question. A polite request can be followed by a period instead of a question mark.

> ➤ **Review Video: <u>Question Marks</u>**
> Visit ***mometrix.com/academy*** *and enter* ***Code:*** **118471**

Direct Question: What is for lunch today? | How are you? | Why is that the answer?

Polite Requests:
Can you please send me the item tomorrow. | Will you please walk with me on the track.

Exclamation Marks
Exclamation marks are used after a word group or sentence that shows much feeling or has special importance. Exclamation marks should not be overused. They are saved for proper exclamatory interjections.

Examples: We're going to the finals! | You have a beautiful car! | That's crazy!

> ➤ **Review Video: <u>Exclamation Point</u>**
> Visit ***mometrix.com/academy*** *and enter* ***Code:*** **199367**

Special Note
Periods for Abbreviations
An abbreviation is a shortened form of a word or phrase.
Examples: 3 P.M. | 2 A.M. | Mr. Jones | Mrs. Stevens | Dr. Smith | Bill Jr. | Pennsylvania Ave.

Commas

The comma is a punctuation mark that can help you understand connections in a sentence. Not every sentence needs a comma. However, if a sentence needs a comma, you need to put it in the right place. A comma in the wrong place (or an absent comma) will make a sentence's meaning unclear. These are some of the rules for commas:

1. Use a comma before a coordinating conjunction joining independent clauses
   Example: *Bob caught three fish, and I caught two fish.*

2. Use a comma after an introductory phrase or an adverbial clause
   Examples:
   After the final out, we went to a restaurant to celebrate.
   Studying the stars, I was surprised at the beauty of the sky.

3. Use a comma between items in a series.
   Example: I will bring *the turkey, the pie, and the coffee.*

4. Use a comma between coordinate adjectives not joined with *and*
   Incorrect: The kind, brown dog followed me home.
   Correct: The *kind, loyal* dog followed me home.

   Not all adjectives are coordinate (i.e., equal or parallel). There are two simple ways to know if your adjectives are coordinate. One, you can join the adjectives with *and*: *The kind and loyal dog.* Two, you can change the order of the adjectives: *The loyal, kind dog.*

5. Use commas for interjections and after *yes* and *no* responses
   Examples:
   Interjection: Oh, I had no idea. | Wow, you know how to play this game.
   Yes and No: *Yes,* I heard you. | *No,* I cannot come tomorrow.

6. Use commas to separate nonessential modifiers and nonessential appositives
   Examples:
   Nonessential Modifier: John Frank, who is coaching the team, was promoted today.
   Nonessential Appositive: Thomas Edison, an American inventor, was born in Ohio.

7. Use commas to set off nouns of direct address, interrogative tags, and contrast
   Examples:
   Direct Address: You, *John,* are my only hope in this moment.
   Interrogative Tag: This is the last time, *correct?*
   Contrast: You are my friend, *not my enemy.*

8. Use commas with dates, addresses, geographical names, and titles
   Examples:
   Date: *July 4, 1776,* is an important date to remember.
   Address: He is meeting me at *456 Delaware Avenue, Washington, D.C.,* tomorrow morning.
   Geographical Name: *Paris, France,* is my favorite city.
   Title: John Smith, *Ph. D.,* will be visiting your class today.

9. Use commas to separate expressions like *he said* and *she said* if they come between a sentence of a quote
   Examples:
   "I want you to know," he began, "that I always wanted the best for you."
   "You can start," Jane said, "with an apology."

> ➢ **Review Video: <u>Commas</u>**
> *Visit **mometrix.com/academy** and enter **Code: 797927***

Semicolons

The semicolon is used to connect major sentence pieces of equal value. Some rules for semicolons include:
1. Use a semicolon between closely connected independent clauses that are not connected with a coordinating conjunction.
   Examples:
   She is outside; we are inside.
   You are right; we should go with your plan.

2. Use a semicolon between independent clauses linked with a transitional word.
   Examples:
   I think that we can agree on this; *however,* I am not sure about my friends.
   You are looking in the wrong places; *therefore,* you will not find what you need.

3. Use a semicolon between items in a series that has internal punctuation.
   Example: I have visited *New York, New York; Augusta, Maine; and Baltimore, Maryland.*

> ➢ **Review Video: <u>Semicolon Usage</u>**
> *Visit **mometrix.com/academy** and enter **Code: 370605***

Colons

The colon is used to call attention to the words that follow it. A colon must come after an independent clause. The rules for colons are as follows:
1. Use a colon after an independent clause to make a list
   Example: I want to learn many languages: Spanish, French, German, and Italian.

2. Use a colon for explanations or to give a quote
   Examples:
   Quote: The man started with an idea: "We are able to do more than we imagine."

   Explanation: There is one thing that stands out on your resume: responsibility.

3. Use a colon after the greeting in a formal letter, to show hours and minutes, and to separate a title and subtitle
   Examples:
   Greeting in a formal letter: Dear Sir: | To Whom It May Concern:

   Time: It is 3:14 P.M.

   Title: The essay is titled "America: A Short Introduction to a Modern Country"

Parentheses

Parentheses are used for additional information. Also, they can be used to put labels for letters or numbers in a series. Parentheses should be not be used very often. If they are overused, parentheses can be a distraction instead of a help.

Examples:

Extra Information: The rattlesnake (see Image 2) is a dangerous snake of North and South America.

Series: Include in the email (1) your name, (2) your address, and (3) your question for the author.

> **Review Video: Parentheses**
*Visit **mometrix.com/academy** and enter **Code: 947743***

Quotation Marks

Use quotation marks to close off direct quotations of a person's spoken or written words. Do not use quotation marks around indirect quotations. An indirect quotation gives someone's message without using the person's exact words. Use single quotation marks to close off a quotation inside a quotation.

Direct Quote: Nancy said, "I am waiting for Henry to arrive."

Indirect Quote: Henry said that he is going to be late to the meeting.

Quote inside a Quote: The teacher asked, "Has everyone read 'The Gift of the Magi'?"

Quotation marks should be used around the titles of short works: newspaper and magazine articles, poems, short stories, songs, television episodes, radio programs, and subdivisions of books or web sites.

Examples:

"Rip van Winkle" (short story by Washington Irving)

"O Captain! My Captain!" (poem by Walt Whitman)

Quotation marks may be used to set off words that are being used in a different way from a dictionary definition. Also, they can be used to highlight irony.

Examples:

The boss warned Frank that he was walking on "thin ice."

(Frank is not walking on real ice. Instead, Frank is being warned to avoid mistakes.)

The teacher thanked the young man for his "honesty."

(Honesty and truth are not always the same thing. In this example, the quotation marks around *honesty* show that the teacher does not believe the young man's explanation.)

> **Review Video: Quotation Marks**
*Visit **mometrix.com/academy** and enter **Code: 884918***

Note: Periods and commas are put inside quotation marks. Colons and semicolons are put outside the quotation marks. Question marks and exclamation points are placed inside quotation marks when they are part of a quote. When the question or exclamation mark goes with the whole sentence, the mark is left outside of the quotation marks.

Examples:

Period and comma: We read "The Gift of the Magi," "The Skylight Room," and "The Cactus."

Semicolon: They watched "The Nutcracker"; then, they went home.

Exclamation mark that is a part of a quote: The crowd cheered, "Victory!"

Question mark that goes with the whole sentence: Is your favorite short story "The Tell-Tale Heart"?

> ➤ **Review Video: <u>Making Commas Flow</u>**
> Visit *mometrix.com/academy* and enter *Code:* **873015**

Apostrophes

An apostrophe is used to show possession or the deletion of letters in contractions. An apostrophe is not needed with the possessive pronouns *his, hers, its, ours, theirs, whose,* and *yours.*

Singular Nouns: David's car | a book's theme | my brother's board game

Plural Nouns with *-s*: the scissors' handle | boys' basketball

Plural Nouns without *-s*: Men's department | the people's adventure

> ➤ **Review Video: <u>Apostrophes</u>**
> Visit *mometrix.com/academy* and enter *Code:* **213068**

Hyphen

The hyphen is used to separate compound words. The following are the rules for hyphens:

1. Compound numbers come with a hyphen
   Example: This team needs *twenty-five* points to win the game.

2. Fractions need a hyphen if they are used as an adjective
   Correct: The recipe says that we need a *three-fourths* cup of butter.
   Incorrect: *One-fourth* of the road is under construction.

3. Compound words used as adjectives that come before a noun need a hyphen
   Correct: The *well-fed* dog took a nap.
   Incorrect: The dog was *well-fed* for his nap.

4. To avoid confusion with some words, use a hyphen
   Examples: semi-irresponsible | Re-collect | Re-claim

Note: This is not a complete set of the rules for hyphens. A dictionary is the best tool for knowing if a compound word needs a hyphen.

> ➤ **Review Video: <u>Hyphens</u>**
> Visit *mometrix.com/academy* and enter *Code:* **981632**

Dashes

Dashes are used to show a break or a change in thought in a sentence or to act as parentheses in a sentence. When typing, use two hyphens to make a dash. Do not put a space before or after the dash. The following are the rules for dashes:

1. To set off parenthetical statements or an appositive that has internal punctuation.
   Example: The three trees—oak, pine, and magnolia—are coming on a truck tomorrow.

2. To show a break or change in tone or thought.
   Example: The first question—how silly of me—does not have a correct answer.

> ➤ **Review Video: Dash**
> *Visit mometrix.com/academy and enter Code:* **351706**

Ellipsis Marks

The ellipsis mark has three periods (...) to show when words have been removed from a quotation. If a full sentence or more is removed from a quoted passage, you need to use four periods to show the removed text and the end punctuation mark. The ellipsis mark should not be used at the beginning of a quotation. Also, the ellipsis should not be used at the end of a quotation. The exception is when some words have been deleted from the end of the final sentence.

The following sentence provides an example:
"...Then he picked up the groceries...paid for them...later he went home...."

> ➤ **Review Video: Ellipses**
> *Visit mometrix.com/academy and enter Code:* **402626**

Brackets

There are two main ways to use brackets:

1. When you need to place parentheses inside of parentheses, you use brackets instead of parentheses.
   Example: The hero of this story, Paul Revere (a silversmith and industrialist [see Ch. 4]), rode through towns of Massachusetts to warn of advancing British troops.

2. You can use brackets when you need to add material that is being quoted.
   Example: The father explained, "My children are planning to attend my alma mater [State University]."

> ➤ **Review Video: Brackets**
> *Visit mometrix.com/academy and enter Code:* **727546**

Improving Sentences

Capitalization

The rules for capitalization are:

1. Capitalize the first word of a sentence and the first word in a direct quotation
   Examples:
   First Word: *Football* is my favorite sport.
   Direct Quote: She asked, "*What* is your name?"

2. Capitalize proper nouns and adjectives that come from proper nouns
   Examples:
   Proper Noun: My parents are from *Europe*.
   Adjective from Proper Noun: My father is *British,* and my mother is *Italian*.

3. Capitalize the names of days, months, and holidays
   Examples:
   Day: Everyone needs to be here on *Wednesday*.
   Month: I am so excited for *December*.
   Holiday: *Independence Day* comes every July.

4. Capitalize the names on a compass for specific areas, not when they give direction
   Examples:
   Specific Area: James is from the *West*.
   Direction: After three miles, turn *south* toward the highway.

5. Capitalize each word in a title (Note: Articles, prepositions, and conjunctions are not capitalized unless they are the first or last word in the title.)
   Examples:
   Titles: <u>Romeo and Juliet</u> is a beautiful drama on love.
   Incorrect: <u>The Taming Of The Shrew</u> is my favorite. (Remember that internal prepositions and articles are not capitalized.)

   Note: Books, movies, plays (more than one act), newspapers, magazines, and long musical pieces are put in italics. The two examples of Shakespeare's plays are underlined to show their use as an example.

> **Review Video: <u>Italicizing and Underlining</u>**
> Visit ***mometrix.com/academy*** *and enter **Code: 327684***

> **Review Video: <u>Consistency in Punctuation</u>**
> Visit ***mometrix.com/academy*** *and enter **Code: 169489***

Subjects and Predicates

<u>Subjects</u>
The *subject* of a sentence names who or what the sentence is about. The complete subject is composed of the simple subject and all of its modifiers. To find the complete subject, ask *Who* or

What and insert the verb to complete the question. The answer is the complete subject. To find the simple subject, remove all of the modifiers in the complete subject.

Examples:
The small red car is the one that he wants for Christmas.
(The complete subject is *the small red car.*)

The young artist is coming over for dinner.
(The complete subject is *the young artist.*)

In imperative sentences, the verb's subject is understood, but not actually present in the sentence. Although the subject ordinarily comes before the verb, in sentences that begin with *There are* or *There was*, the subject follows the verb. The ability to recognize the subject of a sentence helps in editing a variety of problems, such as sentence fragments and subject-verb agreement, as well as the using the correct pronouns.

> **Review Video: Subjects**
> *Visit **mometrix.com/academy** and enter **Code: 444771***

Direct:
John knows the way to the park.
(Who knows the way to the park? Answer: John)

The cookies need ten more minutes.
(What needs ten minutes? Answer: The cookies)

By five o' clock, Bill will need to leave.
(Who needs to leave? Answer: Bill)

Remember: The subject can come after the verb.
There are five letters on the table for him.
(What is on the table? Answer: Five letters)

There were coffee and doughnuts in the house.
(What was in the house? Answer: Coffee and doughnuts)

Implied:
Go to the post office for me.
(Who is going to the post office? Answer: You are.)

Come and sit with me, please?
(Who needs to come and sit? Answer: You do.)

Predicates

In a sentence, you always have a predicate and a subject. A predicate is what remains when you have found the subject. The subject tells what the sentence is about, and the predicate explains or describes the subject. Think about the sentence: *He sings.* In this sentence, we have a subject (He) and a predicate (sings). This is all that is needed for a sentence to be complete. Would we like more information? Of course, we would like to know more. However, if this all the information that you are given, you have a complete sentence.

Now, let's look at another sentence:
John and Jane sing on Tuesday nights at the dance hall.

What is the subject of this sentence?
Answer: John and Jane.

What is the predicate of this sentence?
Answer: Everything else in the sentence besides John and Jane.

> ➢ **Review Video: <u>What is a Predicate?</u>**
> *Visit **mometrix.com/academy** and enter **Code: 511780***

> ➢ **Review Video: <u>Complete Predicates</u>**
> *Visit **mometrix.com/academy** and enter **Code: 293942***

Subject-Verb Agreement

Verbs agree with their subjects in number. In other words, singular subjects need singular verbs. Plural subjects need plural verbs. Singular is for one person, place, or thing. Plural is for more than one person, place, or thing. Subjects and verbs must also agree in person: first, second, or third. The present tense ending *-s* is used on a verb if its subject is third person singular; otherwise, the verb takes no ending.

<u>Number Agreement Examples:</u>
Single Subject and Verb: *Dan calls home.*
(Dan is one person. So, the singular verb *calls* is needed.)

Plural Subject and Verb: *Dan and Bob call home.*
(More than one person needs the plural verb *call*.)

<u>Person Agreement Examples:</u>
First Person: I *am* walking.
Second Person: You *are* walking.
Third Person: He *is* walking.

> ➢ **Review Video: <u>Subject Verb Agreement</u>**
> *Visit **mometrix.com/academy** and enter **Code: 479190***

Problems with Subject-Verb Agreement

- <u>Words between Subject and Verb</u>
The joy of my life returns home tonight.
(**Singular Subject**: joy. **Singular Verb**: returns)
The phrase *of my life* does not influence the verb *returns*.

The question that still remains unanswered is "Who are you?"
(**Singular Subject**: question. **Singular Verb**: is)
Don't let the phrase "*that still remains…*" trouble you. The subject *question* goes with *is*.

- **Compound Subjects**

You and Jon are invited to come to my house.
(**Plural Subject**: You and Jon. **Plural Verb**: are)

The pencil and paper belong to me.
(**Plural Subject**: pencil and paper. **Plural Verb**: belong)

- **Subjects Joined by *Or* and *Nor***

Today or tomorrow is the day.
(**Subject**: Today / tomorrow. **Verb**: is)

Stan or Phil wants to read the book.
(**Subject**: Stan / Phil. **Verb**: wants)

Neither the books nor the *pen is* on the desk.
(**Subject**: Books / Pen. **Verb**: is)

Either the blanket or *pillows arrive* this afternoon.
(**Subject**: Blanket / Pillows. **Verb**: arrive)

Note: Singular subjects that are joined with the conjunction *or* need a singular verb. However, when one subject is singular and another is plural, you make the verb agree with the closer subject. The example about books and the pen has a singular verb because the pen (singular subject) is closer to the verb.

- **Indefinite Pronouns: Either, Neither, and Each**

Is either of you ready for the game?
(**Singular Subject**: Either. **Singular Verb**: is)

Each man, woman, and child is unique.
(**Singular Subject**: Each. **Singular Verb**: is)

- **The adjective *Every* and compounds: Everybody, Everyone, Anybody, Anyone**

Every day passes faster than the last.
(**Singular Subject**: Every day. **Singular Verb**: passes)

Anybody is welcome to bring a tent.
(**Singular Subject**: Anybody. **Singular Verb**: is)

- **Collective Nouns**

The family eats at the restaurant every Friday night.
(The members of the family are one at the restaurant.)

The team are leaving for their homes after the game.
(The members of the team are leaving as individuals to go to their own homes.)

- **Who, Which, and That as Subject**

This is the man who is helping me today.
He is a good man who serves others before himself.
This painting that is hung over the couch is very beautiful.

- <u>Plural Form and Singular Meaning</u>

Some nouns that are singular in meaning but plural in form: news, mathematics, physics, and economics

> The news is coming on now.
> Mathematics is my favorite class.

Some nouns that are plural in meaning: athletics, gymnastics, scissors, and pants

> Do these pants come with a shirt?
> The scissors are for my project.

Note: Look to your dictionary for help when you aren't sure whether a noun with a plural form has a singular or plural meaning.

Addition, Multiplication, Subtraction, and Division are normally singular.

> One plus one is two.
> Three times three is nine.

Complements

A complement is a noun, pronoun, or adjective that is used to give more information about the verb in the sentence.

<u>Direct Objects</u>
A direct object is a noun that takes or receives the action of a verb. Remember: a complete sentence does not need a direct object. A sentence needs only a subject and a verb. When you are looking for a direct object, find the verb and ask *who* or *what*.

> Example: I took the blanket. (Who or what did I take? *The blanket*)
> Jane read books. (Who or what does Jane read? *Books*)

<u>Indirect Objects</u>
An indirect object is a word or group of words that show how an action had an influence on someone or something. If there is an indirect object in a sentence, then you always have a direct object in the sentence. When you are looking for the indirect object, find the verb and ask *to/for whom or what*.

> Examples: We taught the old dog a new trick.
> (To/For Whom or What was taught? *The old dog*)
>
> I gave them a math lesson.
> (To/For Whom or What was given? *Them*)

<u>Predicate Nouns</u> are nouns that modify the subject and finish linking verbs.

> Example: My father is a lawyer.
> Father is the subject. Lawyer is the predicate noun.

<u>Predicate Adjectives</u> are adjectives that modify the subject and finish linking verbs.

> Example: Your mother is patient.
> Mother is the subject. Patient is the predicate adjective.

Pronoun Usage

Pronoun-antecedent agreement – The antecedent is the noun that has been replaced by a pronoun. A pronoun and the antecedent agree when they are singular or plural.

Singular agreement: *John* came into town, and *he* played for us.
(The word *He* replaces *John*.)

Plural agreement: *John and Rick* came into town, and *they* played for us.
(The word *They* replaces *John* and *Rick*.)

To know the correct pronoun for a compound subject, try each pronoun separately with the verb. Your knowledge of pronouns will tell you which one is correct.
Example: Bob and (I, me) will be going.
(Answer: Bob and I will be going.)

Test: (1) *I will be going* or (2) *Me will be going*. The second choice cannot be correct because *me* is not used as a subject of a sentence. Instead, *me* is used as an object.

When a pronoun is used with a noun immediately following (as in "we boys"), try the sentence without the added noun.
Example: (We/Us) boys played football last year.
(Answer: We boys played football last year.)

Test: (1) *We* played football last year or (2) *Us* played football last year. Again, the second choice cannot be correct because *us* is not used as a subject of a sentence. Instead, *us* is used as an object.

> ➤ **Review Video: Using the Correct Pronoun**
> *Visit **mometrix.com/academy** and enter **Code: 662744***

Pronoun reference – A pronoun should point clearly to the antecedent. Here is how a pronoun reference can be unhelpful if it is not directly stated or puzzling.

Unhelpful: Ron and Jim went to the store, and he bought soda.
(Who bought soda? Ron or Jim?)

Helpful: Jim went to the store, and he bought soda.
(The sentence is clear. Jim bought the soda.)

Personal pronouns – Some pronouns change their form by their placement in a sentence. A pronoun that is a subject in a sentence comes in the subjective case. Pronouns that serve as objects appear in the objective case. Finally, the pronouns that are used as possessives appear in the possessive case.

Subjective case: *He* is coming to the show.
(The pronoun *He* is the subject of the sentence.)

Objective case: Josh drove *him* to the airport.
(The pronoun *him* is the object of the sentence.)

Possessive case: The flowers are *mine.*
(The pronoun *mine* shows ownership of the flowers.)

Who or whom – *Who*, a subjective-case pronoun, can be used as a subject. *Whom*, an objective case pronoun, can be used as an object. The words *who* and *whom* are common in subordinate clauses or in questions.

Subject: He knows who wants to come.
(*Who* is the subject of the verb *wants.*)

Object: He knows whom we want at the party.
(*Whom* is the object of *we want.*)

Clauses

There are two groups of clauses: independent and dependent. Unlike phrases, a clause has a subject and a verb. So, what is the difference between a clause that is independent and one that is dependent? An independent clause gives a complete thought. A dependent clause does not share a complete thought. Instead, a dependent clause has a subject and a verb, but it needs an independent clause. Subordinate (i.e., dependent) clauses look like sentences. They may have a subject, a verb, and objects or complements. They are used within sentences as adverbs, adjectives, or nouns.

Examples:
Independent Clause: I am running outside.
(The sentence has a subject *I* and a verb *am running.*)

Dependent Clause: I am running <u>because I want to stay in shape</u>.

The clause *I am running* is an independent clause. The underlined clause is dependent. Remember: a dependent clause does not give a complete thought. Think about the dependent clause: *because I want to stay in shape.*

Without any other information, you think: So, you want to stay in shape. What are you are doing to stay in shape? Answer: *I am running.*

<u>Types of Dependent Clauses</u>
An **adjective clause** is a dependent clause that modifies nouns and pronouns. Adjective clauses begin with a relative pronoun (*who, whose, whom, which,* and *that*) or a relative adverb (*where, when,* and *why*). Also, adjective clauses come after the noun that the clause needs to explain or rename. This is done to have a clear connection to the independent clause.
Examples:
I learned the reason *why I won the award.*
This is the place *where I started my first job.*

An adjective clause can be an essential or nonessential clause. An essential clause is very important to the sentence. Essential clauses explain or define a person or thing. Nonessential clauses give more information about a person or thing. However, they are not necessary to the sentence.

Examples:
Essential: A person *who works hard at first* can rest later in life.
Nonessential: Neil Armstrong, *who walked on the moon*, is my hero.

> ➤ **Review Video: Adjective Clauses and Phrases**
> Visit *mometrix.com/academy* and enter *Code:* **643738**

An **adverb clause** is a dependent clause that modifies verbs, adjectives, and other adverbs. To show a clear connection to the independent clause, put the adverb clause immediately before or after the independent clause. An adverb clause can start with *after, although, as, as if, before, because, if, since, so, so that, unless, when, where,* or *while.*
Examples:
When you walked outside, I called the manager.
I want to go with you *unless you want to stay.*

> ➤ **Review Video: Adverb Clauses and Adverbial Phrases**
> Visit *mometrix.com/academy* and enter *Code:* **728468**

A **noun clause** is a dependent clause that can be used as a subject, object, or complement. Noun clauses can begin with *how, that, what, whether, which, who,* or *why.* These words can also come with an adjective clause. Remember that the entire clause makes a noun or an adjective clause, not the word that starts a clause. So, be sure to look for more than the word that begins the clause. To show a clear connection to the independent clause, be sure that a noun clause comes after the verb. The exception is when the noun clause is the subject of the sentence.
Examples:
The fact *that you were alone* alarms me.
What you learn from each other depends on your honesty with others.

> ➤ **Review Video: Clauses**
> Visit *mometrix.com/academy* and enter *Code:* **940170**

Phrases

A phrase is not a complete sentence. So, a phrase cannot be a statement and cannot give a complete thought. Instead, a phrase is a group of words that can be used as a noun, adjective, or adverb in a sentence. Phrases strengthen sentences by adding explanation or renaming something.

Prepositional Phrases – A phrase that can be found in many sentences is the prepositional phrase. A prepositional phrase begins with a preposition and ends with a noun or pronoun that is used as an object. Normally, the prepositional phrase works as an adjective or an adverb.

Examples:
The picnic is *on the blanket.*
I am sick *with a fever* today.
Among the many flowers, a four-leaf clover was found by John.

Verbals and Verbal Phrases
A verbal looks like a verb, but it is not used as a verb. Instead, a verbal is used as a noun, adjective, or adverb. Be careful with verbals. They do not replace a verb in a sentence.

Correct: Walk a mile daily.
(*Walk* is the verb of this sentence. As in, "*You* walk a mile daily.")

Incorrect: To walk a mile.
(*To walk* is a type of verbal. But, verbals cannot be a verb for a sentence.)

A verbal phrase is a verb form that does not function as the verb of a clause. There are three major types of verbal phrases: participial, gerund, and infinitive phrases.

> ➢ **Review Video: <u>Verbals</u>**
> *Visit mometrix.com/academy and enter Code:* **915480**

Participles
A participle is a verbal that is used as an adjective. The present participle always ends with *-ing*. Past participles end with *-d, -ed, -n,* or *-t.*

Examples: Verb: *dance* | Present Participle: *dancing* | Past Participle: *danced*

Participial phrases are made of a participle and any complements or modifiers. Often, they come right after the noun or pronoun that they modify.

Examples:
Shipwrecked on an island, the boys started to fish for food.
Having been seated for five hours, we got out of the car to stretch our legs.
Praised for their work, the group accepted the first place trophy.

Gerunds
A gerund is a verbal that is used as a noun. Gerunds can be found by looking for their *-ing* endings. However, you need to be careful that you have found a gerund, not a present participle. Since gerunds are nouns, they can be used as a subject of a sentence and the object of a verb or preposition.

Gerund Phrases are built around present participles (i.e., *-ing* endings to verbs) and they are always used as nouns. The gerund phrase has a gerund and any complements or modifiers.

Examples:
We want to be known for *teaching the poor*. (Object of Preposition)
Coaching this team is the best job of my life. (Subject)
We like *practicing our songs* in the basement. (Object of the verb: *like*)

Infinitives
An infinitive is a verbal that can be used as a noun, an adjective, or an adverb. An infinitive is made of the basic form of a verb with the word *to* coming before the verb.

Infinitive Phrases are made of an infinitive and all complements and modifiers. They are used as nouns, adjectives, or adverbs.

Examples:
To join the team is my goal in life. (Noun)
The animals have enough food *to eat for the night*. (Adjective)
People lift weights *to exercise their muscles*. (Adverb)

> ➤ **Review Video: <u>Gerund, Infinitive, and Participle</u>**
> *Visit **mometrix.com/academy** and enter **Code: 634263***

<u>Appositive Phrases</u>
An appositive is a word or phrase that is used to explain or rename nouns or pronouns. In a sentence they can be noun phrases, prepositional phrases, gerund phrases, or infinitive phrases.

Examples:
Terriers, *hunters at heart*, have been dressed up to look like lap dogs.
(The phrase *hunters at heart* renames the noun *terriers*.)

His plan, *to save and invest his money*, was proven as a safe approach.
(The italicized infinitive phrase renames the plan.)

Appositive phrases can be essential or nonessential. An appositive phrase is essential if the person, place, or thing being described or renamed is too general.
Essential: Two Founding Fathers George Washington and Thomas Jefferson served as presidents.

Nonessential: George Washington and Thomas Jefferson, two Founding Fathers, served as presidents.

<u>Absolute Phrases</u>
An absolute phrase is a phrase with a participle that comes after a noun. The absolute phrase is never the subject of a sentence. Also, the phrase does not explain or add to the meaning of a word in a sentence. Absolute phrases are used independently from the rest of the sentence. However, they are still a phrase, and phrases cannot give a complete thought.

Examples:
The alarm ringing, he pushed the snooze button.
The music paused, she continued to dance through the crowd.

Note: Appositive and absolute phrases can be confusing in sentences. So, don't be discouraged if you have a difficult time with them.

Modes of Sentence Patterns

Sentence patterns fall into five common modes with some exceptions. They are:
- Subject + linking verb + subject complement
- Subject + transitive verb + direct object
- Subject + transitive verb + indirect object + direct object
- Subject + transitive verb + direct object + object complement
- Subject + intransitive verb

Common exceptions to these patterns are questions and commands, sentences with delayed subjects, and passive transformations.

Types of Sentences

For a sentence to be complete, it must have a subject and a verb or predicate. A complete sentence will express a complete thought, otherwise it is known as a fragment. An example of a fragment is: *As the clock struck midnight.* A complete sentence would be: *As the clock struck midnight, she ran home.* The types of sentences are declarative, imperative, interrogative, and exclamatory.

> ➢ **Review Video: <u>Complete Sentences</u>**
> Visit *mometrix.com/academy* and enter *Code:* **603161**

A declarative sentence states a fact and ends with a period. The following is an example:
> *The football game starts at seven o'clock.*

An imperative sentence tells someone to do something and ends with a period. The following is an example:
> *Go to the store and buy milk.*

An interrogative sentence asks a question and ends with a question mark. The following is an example:
> *Are you going to the game on Friday?*

An exclamatory sentence shows strong emotion and ends with an exclamation point. The following is an example:
> *I can't believe we won the game!*

Sentence Structures

The four major types of sentence structure are:
1. Simple Sentences – Simple sentences have one independent clause with no subordinate clauses. A simple sentence can have compound elements (e.g., a compound subject or verb). Examples:
   Judy watered the lawn. (Singular Subject & Singular Predicate)
   Judy and Alan watered the lawn. (Compound Subject: Judy and Alan)

2. Compound Sentences – Compound sentences have two or more independent clauses with no dependent clauses. Usually, the independent clauses are joined with a comma and a coordinating conjunction, or they can be joined with a semicolon. Example:
   The time has come, and we are ready.
   I woke up at dawn; then I went outside to watch the sun rise.

3. Complex Sentences – A complex sentence has one independent clause and one or more dependent clauses. Examples:
   Although he had the flu, Harry went to work.
   Marcia got married after she finished college.

4. Compound-Complex Sentences – A compound-complex sentence has at least two independent clauses and at least one dependent clause.

Examples:
John is my friend who went to India, and he brought souvenirs for us.
You may not know, but we heard the music that you played last night.

> ➤ **Review Video: <u>Sentence Structure</u>**
> *Visit **mometrix.com/academy** and enter **Code: 700478***

Sentence Fragments

A part of a sentence should not be treated like a complete sentence. A sentence must be made of at least one independent clause. An independent clause has a subject and a verb. Remember that the independent clause can stand alone as a sentence. Some fragments are independent clauses that begin with a subordinating word (e.g., as, because, so, etc.). Other fragments may not have a subject, a verb, or both.

A sentence fragment can be repaired in several ways. One way is to put the fragment with a neighbor sentence. Another way is to be sure that punctuation is not needed. You can also turn the fragment into a sentence by adding any missing pieces. Sentence fragments are allowed for writers who want to show off their art. However, for your exam, sentence fragments are not allowed.

Fragment: Because he wanted to sail for Rome.
Correct: He dreamed of Europe because he wanted to sail for Rome.

Run-on Sentences

Run-on sentences are independent clauses that have not been joined by a conjunction. When two or more independent clauses appear in one sentence, they must be joined in one of these ways:
1. Correction with a comma and a coordinating conjunction.
   Incorrect: I went on the trip and I had a good time.
   Correct: I went on the trip, and I had a good time.

2. Correction with a semicolon, a colon, or a dash. Used when independent clauses are closely related and their connection is clear without a coordinating conjunction.
   Incorrect: I went to the store and I bought some eggs.
   Correct: I went to the store; I bought some eggs.

3. Correction by separating sentences. This correction may be used when both independent clauses are long. Also, this can be used when one sentence is a question and one is not.
Incorrect: The drive to New York takes ten hours it makes me very tired.
Correct: The drive to New York takes ten hours. So, I become very tired.

4. Correction by changing parts of the sentence. One way is to turn one of the independent clauses into a phrase or subordinate clause.
Incorrect: The drive to New York takes ten hours it makes me very tired.
Correct: During the ten hour drive to New York, I become very tired.

Note: Normally, one of these choices will be a clear correction to a run-on sentence. The fourth way can be the best correction but needs the most work.

> **Review Video: <u>Fragments and Run-on Sentences</u>**
> *Visit **mometrix.com/academy** and enter **Code: 541989***

Dangling and Misplaced Modifiers

<u>Dangling Modifiers</u>
A dangling modifier is a verbal phrase that does not have a clear connection to a word. A dangling modifier can also be a dependent clause (the subject and/or verb are not included) that does not have a clear connection to a word.

Examples:
Dangling: *Reading each magazine article*, the stories caught my attention.
Corrected: Reading each magazine article, *I* was entertained by the stories.

In this example, the word *stories* cannot be modified by *Reading each magazine article*. People can read, but stories cannot read. So, the pronoun *I* is needed for the modifying phrase *Reading each magazine article*.

Dangling: Since childhood, my grandparents have visited me for Christmas.
Corrected: Since childhood, I have been visited by my grandparents for Christmas.

In this example, the dependent adverb clause *Since childhood* cannot modify grandparents. So, the pronoun *I* is needed for the modifying adverb clause.

<u>Misplaced Modifiers</u>
In some sentences, a modifier can be put in more than one place. However, you need to be sure that there is no confusion about which word is being explained or given more detail.

Incorrect: He read the book to a crowd that was filled with beautiful pictures.
Correct: He read the book that was filled with beautiful pictures to a crowd.

The crowd is not filled with pictures. The book is filled with pictures.

Incorrect: John only ate fruits and vegetables for two weeks.
Correct: John ate *only* fruits and vegetables for two weeks.

John may have done nothing else for two weeks but eat fruits and vegetables and sleep. However, it is reasonable to think that John had fruits and vegetables for his meals. Then, he continued to work on other things.

> ➢ **Review Video: <u>Misplaced Modifiers</u>**
> *Visit **mometrix.com/academy** and enter **Code:** **312681***

<u>Split Infinitives</u>
A split infinitive occurs when a modifying word comes between the word *to* and the verb that pairs with *to*.
Example: To *clearly* explain vs. *To explain* clearly | To *softly* sing vs. *To sing* softly

Though still considered improper by some, split infinitives may provide better clarity and simplicity than the alternatives. As such, avoiding them should not be considered a universal rule.

Double Negatives

Standard English allows two negatives when a positive meaning is intended. For example, "The team was not displeased with their performance." Double negatives that are used to emphasize negation are not part of Standard English.

Negative modifiers (e.g., never, no, and not) should not be paired with other negative modifiers or negative words (e.g., none, nobody, nothing, or neither). The modifiers *hardly, barely,* and *scarcely* are also considered negatives in Standard English. So, they should not be used with other negatives.

Parallelism and Subordination

<u>Parallelism</u>
Parallel structures are used in sentences to highlight similar ideas and to connect sentences that give similar information. Parallelism pairs parts of speech, phrases, or clauses together with a matching piece. To write, *I enjoy <u>reading</u> and <u>to study</u>* would be incorrect. An infinitive does not match with a gerund. Instead, you should write *I enjoy <u>reading</u> and <u>studying</u>*.

Be sure that you continue to use certain words (e.g., articles, linking verbs, prepositions, infinitive sign (to), and the introductory word for a dependent clause) in sentences.

Incorrect: Will you bring the paper and pen with you?
Correct: Will you bring *the* paper and *a* pen with you?

Incorrect: The animals can come to eat and play.
Correct: The animals can come *to* eat and *to* play.

Incorrect: You are the person who remembered my name and cared for me.
Correct: You are the person *who* remembered my name and *who* cared for me.

<u>Subordination</u>

When two items are not equal to each other, you can join them by making the more important piece an independent clause. The less important piece can become subordinate. To make the less important piece subordinate, you make it a phrase or a dependent clause. The piece of more importance should be the one that readers want or will need to remember.

Example:

(1) The team had a perfect regular season. (2) The team lost the championship.

Despite having a perfect regular season, *the team lost the championship.*

> **Review Video: <u>Rhetorical Schemes</u>**
> *Visit **mometrix.com/academy** and enter **Code: 470887***

Word Usage

Word usage, or diction, refers to the use of words with meanings and forms that are appropriate for the context and structure of a sentence. A common error in word usage occurs when a word's meaning does not fit the context of the sentence.

Incorrect: Susie likes chips better then candy.
Correct: Susie likes chips better than candy.

Incorrect: The cat licked it's coat.
Correct: The cat licked its coat.

> **Review Video: <u>Word Usage</u>**
> *Visit **mometrix.com/academy** and enter **Code: 197863***

Word Confusion

Which is used for things only.
     Example: John's dog, *which was called Max,* is large and fierce.

That is used for people or things.
     Example: Is this the only book *that Louis L'Amour wrote?*
     Example: Is Louis L'Amour the author *that wrote Western novels?*

Who is used for people only.
     Example: Mozart was the composer *who wrote those operas.*

The Math Test

Number and Quantity

Numbers are the basic building blocks of mathematics. Specific features of numbers are identified by the following terms:

Integer – any positive or negative whole number, including zero. Integers do not include fractions $\left(\frac{1}{3}\right)$, decimals (0.56), or mixed numbers $\left(7\frac{3}{4}\right)$.

Prime number – any whole number greater than 1 that has only two factors, itself and 1; that is, a number that can be divided evenly only by 1 and itself.

Composite number – any whole number greater than 1 that has more than two different factors; in other words, any whole number that is not a prime number. For example: The composite number 8 has the factors of 1, 2, 4, and 8.

Even number – any integer that can be divided by 2 without leaving a remainder. For example: 2, 4, 6, 8, and so on.

Odd number – any integer that cannot be divided evenly by 2. For example: 3, 5, 7, 9, and so on.

Decimal number – any number that uses a decimal point to show the part of the number that is less than one. Example: 1.234.

Decimal point – a symbol used to separate the ones place from the tenths place in decimals or dollars from cents in currency.

Decimal place – the position of a number to the right of the decimal point. In the decimal 0.123, the 1 is in the first place to the right of the decimal point, indicating tenths; the 2 is in the second place, indicating hundredths; and the 3 is in the third place, indicating thousandths.

The decimal, or base 10, system is a number system that uses ten different digits (0, 1, 2, 3, 4, 5, 6, 7, 8, 9). An example of a number system that uses something other than ten digits is the binary, or base 2, number system, used by computers, which uses only the numbers 0 and 1. It is thought that the decimal system originated because people had only their 10 fingers for counting.

Rational numbers include all integers, decimals, and fractions. Any terminating or repeating decimal number is a rational number.

Irrational numbers cannot be written as fractions or decimals because the number of decimal places is infinite and there is no recurring pattern of digits within the number. For example, pi (π) begins with 3.141592 and continues without terminating or repeating, so pi is an irrational number.

Real numbers are the set of all rational and irrational numbers.

> ➢ **Review Video: <u>Numbers and Their Classification</u>**
> *Visit **mometrix.com/academy** and enter **Code: 461071***

Place Value

Write the place value of each digit in the following number: 14,059.826

1: ten thousands
4: thousands
0: hundreds
5: tens
9: ones
8: tenths
2: hundredths
6: thousandths

Writing Numbers in Word Form

<u>Example 1</u>
Write each number in words.

29: twenty-nine
478: four hundred seventy-eight
9,435: nine thousand four hundred thirty-five
98,542: ninety-eight thousand five hundred forty-two
302, 876: three hundred two thousand eight hundred seventy-six

<u>Example 2</u>
Write each decimal in words.

0.06: six hundredths
0.6: six tenths
6.0: six

0.009: nine thousandths;
0.113: one hundred thirteen thousandths;
0.901: nine hundred and one thousandths

The Number Line

A number line is a graph to see the distance between numbers. Basically, this graph shows the relationship between numbers. So, a number line may have a point for zero and may show negative numbers on the left side of the line. Also, any positive numbers are placed on the right side of the line.

Example 1
Name each point on the number line below:

Use the dashed lines on the number line to identify each point. Each dashed line between two whole numbers is $\frac{1}{4}$. The line halfway between two numbers is $\frac{1}{2}$.

Rational Numbers from Least to Greatest

Example
Order the following rational numbers from least to greatest: 0.55, 17%, $\sqrt{25}$, $\frac{64}{4}$, $\frac{25}{50}$, 3.

Recall that the term *rational* simply means that the number can be expressed as a ratio or fraction. The set of rational numbers includes integers and decimals. Notice that each of the numbers in the problem can be written as a decimal or integer:
$17\% = 0.17$

$\sqrt{25} = 5$

$\frac{64}{4} = 16$

$\frac{25}{50} = \frac{1}{2} = 0.5$

So, the answer is 17%, $\frac{25}{50}$, 0.55, 3, $\sqrt{25}$, $\frac{64}{4}$.

Rational Numbers from Greatest to Least

Example

Order the following rational numbers from greatest to least: $0.3, 27\%, \sqrt{100}, \frac{72}{9}, \frac{1}{9}, 4.5$

Recall that the term *rational* simply means that the number can be expressed as a ratio or fraction. The set of rational numbers includes integers and decimals. Notice that each of the numbers in the problem can be written as a decimal or integer:

$27\% = 0.27$

$\sqrt{100} = 10$

$\frac{72}{9} = 8$

$\frac{1}{9} \approx 0.11$

So, the answer is $\sqrt{100}, \frac{72}{9}, 4.5, 0.3, 27\%, \frac{1}{9}$.

Fractions

A fraction is a number that is expressed as one integer written above another integer, with a dividing line between them $\left(\frac{x}{y}\right)$. It represents the quotient of the two numbers "x divided by y." It can also be thought of as x out of y equal parts.

The top number of a fraction is called the numerator, and it represents the number of parts under consideration. The 1 in $\frac{1}{4}$ means that 1 part out of the whole is being considered in the calculation. The bottom number of a fraction is called the denominator, and it represents the total number of equal parts. The 4 in $\frac{1}{4}$ means that the whole consists of 4 equal parts. A fraction cannot have a denominator of zero; this is referred to as "undefined."

> ➤ **Review Video: Fractions**
> *Visit mometrix.com/academy and enter Code:* **262335**

Fractions can be manipulated, without changing the value of the fraction, by multiplying or dividing (but not adding or subtracting) both the numerator and denominator by the same number. If you divide both numbers by a common factor, you are reducing or simplifying the fraction. Two fractions that have the same value, but are expressed differently are known as equivalent fractions. For example, $\frac{2}{10}, \frac{3}{15}, \frac{4}{20}$, and $\frac{5}{25}$ are all equivalent fractions. They can also all be reduced or simplified to $\frac{1}{5}$.

> ➤ **Review Video: Ordering Fractions**
> *Visit mometrix.com/academy and enter Code:* **930652**

Proper Fractions and Mixed Numbers
A fraction whose denominator is greater than its numerator is known as a proper fraction, while a fraction whose numerator is greater than its denominator is known as an improper fraction. Proper fractions have values less than one and improper fractions have values greater than one.

> **Review Video: Improper Fractions and Mixed Numbers**
> *Visit mometrix.com/academy and enter Code: 731507*

A mixed number is a number that contains both an integer and a fraction. Any improper fraction can be rewritten as a mixed number. Example: $\frac{8}{3} = \frac{6}{3} + \frac{2}{3} = 2 + \frac{2}{3} = 2\frac{2}{3}$. Similarly, any mixed number can be rewritten as an improper fraction. Example: $1\frac{3}{5} = 1 + \frac{3}{5} = \frac{5}{5} + \frac{3}{5} = \frac{8}{5}$.

> **Review Video: Changing Mixed Numbers to Improper Fractions**
> *Visit mometrix.com/academy and enter Code: 972516*

> **Review Video: Converting Improper Fractions to Mixed Numbers and Decimals**
> *Visit mometrix.com/academy and enter Code: 440122*

> **Review Video: Converting Mixed Numbers to Decimals and Improper Fractions**
> *Visit mometrix.com/academy and enter Code: 440122*

Common Denominators with Fractions
When two fractions are manipulated so that they have the same denominator, this is known as finding a common denominator. The number chosen to be that common denominator should be the least common multiple of the two original denominators. Example: $\frac{3}{4}$ and $\frac{5}{6}$; the least common multiple of 4 and 6 is 12. Manipulating to achieve the common denominator: $\frac{3}{4} = \frac{9}{12}$; $\frac{5}{6} = \frac{10}{12}$.

Decimals

Decimal Illustration
Use a model to represent the decimal: 0.24. Write 0.24 as a fraction.
The decimal 0.24 is twenty four hundredths. One possible model to represent this fraction is to draw 100 pennies, since each penny is worth 1 one hundredth of a dollar. Draw one hundred circles to represent one hundred pennies. Shade 24 of the pennies to represent the decimal twenty-four hundredths.

To write the decimal as a fraction, write a fraction: $\frac{\#\ shaded\ spaces}{\#\ total\ spaces}$. The number of shaded spaces is 24, and the total number of spaces is 100, so as a fraction 0.24 equals $\frac{24}{100}$. This fraction can then be reduced to $\frac{6}{25}$.

> **Review Video: <u>Decimals</u>**
> *Visit **mometrix.com/academy** and enter Code: **837268***

> **Review Video: <u>Ordering Decimals</u>**
> *Visit **mometrix.com/academy** and enter Code: **560690***

> **Review Video: <u>Converting Decimals to Improper Fractions and Mixed numbers</u>**
> *Visit **mometrix.com/academy** and enter Code: **696924***

Percentages

Percentages can be thought of as fractions that are based on a whole of 100; that is, one whole is equal to 100%. The word percent means "per hundred." Fractions can be expressed as percents by finding equivalent fractions with a denomination of 100. Example: $\frac{7}{10} = \frac{70}{100} = 70\%$; $\frac{1}{4} = \frac{25}{100} = 25\%$.

To express a percentage as a fraction, divide the percentage number by 100 and reduce the fraction to its simplest possible terms. Example: $60\% = \frac{60}{100} = \frac{3}{5}$; $96\% = \frac{96}{100} = \frac{24}{25}$.

> **Review Video: <u>Percentages</u>**
> *Visit **mometrix.com/academy** and enter Code: **141911***

> **Review Video: <u>Calculation of a Percentage</u>**
> *Visit **mometrix.com/academy** and enter Code: **456247***

> **Review Video: <u>Computation with Percentages</u>**
> *Visit **mometrix.com/academy** and enter Code: **693099***

> **Review Video: <u>Finding the Percentage Decrease</u>**
> *Visit **mometrix.com/academy** and enter Code: **572167***

> **Review Video: <u>Finding the Percentage Increase</u>**
> *Visit **mometrix.com/academy** and enter Code: **176476***

Converting Percents, Fractions, and Decimals

Converting decimals to percentages and percentages to decimals is as simple as moving the decimal point. To convert from a decimal to a percent, move the decimal point two places to the right. To convert from a percent to a decimal, move it two places to the left. Example: $0.23 = 23\%$; $5.34 = 534\%$; $0.007 = 0.7\%$; $700\% = 7.00$; $86\% = 0.86$; $0.15\% = 0.0015$.

It may be helpful to remember that the percentage number will always be larger than the equivalent decimal number.

> ➤ **Review Video: <u>Converting Decimals to Fractions and Percentages</u>**
> *Visit **mometrix.com/academy** and enter **Code: 986765***

<u>Example 1</u>

15% can be written as a fraction and as a decimal. 15% written as a fraction is $\frac{15}{100}$ which equals $\frac{3}{20}$. 15% written as a decimal is 0.15.

To convert a percent to a fraction, follow these steps:

1) Write the percent over 100 because percent means "per one hundred." So, 15% can be written as $\frac{15}{100}$.

2) Fractions should be written in simplest form, which means that the numbers in the numerator and denominator should be reduced if possible. Both 15 and 100 can be divided by 5.

3) Therefore, $\frac{15 \div 5}{100 \div 5} = \frac{3}{20}$.

To convert a percent to a decimal, follow these steps:

1) Write the percent over 100 because percent means "per one hundred." So, 15% can be written as $\frac{15}{100}$.

2) 15 divided by 100 equals 0.15, so $15\% = 0.15$. In other words, when converting from a percent to a decimal, drop the percent sign and move the decimal two places to the left.

<u>Example 2</u>

Write 24.36% as a fraction and then as a decimal. Explain how you made these conversions.

24.36% written as a fraction is $\frac{24.36}{100}$, or $\frac{2436}{10,000}$, which reduces to $\frac{609}{2500}$. 24.36% written as a decimal is 0.2436. Recall that dividing by 100 moves the decimal two places to the left.

> ➤ **Review Video: <u>Converting Percentages to Decimals and Fractions</u>**
> *Visit **mometrix.com/academy** and enter **Code: 287297***

<u>Example 3</u>

Convert $\frac{4}{5}$ to a decimal and to a percent.

To convert a fraction to a decimal, simply divide the numerator by the denominator in the fraction. The numerator is the top number in the fraction and the denominator is the bottom number in a fraction. So $\frac{4}{5} = 4 \div 5 = 0.80 = 0.8$.

Percent means "per hundred." $\frac{4 \times 20}{5 \times 20} = \frac{80}{100} = 80\%$.

Example 4

Convert $3\frac{2}{5}$ to a decimal and to a percent.

The mixed number $3\frac{2}{5}$ has a whole number and a fractional part. The fractional part $\frac{2}{5}$ can be written as a decimal by dividing 5 into 2, which gives 0.4. Adding the whole to the part gives 3.4. Alternatively, note that $3\frac{2}{5} = 3\frac{4}{10} = 3.4$

To change a decimal to a percent, multiply it by 100.

$3.4(100) = 340\%$. Notice that this percentage is greater than 100%. This makes sense because the original mixed number $3\frac{2}{5}$ is greater than 1.

> ➤ **Review Video: <u>Converting Fractions to Percentages and Decimals</u>**
> *Visit **mometrix.com/academy** and enter **Code: 306233***

Operations

There are four basic mathematical operations:

Addition and Subtraction

Addition increases the value of one quantity by the value of another quantity. Example: $2 + 4 = 6$; $8 + 9 = 17$. The result is called the sum. With addition, the order does not matter. $4 + 2 = 2 + 4$.

> ➤ **Review Video: <u>Word Problems and Addition</u>**
> *Visit **mometrix.com/academy** and enter **Code: 612687***

Subtraction is the opposite operation to addition; it decreases the value of one quantity by the value of another quantity. Example: $6 - 4 = 2$; $17 - 8 = 9$. The result is called the difference. Note that with subtraction, the order does matter. $6 - 4 \neq 4 - 6$.

> ➤ **Review Video: <u>Word Problems and Subtraction</u>**
> *Visit **mometrix.com/academy** and enter **Code: 963988***

Multiplication and Division

Multiplication can be thought of as repeated addition. One number tells how many times to add the other number to itself. Example: 3×2 (three times two) $= 2 + 2 + 2 = 6$. With multiplication, the order does not matter. $2 \times 3 = 3 \times 2$ or $3 + 3 = 2 + 2 + 2$.

> ➤ **Review Video: <u>Word Problems and Multiplication</u>**
> *Visit **mometrix.com/academy** and enter **Code: 841828***

Division is the opposite operation to multiplication; one number tells us how many parts to divide the other number into. Example: $20 \div 4 = 5$; if 20 is split into 4 equal parts, each part is 5. With division, the order of the numbers does matter. $20 \div 4 \neq 4 \div 20$.

> ➤ **Review Video: <u>Word Problems and Division</u>**
> *Visit **mometrix.com/academy** and enter **Code: 442669***

<u>Order of Operations</u>
Order of Operations is a set of rules that dictates the order in which we must perform each operation in an expression so that we will evaluate it accurately. If we have an expression that includes multiple different operations, Order of Operations tells us which operations to do first. The most common mnemonic for Order of Operations is PEMDAS, or "Please Excuse My Dear Aunt Sally." PEMDAS stands for Parentheses, Exponents, Multiplication, Division, Addition, and Subtraction. It is important to understand that multiplication and division have equal precedence, as do addition and subtraction, so those pairs of operations are simply worked from left to right in order.

Example: Evaluate the expression 5+20÷4×(2+3)^2-6 using the correct order of operations.
P: Perform the operations inside the parentheses, (2+3)=5.
E: Simplify the exponents, $(5)^2$=25.
The equation now looks like this: 5+20÷4×25-6.
MD: Perform multiplication and division from left to right, 20÷4=5; then 5×25=125.
The equation now looks like this: 5+125-6.
AS: Perform addition and subtraction from left to right, 5+125=130; then 130-6=124.

> ➤ **Review Video: <u>Order of Operations</u>**
> *Visit **mometrix.com/academy** and enter **Code: 259675***

Parentheses

Parentheses are used to designate which operations should be done first when there are multiple operations. Example: $4 - (2 + 1) = 1$; the parentheses tell us that we must add 2 and 1, and then subtract the sum from 4, rather than subtracting 2 from 4 and then adding 1 (this would give us an answer of 3).

Exponents

An exponent is a superscript number placed next to another number at the top right. It indicates how many times the base number is to be multiplied by itself. Exponents provide a shorthand way to write what would be a longer mathematical expression. Example: $a^2 = a \times a$; $2^4 = 2 \times 2 \times 2 \times 2$. A number with an exponent of 2 is said to be "squared," while a number with an exponent of 3 is said to be "cubed." The value of a number raised to an exponent is called its power. So, 8^4 is read as "8 to the 4th power," or "8 raised to the power of 4." A negative exponent is the same as the reciprocal of a positive exponent. Example: $a^{-2} = \frac{1}{a^2}$.

> ➤ **Review Video: <u>Exponents and Roots</u>**
> *Visit **mometrix.com/academy** and enter **Code: 114162***

Absolute Value

A precursor to working with negative numbers is understanding what absolute values are. A number's *Absolute Value* is simply the distance away from zero a number is on the number line. The absolute value of a number is always positive and is written $|x|$.

<u>Example</u>
Show that $|3| = |-3|$.

The absolute value of 3, written as $|3|$, is 3 because the distance between 0 and 3 on a number line is three units. Likewise, the absolute value of –3, written as $|-3|$, is 3 because the distance between 0 and –3 on a number line is three units. So, $|3| = |-3|$.

> ➢ **Review Video:** <u>**Absolute Value**</u>
> *Visit **mometrix.com/academy** and enter **Code: 314669***

Operations with Positive and Negative Numbers

<u>Addition</u>
When adding signed numbers, if the signs are the same simply add the absolute values of the addends and apply the original sign to the sum. For example, $(+4) + (+8) = +12$ and $(-4) + (-8) = -12$. When the original signs are different, take the absolute values of the addends and subtract the smaller value from the larger value, then apply the original sign of the larger value to the difference. For instance, $(+4) + (-8) = -4$ and $(-4) + (+8) = +4$.

<u>Subtraction</u>
For subtracting signed numbers, change the sign of the number after the minus symbol and then follow the same rules used for addition. For example, $(+4) - (+8) = (+4) + (-8) = -4$.

<u>Multiplication</u>
If the signs are the same the product is positive when multiplying signed numbers. For example, $(+4) \times (+8) = +32$ and $(-4) \times (-8) = +32$. If the signs are opposite, the product is negative. For example, $(+4) \times (-8) = -32$ and $(-4) \times (+8) = -32$. When more than two factors are multiplied together, the sign of the product is determined by how many negative factors are present. If there are an odd number of negative factors then the product is negative, whereas an even number of negative factors indicates a positive product. For instance, $(+4) \times (-8) \times (-2) = +64$ and $(-4) \times (-8) \times (-2) = -64$.

<u>Division</u>
The rules for dividing signed numbers are similar to multiplying signed numbers. If the dividend and divisor have the same sign, the quotient is positive. If the dividend and divisor have opposite signs, the quotient is negative. For example, $(-4) \div (+8) = -0.5$.

Operations with Decimals

Adding and Subtracting Decimals

When adding and subtracting decimals, the decimal points must always be aligned. Adding decimals is just like adding regular whole numbers. Example: $4.5 + 2 = 6.5$.

If the problem-solver does not properly align the decimal points, an incorrect answer of 4.7 may result. An easy way to add decimals is to align all of the decimal points in a vertical column visually. This will allow one to see exactly where the decimal should be placed in the final answer. Begin adding from right to left. Add each column in turn, making sure to carry the number to the left if a column adds up to more than 9. The same rules apply to the subtraction of decimals.

> ➤ **Review Video: <u>Adding and Subtracting Decimals</u>**
> Visit *mometrix.com/academy* and enter *Code:* **381101**

Multiplying Decimals

A simple multiplication problem has two components: a multiplicand and a multiplier. When multiplying decimals, work as though the numbers were whole rather than decimals. Once the final product is calculated, count the number of places to the right of the decimal in both the multiplicand and the multiplier. Then, count that number of places from the right of the product and place the decimal in that position.

For example, 12.3×2.56 has three places to the right of the respective decimals. Multiply 123×256 to get 31488. Now, beginning on the right, count three places to the left and insert the decimal. The final product will be 31.488.

> ➤ **Review Video: <u>Multiplying Decimals</u>**
> Visit *mometrix.com/academy* and enter *Code:* **731574**

Dividing Decimals

Every division problem has a divisor and a dividend. The dividend is the number that is being divided. In the problem $14 \div 7$, 14 is the dividend and 7 is the divisor. In a division problem with decimals, the divisor must be converted into a whole number. Begin by moving the decimal in the divisor to the right until a whole number is created. Next, move the decimal in the dividend the same number of spaces to the right. For example, 4.9 into 24.5 would become 49 into 245. The decimal was moved one space to the right to create a whole number in the divisor, and then the same was done for the dividend. Once the whole numbers are created, the problem is carried out normally: $245 \div 49 = 5$.

> ➤ **Review Video: <u>Dividing Decimals</u>**
> Visit *mometrix.com/academy* and enter *Code:* **560690**

Operations with Fractions

Adding and Subtracting Fractions
If two fractions have a common denominator, they can be added or subtracted simply by adding or subtracting the two numerators and retaining the same denominator. Example: $\frac{1}{2} + \frac{1}{4} = \frac{2}{4} + \frac{1}{4} = \frac{3}{4}$.
If the two fractions do not already have the same denominator, one or both of them must be manipulated to achieve a common denominator before they can be added or subtracted.

> ➤ **Review Video: <u>Adding and Subtracting Fractions</u>**
> *Visit mometrix.com/academy and enter Code:* **378080**

Multiplying Fractions
Two fractions can be multiplied by multiplying the two numerators to find the new numerator and the two denominators to find the new denominator. Example: $\frac{1}{3} \times \frac{2}{3} = \frac{1 \times 2}{3 \times 3} = \frac{2}{9}$.

> ➤ **Review Video: <u>Multiplying and Dividing Fractions</u>**
> *Visit mometrix.com/academy and enter Code:* **473632**

Dividing Fractions
Two fractions can be divided by flipping the numerator and denominator of the second fraction and then proceeding as though it were a multiplication. Example: $\frac{2}{3} \div \frac{3}{4} = \frac{2}{3} \times \frac{4}{3} = \frac{8}{9}$.

> ➤ **Review Video: <u>Integers, Decimals, and Fractions</u>**
> *Visit mometrix.com/academy and enter Code:* **747659**

Factors and Multiples

Factors are numbers that are multiplied together to obtain a product. For example, in the equation $2 \times 3 = 6$, the numbers 2 and 3 are factors. A prime number has only two factors (1 and itself), but other numbers can have many factors.

> ➤ **Review Video: <u>Factors</u>**
> *Visit mometrix.com/academy and enter Code:* **920086**

A common factor is a number that divides exactly into two or more other numbers. For example, the factors of 12 are 1, 2, 3, 4, 6, and 12, while the factors of 15 are 1, 3, 5, and 15. The common factors of 12 and 15 are 1 and 3.
A prime factor is also a prime number. Therefore, the prime factors of 12 are 2 and 3. For 15, the prime factors are 3 and 5.

> ➤ **Review Video: <u>Prime Numbers, Factoring, and Prime Factorization</u>**
> *Visit mometrix.com/academy and enter Code:* **920086**

The greatest common factor (GCF) is the largest number that is a factor of two or more numbers. For example, the factors of 15 are 1, 3, 5, and 15; the factors of 35 are 1, 5, 7, and 35. Therefore, the greatest common factor of 15 and 35 is 5.

> ➢ **Review Video: <u>Greatest Common Factor</u>**
> *Visit **mometrix.com/academy** and enter **Code: 838699***

The least common multiple (LCM) is the smallest number that is a multiple of two or more numbers. For example, the multiples of 3 include 3, 6, 9, 12, 15, etc.; the multiples of 5 include 5, 10, 15, 20, etc. Therefore, the least common multiple of 3 and 5 is 15.

> ➢ **Review Video: <u>Multiples</u>**
> *Visit **mometrix.com/academy** and enter **Code: 626738***

Ratios

A ratio is a comparison of two quantities in a particular order. Example: If there are 14 computers in a lab, and the class has 20 students, there is a student to computer ratio of 20 to 14, commonly written as 20:14.

Two more comparisons used frequently in algebra are ratios and proportions. A *Ratio* is a comparison of two quantitites, expressed in a number of different ways. Ratios can be listed as "a to b", "a:b", or "a/b". Examples of ratios are miles per hour (miles/hour), meters per second (meters/second), miles per gallon (miles/gallon), etc..

> ➢ **Review Video: <u>Ratios</u>**
> *Visit **mometrix.com/academy** and enter **Code: 996914***

Proportions and Cross Products

A proportion is a relationship between two quantities that dictates how one changes when the other changes. A direct proportion describes a relationship in which a quantity increases by a set amount for every increase in the other quantity, or decreases by that same amount for every decrease in the other quantity. Example: For every 1 sheet cake, 18 people can be served cake. The number of sheet cakes, and the number of people that can be served from them is directly proportional.

A statement of two equal ratios is a *Proportion*, such as $\frac{m}{b} = \frac{w}{z}$. If Fred travels 2 miles in 1 hour and Jane travels 4 miles in 2 hours, their speeds are said to be proportional because $\frac{2}{1} = \frac{4}{2}$. In a proportion, the product of the numerator of the first ratio and the denominator of the second ratio is equal to the product of the denominator of the first ratio and the numerator of the second ratio. Using the previous example we see that $m \times z = b \times w$, thus $2 \times 2 = 1 \times 4$.

> ➢ **Review Video: <u>Proportions</u>**
> *Visit **mometrix.com/academy** and enter **Code: 505355***

Inverse proportion is a relationship in which an increase in one quantity is accompanied by a decrease in the other, or vice versa. Example: the time required for a car trip decreases as the speed increases, and increases as the speed decreases, so the time required is inversely proportional to the speed of the car.

Roots and Square Roots

A root, such as a square root, is another way of writing a fractional exponent. Instead of using a superscript, roots use the radical symbol ($\sqrt{}$) to indicate the operation. A radical will have a number underneath the bar, and may sometimes have a number in the upper left: $\sqrt[n]{a}$, read as "the nth root of a."

The relationship between radical notation and exponent notation can be described by this equation: $\sqrt[n]{a} = a^{1/n}$. The two special cases of n = 2 and n = 3 are called square roots and cube roots. If there is no number to the upper left, it is understood to be a square root (n = 2). Nearly all of the roots you encounter will be square roots. A square root is the same as a number raised to the one-half power. When we say that a is the square root of b (a = $\sqrt{b}$), we mean that a multiplied by itself equals b: (a × a = b).

A perfect square is a number that has an integer for its square root. There are 10 perfect squares from 1 to 100: 1, 4, 9, 16, 25, 36, 49, 64, 81, 100 (the squares of integers 1 through 10).

Coefficients and the Distributive Property

Coefficients
A coefficient is a number or symbol that is multiplied by a variable. For example, in the expression 2(ab), the number 2 is the coefficient of (ab). The expression can be written in other ways to have a different coefficient. For example, the expression can be 2a(b). This means that 2a is the coefficient of (b).

Distributive Property
The distributive property can be used to multiply each addend in parentheses. Then, the products are added to reach the result. The formula for the distributive property looks like this: a(b+c) = ab+ac.
Example: 6(2+4)
First, multiply 6 and 2. The answer is 12.
Then, multiply 6 and 4. The answer is 24.
Last, we add 12 and 24. The final answer is 36.

> ➤ **Review Video: <u>Distributive Property</u>**
> *Visit **mometrix.com/academy** and enter **Code: 418491***

Other Properties

Below is a list of the field properties of number systems for quick reference.

- Subtraction:
  - $a - b = a + (-b)$
- Additive Identity:
  - $a + 0 = a$
  - $0 + a = a$
- Additive Inverse:
  - $a + (-a) = 0$
  - $(-a) + a = 0$
- Associative:
  - $(a + b) + c = a + (b + c)$ for addition
  - $(ab)c = a(bc)$ for multiplication
- Closure:
  - $a + b$ is a real number for addition
  - ab is a real number for multiplication
- Commutative:
  - $a + b = b + a$ for addition
  - $ab = ba$ for multiplication
- Distributive:
  - $a(b + c) = ab + ac$
  - $(a + b)c = ac + bc$
- Multiplicative Identity:
  - $a \cdot 1 = a$
  - $1 \cdot a = a$
- Multiplicative Inverse:
  - $a \cdot a^{-1} = 1$
  - $a^{-1} \cdot a = 1$
- Division:
  - $a \div b = \frac{a}{b} = a \cdot b^{-1} = a \cdot \frac{1}{b}$

> **Review Video:** <u>Associative Property</u>
> *Visit **mometrix.com/academy** and enter **Code: 483176***

Scientific Notation

Scientific notation is a way of writing long numbers in a shorter form. The form $a \times 10^n$ is used in scientific notation. This form means that a is greater than or equal to 1 but less than 10. Also, n is the number of places the decimal must move to get from the original number to a.

Example: The number 230,400,000 is long to write. To see this value in scientific notation, place a decimal point between the first and second numbers. This includes all digits through the last non-zero digit ($a = 2.304$).

To find the correct power of 10, count the number of places the decimal point had to move ($n = 8$). The number is positive if the decimal moved to the left. Thus, the number is negative if it moved to the right. So, 230,400,000 can be written as 2.304×10^8.

Now, let's look at the number 0.00002304. We have the same value for *a*. However, this time the decimal moved 5 places to the right (n = -5). So, 0.00002304 can be written as 2.304 × 10⁻⁵. This notation makes it easy to compare very large or very small numbers. By comparing exponents, you can see that 3.28 × 10⁴ is smaller than 1.51×10⁵ because 4 is less than 5.

> ➢ **Review Video: <u>Scientific Notation</u>**
> *Visit **mometrix.com/academy** and enter **Code: 124106***

> ➢ **Review Video: <u>Changing a Number from Standard Form to Scientific Notation</u>**
> *Visit **mometrix.com/academy** and enter **Code: 182520***

Addition and Subtraction
To add and subtract numbers in scientific notation, you need the numbers to have the same power of 10. Next, you can add the constants. Then, you can use the power of 10 with the result.

If the constant is greater than 10 or less than 1, you need to move the decimal place. For constants less than 1, the decimal is moved to the right. For constants greater than 10, the decimal is moved to the left. Also, the power of 10 needs to change as you move the decimal place.

<u>Example 1</u>
In the problem $(4.8 \times 10^4) + (2.2 \times 10^4)$, the numbers have the same power of 10. So, add 4.8 and 2.2. So, you have 7 as the result. Now, the number can be written as (7×10^4).

<u>Example 2</u>
In the problem $(3.1 \times 10^8) - (2.4 \times 10^8)$, the numbers have the same power of 10. So, subtract 3.4 and 1.1. So, you have 0.7 as the result. Remember that you cannot have a constant that is less than 1. So, you need to move the decimal place one time to the right: (7×10^8). Also, the power of 10 has to change. Now, the number can be written as (7×10^{-1}).

The power of 10 is -1 because we moved the decimal place one time to the right. Now you have $(7 \times 10^{-1}) \times 10^8$. The reason is that we still have the power of 10 as 8. Now, you can add the -1 to the +8 for an answer of (7×10^7).

<u>Example 3</u>
In the problem$(5.3 \times 10^6) + (2.7 \times 10^7)$, the numbers do not have the same power of 10. So, you need one of the terms to have the same power. So, take (5.3×10^6) and change it to (0.53×10^7). Now, you can add 0.53 and 2.7. So, the number can be written as (3.23×10^7).

Multiplication
In the problem $(2.4 \times 10^3) \times (5.7 \times 10^5)$, you need to multiply 2.4 and 5.7. Then, you need to add the powers of 10 which are 3 and 5 for this example. So, you have (13.68×10^8). Remember that this cannot be an answer for scientific notation. The 13.68 for a constant is higher than 10. So, move the decimal to the left one time and change the exponent. Now, you have (1.368×10^9) as the answer.

Division
In the problem $(5.6 \times 10^6) \div (2.3 \times 10^2)$, you need to divide 5.6 and 2.3. Then, you need to subtract the powers of 10 which are 6 and 2 for this example. So, you have (2.43×10^4).

Algebra

Matrices

Matrix Basics

A **matrix** (plural: matrices) is a rectangular array of numbers or variables, often called **elements**, which are arranged in columns and rows. A matrix is generally represented by a capital letter, with its elements represented by the corresponding lowercase letter with two subscripts indicating the row and column of the element. For example, n_{ab} represents the element in row a column b of matrix N.

$$N = \begin{bmatrix} n_{11} & n_{12} & n_{13} \\ n_{21} & n_{22} & n_{23} \end{bmatrix}$$

A matrix can be described in terms of the number of rows and columns it contains in the format $a \times b$, where a is the number of rows and b is the number of columns. The matrix shown above is a 2×3 matrix. Any $a \times b$ matrix where $a = b$ is a square matrix.

Addition and Subtraction with Matrices

There are two categories of basic operations with regard to matrices: operations between a matrix and a scalar, and operations between two matrices.

Scalar Operations

A scalar being added to a matrix is treated as though it were being added to each element of the matrix:

$$M + 4 = \begin{bmatrix} m_{11} + 4 & m_{12} + 4 \\ m_{21} + 4 & m_{22} + 4 \end{bmatrix}$$

The same is true for the other three operations. Subtraction:

$$M - 4 = \begin{bmatrix} m_{11} - 4 & m_{12} - 4 \\ m_{21} - 4 & m_{22} - 4 \end{bmatrix}$$

Matrix Addition and Subtraction

All four of the basic operations can be used with operations between matrices (although division is usually discarded in favor of multiplication by the inverse), but there are restrictions on the situations in which they can be used. Matrices that meet all the qualifications for a given operation are called **conformable matrices**. However, conformability is specific to the operation; two matrices that are conformable for addition are not necessarily conformable for multiplication.

For two matrices to be conformable for addition or subtraction, they must be of the same dimension; otherwise the operation is not defined. If matrix M is a 3×2 matrix and matrix N is a 2×3 matrix, the operations $M + N$ and $M - N$ are meaningless. If matrices M and N are the same size, the operation is as simple as adding or subtracting all of the corresponding elements:

$$\begin{bmatrix} m_{11} & m_{12} \\ m_{21} & m_{22} \end{bmatrix} + \begin{bmatrix} n_{11} & n_{12} \\ n_{21} & n_{22} \end{bmatrix} = \begin{bmatrix} m_{11} + n_{11} & m_{12} + n_{12} \\ m_{21} + n_{21} & m_{22} + n_{22} \end{bmatrix}$$

$$\begin{bmatrix} m_{11} & m_{12} \\ m_{21} & m_{22} \end{bmatrix} - \begin{bmatrix} n_{11} & n_{12} \\ n_{21} & n_{22} \end{bmatrix} = \begin{bmatrix} m_{11} - n_{11} & m_{12} - n_{12} \\ m_{21} - n_{21} & m_{22} - n_{22} \end{bmatrix}$$

The result of addition or subtraction is a matrix of the same dimension as the two original matrices involved in the operation.

Polynomial Algebra

Equations are made up of monomials and polynomials. A *Monomial* is a single variable or product of constants and variables, such as x, $2x$, or $\frac{2}{x}$. There will never be addition or subtraction symbols in a monomial. Like monomials have like variables, but they may have different coefficients. *Polynomials* are algebraic expressions which use addition and subtraction to combine two or more monomials. Two terms make a binomial; three terms make a trinomial; etc.. The *Degree of a Monomial* is the sum of the exponents of the variables. The *Degree of a Polynomial* is the highest degree of any individual term.

Add Polynomials
To add polynomials, you need to add like terms. These terms have the same variable part. An example is $4x^2$ and $3x^2$ have x^2 terms. To find the sum of like terms, find the sum of the coefficients. Then, keep the same variable part. You can use the distributive property to distribute the plus sign to each term of the polynomial. For example:
$(4x^2 - 5x + 7) + (3x^2 + 2x + 1) =$
$(4x^2 - 5x + 7) + 3x^2 + 2x + 1 =$
$(4x^2 + 3x^2) + (-5x + 2x) + (7 + 1) =$
$7x^2 - 3x + 8$

Subtract Polynomials
To subtract polynomials, you need to subtract like terms. To find the difference of like terms, find the difference of the coefficients. Then, keep the same variable part. You can use the distributive property to distribute the minus sign to each term of the polynomial. For example:
$(-2x^2 - x + 5) - (3x^2 - 4x + 1) =$
$(-2x^2 - x + 5) - 3x^2 + 4x - 1 =$
$(-2x^2 - 3x^2) + (-x + 4x) + (5 - 1) =$
$-5x^2 + 3x + 4$

Multiply Polynomials

To multiply two binomials, follow the *FOIL* method. FOIL stands for:

- First: Multiply the first term of each binomial
- Outer: Multiply the outer terms of each binomial
- Inner: Multiply the inner terms of each binomial
- Last: Multiply the last term of each binomial

Using FOIL $(Ax + By)(Cx + Dy) = ACx^2 + ADxy + BCxy + BDy^2$.

Example: $(3x + 6)(4x - 2)$

First: $3x \times 4x = 12x^2$

Outer: $3x \times -2 = -6x$ | Current Expression: $12x^2 - 6x$

Inner: $6 \times 4x = 24x$ | Current Expression: $12x^2 - 6x + 24x$

Last: $6 \times -2 = -12$ | Final Expression: $12x^2 - 6x + 24x - 12$

Now, combine like terms. For this example, that is $-6x + 24x$. Then, the expression looks like: $12x^2 + 18x - 12$. Each number is a multiple of 6. So, the expression becomes $6(2x^2 + 3x - 2)$, and the polynomial has been expanded.

Divide Polynomials

To divide polynomials, start with placing the terms of each polynomial in order of one variable. You may put them in ascending or descending order. Also, be consistent with both polynomials. To get the first term of the quotient, divide the first term of the dividend by the first term of the divisor. Next, multiply the first term of the quotient by the entire divisor. Then, subtract that product from the dividend and repeat for the following terms.

You want to end with a remainder of zero or a remainder with a degree that is less than the degree of the divisor. If the quotient has a remainder, write the answer as a mixed expression in the form: quotient $+ \frac{\text{remainder}}{\text{divisor}}$.

Example: Divide $4x^5 + 3x^2 - x$ by x

$$\frac{4x^5}{x} + \frac{3x^2}{x} - \frac{x}{x} = 4x^4 + 3x - 1$$

Below are patterns of some special products to remember: *perfect trinomial squares*, the *difference between two squares*, the *sum and difference of two cubes*, and *perfect cubes*.

- Perfect Trinomial Squares: $x^2 + 2xy + y^2 = (x + y)^2$ or $x^2 - 2xy + y^2 = (x - y)^2$
- Difference between Two Squares: $x^2 - y^2 = (x + y)(x - y)$
- Sum of Two Cubes: $x^3 + y^3 = (x + y)(x^2 - xy + y^2)$
  Note: the second factor is NOT the same as a perfect trinomial square. So, do not try to factor it further.
- Difference between Two Cubes: $x^3 - y^3 = (x - y)(x^2 + xy + y^2)$
  Again, the second factor is NOT the same as a perfect trinomial square.
- Perfect Cubes: $x^3 + 3x^2y + 3xy^2 + y^3 = (x + y)^3$ and $x^3 - 3x^2y + 3xy^2 - y^3 = (x - y)^3$

<u>Factor a Polynomial</u>
1. Check for a common monomial factor.
2. Factor out the greatest common monomial factor
3. Look for patterns of special products: differences of two squares, the sum or difference of two cubes for binomial factors, or perfect trinomial squares for trinomial factors.

Example
Solve the equation $2x^2 - 5x - 12 = 0$ by factoring.

The expression $2x^2 - 5x - 12$ splits into two factors of the form $(2x + a)(x + b)$. To find *a* and *b*, you must find two factors of -12 that sum to -5 after one of them is doubled.

-12 can be factored in the following ways: 1 and -12 | 2 and -6 | 3 and -4 | 4 and -3 | 6 and -2 | 12 and -1.

Of these factors, only 3 and -4 will sum to -5 after we double one of them. Since -4 is the factor that must be doubled, it should go in position *b*, where it will be multiplied by $2x$ when the FOIL method is used. The factored expression is $(2x + 3)(x - 4)$. So, you are left with $(2x + 3)(x - 4) = 0$.

By the zero product property, each value of *x* that will make one of the factors equal zero is a solution to this equation. The first factor equals zero when $x = -1.5$, and the second factor equals zero when x = 4. So, those are the solutions.

Note: The factor may be a trinomial but not a perfect trinomial square. So, look for a factorable form: $x^2 + (a + b)x + ab = (x + a)(x + b)$
or $(ac)x^2 + (ad + bc)x + bd = (ax + b)(cx + d)$

Some factors may have four terms. So, look for groups to factor. After you have found the factors, write the original polynomial as the product of all the factors. Make sure that all of the polynomial factors are prime. Monomial factors may be prime or composite. Check your work by multiplying the factors to make sure you get the original polynomial.

> ➢ **Review Video: <u>Polynomials</u>**
> Visit *mometrix.com/academy* and enter *Code:* **305005**

Rational Expressions

Rational Expressions are fractions with polynomials in the numerator and the denominator. The value of the polynomial in the denominator cannot be equal to zero.

<u>Add or Subtract with Rational Expressions</u>
1. Find the common denominator.
2. Rewrite each fraction as an equivalent fraction with the common denominator
3. Add or subtract the numerators to get the numerator of the answer
4. Keep the common denominator as the denominator of the answer

- 65 -

<u>Multiplication with Rational Expressions</u>
1. Factor each polynomial and cancel like factors. These are the factors that are in the numerator and the denominator.
2. Multiply all remaining factors in the numerator to get the numerator of the product
3. Multiply the remaining factors in the denominator to get the denominator of the product
4. Remember: cancel entire factors, not individual terms

<u>Division with Rational Expressions</u>
1. Take the reciprocal of the divisor. This is the rational expression that you are dividing by.
2. Multiply by the dividend.

Solving Quadratic Equations

The *Quadratic Formula* is used to solve quadratic equations when other methods are more difficult. To use the quadratic formula to solve a quadratic equation, begin by rewriting the equation in standard form $ax^2 + bx + c = 0$, where a, b, and c are coefficients. Once you have identified the values of the coefficients, substitute those values into the quadratic formula $= \frac{-b \pm \sqrt{b^2 - 4ac}}{2a}$. Evaluate the equation and simplify the expression.

Again, check each root by substituting into the original equation. In the quadratic formula, the portion of the formula under the radical ($b^2 - 4ac$) is called the *Discriminant*. If the discriminant is zero, there is only one root: zero. If the discriminant is positive, there are two different real roots. If the discriminant is negative, there are no real roots.

> ➤ **Review Video: <u>Using the Quadratic Formula</u>**
> *Visit **mometrix.com/academy** and enter **Code: 163102***

To solve a quadratic equation by *Factoring*, begin by rewriting the equation in standard form, if necessary. Factor the side with the variable then set each of the factors equal to zero and solve the resulting linear equations. Check your answers by substituting the roots you found into the original equation. If, when writing the equation in standard form, you have an equation in the form $x^2 + c = 0$ or $x^2 - c = 0$, set $x^2 = -c$ or $x^2 = c$ and take the square root of c. If $c = 0$, the only real root is zero. If c is positive, there are two real roots—the positive and negative square root values. If c is negative, there are no real roots because you cannot take the square root of a negative number.

To solve a quadratic equation by *Completing the Square*, rewrite the equation so that all terms containing the variable are on the left side of the equal sign, and all the constants are on the right side of the equal sign. Make sure the coefficient of the squared term is 1. If there is a coefficient with the squared term, divide each term on both sides of the equal side by that number. Next, work with the coefficient of the single-variable term. Square half of this coefficient, and add that value to both sides. Now you can factor the left side (the side containing the variable) as the square of a binomial. $x^2 + 2ax + a^2 = C \Rightarrow (x + a)^2 = C$, where x is the variable, and a and C are constants. Take the square root of both sides and solve for the variable. Substitute the value of the variable in the original problem to check your work.

Inequalities

In algebra and higher areas of math, you will work with problems that do not equal each other. The statement comparing such expressions with symbols such as < (less than) or > (greater than) is called an *Inequality*.

One way to remember these symbols is to see that the sign for "less than" looks like an *L* for *Less*. Also, the sign for "greater than" looks like half of an *R* in g*R*eater. The terms *less than or equal to*, *at most*, or *no more than* are for the symbol ≤. Also, the terms *greater than or equal to*, *at least*, and *no less than* are for the symbol ≥.

> **Review Video: <u>Equations and Inequalities</u>**
> *Visit **mometrix.com/academy** and enter Code:* **869843**

Graphing and Solving Inequalities
Solving inequalities can be done with the same rules as for solving equations. However, when multiplying or dividing by a negative number, the direction of the inequality sign must be flipped or reversed.

Example 1
An example of an inequality is $7x > 5$. To solve for x, divide both sides by 7, and the solution is $x > \frac{5}{7}$. Graphs of the solution set of inequalities are given on a number line. Open circles are used to show that an expression approaches a number. However, the open circle points out that it is not equal to that number.

Example 2
Graph $10 > -2x + 4$.
In order to graph the inequality $10 > -2x + 4$, you need to solve for x. The opposite of addition is subtraction. So, subtract 4 from both sides. This gives you $6 > -2x$.

Next, the opposite of multiplication is division. So, divide both sides by -2. Don't forget to flip the inequality symbol because you are dividing by a negative number. Now, you have $-3 < x$. You can rewrite this as $x > -3$.

To graph an inequality, you make a number line. Then, put a circle around the value that is being compared to x. If you are graphing a *greater than* or *less than* inequality, the circle remains open. This stands for all of the values except -3. If the inequality is *greater than or equal to* or *less than or equal to*, you draw a closed circle around the value. This would stand for all of the values including the number.

Finally, look over the values that the solution stands for. Then, shade the number line in the needed direction. This example calls for graphing all of the values greater than -3. This is all of the numbers to the right of -3. So, you shade this area on the number line.

> **Review Video: <u>Linear Inequalities</u>**
> *Visit **mometrix.com/academy** and enter Code:* **439421**

> **Review Video: <u>Graphing Solutions to Linear Inequalities</u>**
> *Visit **mometrix.com/academy** and enter Code:* **391281**

Other Inequalities

Conditional Inequalities are those with certain values for the variable that will make the condition true. So, other values for the variable where the condition will be false. *Absolute Inequalities* can have any real number as the value for the variable to make the condition true. So, there is no real number value for the variable that will make the condition false.

Double Inequalities are when two inequality statements are part of the same variable expression. An example of this is $-c < ax + b < c$.

> ➤ **Review Video:** <u>**Solving Absolute Value Inequalities**</u>
> *Visit **mometrix.com/academy** and enter **Code: 997008***

Important Concepts

Substitute an Integer

Polynomial Expressions
Solve the expression $(x^2+4)+(3x^2+4x+2)$, when x=5.

First, substitute in 5 for each occurrence of 'x': $(5^2 + 4) + (3(5)^2 + 4(5) + 2) =$
Second, solve for the parentheses: $(25 + 4) + (75 + 20 + 2) =$
Third, add the totals: $29 + 97 = 126$

Linear Expressions
Solve the expression $(x - 4) + (4x + 10)$, when x=6.

First, put in 6 for every x: $(6 - 4) + (4(6) + 10)$
Second, solve the parentheses: $(2) + (34) =$
Third, add 2 and 34: $(2) + (34) = 36$

Rational Expressions
Solve the expression: $\frac{x+7}{10-x}$, when x=9
First, put in 9 for every x: $\frac{9+7}{10-9}$
Second, solve the numerator and the denominator: $\frac{16}{1}$
Third, divide 16 and 1: $\frac{16}{1}=16$.

Writing an Expression from Word-to-Symbol
To write an expression, you must first put variables with the unknown values in the problem. Then, translate the words and phrases into expressions that have numbers and symbols.

Inequalities
To write out an inequality, you may need to translate a sentence into an inequality. This translation is putting the words into symbols. When translating, choose a variable to stand for the unknown value. Then, change the words or phrases into symbols. For example, the sum of 2 and a number is at most 12. So, you would write: $2 + b \leq 12$.

Example: A farm sells vegetables and dairy products. One third of the sales from dairy products plus half of the sales from vegetables should be greater than the monthly payment (P) for the farm.

Let d stand for the sales from dairy products. Let v stand for the sales from vegetables. One third of the sales from dairy products is the expression $\frac{d}{3}$. One half of the sales from vegetables is the expression $\frac{v}{2}$. The sum of these expressions should be greater than the monthly payment for the farm. An inequality for this is $\frac{d}{3} + \frac{v}{2} > P$.

> ➤ **Review Video: <u>Solving Inequalities Using All Four Basic Operations</u>**
> *Visit **mometrix.com/academy** and enter **Code: 401111***

Rational Expressions
John and Luke play basketball every week. John can make 5 free throws per minute faster than Luke can make three-point shots. On one day, John made 30 free throws in the same time that it took Luke to make 10 three-point shots. So, how fast are Luke and John scoring points?

First, set up what you know. You know that John made 30 free throws, and he had a rate of 5 free throws per minute faster than Luke's three point shots: $\frac{30}{x+5}$. The x is for Luke's speed. Also, you know that Luke made 20 three point shots in the same amount of time that John scored his free throws: $\frac{20}{x}$. So, we can set up proportions because their times are equal.

$$\frac{30}{x + 5} = \frac{20}{x}$$

Cross factor the proportion: $30x = 20(x + 5)$

Then, distribute the 20 across the parentheses: $30x = 20x + 100$
Now, you can subtract 20x from both sides of the equation, and you are left with: $10x = 100$

So, you can divide both sides by 10: $\frac{10x}{10} = \frac{100}{10}$
Now, you are left with: $x = 10$. So, Luke's speed was 10 three-point shots per minute. Then, John's speed was 15 free throws per minute.

Polynomial Expressions
Fred buys some CDs for $12 each. He also buys two DVDs. The total that Fred spent is $60. So, write an equation that shows the connection between the number of CDs and the average cost of a DVD.

Let c stand for the number of CDs that Fred buys. Also, let d stand for the average cost of one of the DVDs that Fred buys. The expression 12c gives the cost of the CDs. Also, the expression 2d gives the cost of the DVDs. So, the equation 12c + 2d = 60 states the number of CDs and the average cost of a DVD.

Solve Equations in One Variable

Manipulating Equations

Sometimes you will have variables missing in equations. So, you need to find the missing variable. To do this, you need to remember one important thing: whatever you do to one side of an equation, you need to do to the other side. If you subtract 100 from one side of an equation, you need to subtract 100 from the other side of the equation. This will allow you to change the form of the equation to find missing values.

Example

Ray earns \$10 an hour. This can be given with the expression $10x$, where x is equal to the number of hours that Ray works. This is the independent variable. The independent variable is the amount that can change. The money that Ray earns is in y hours. So, you would write the equation: $10x = y$. The variable y is the dependent variable. This depends on x and cannot be changed. Now, let's say that Ray makes \$360. How many hours did he work to make \$360?

$$10x = 360$$

Now, you want to know how many hours that Ray worked. So, you want to get x by itself. To do that, you can divide both sides of the equation by 10.

$$\frac{10x}{10} = \frac{360}{10}$$

So, you have: $x = 36$. Now, you know that Ray worked 36 hours to make \$360.

Solving One Variable Linear Equations

Another way to write an equation is $ax + b = 0$ where $a \neq 0$. This is known as a *One Variable Linear Equation*. A solution to an equation is called a *Root*.
Example: $5x + 10 = 0$
If we solve for x, the solution is $x = -2$. In other words, the root of the equation is -2.
The first step is to subtract 10 from both sides. This gives $5x = -10$.

Next, divide both sides by the coefficient of the variable. For this example, that is 5. So, you should have $x = -2$. You can make sure that you have the correct answer by placing -2 back into the original equation. So, the equation now looks like this: $(5)(-2) + 10 = -10 + 10 = 0$.

> ➤ **Review Video: <u>Solving Equations Using Addition and Subtraction</u>**
> *Visit **mometrix.com/academy** and enter **Code: 447444***

> ➤ **Review Video: <u>Solving Equations Using Multiplication and Division</u>**
> *Visit **mometrix.com/academy** and enter **Code: 817870***

> ➤ **Review Video: <u>Solving Equations Using All Four Basic Operations</u>**
> *Visit **mometrix.com/academy** and enter **Code: 465867***

The *Solution Set* is the set of all solutions to an equation. In the last example, the solution set would be -2. If there were more solutions, then they would also be included in the solution set. Usually, there are more solutions in multivariable equations. When an equation has no true solutions, this is known as an *Empty Set*. Equations with identical solution sets are *Equivalent Equations*. An *Identity* is a term whose value or determinant is equal to 1.

To solve a *Radical Equation*, start by placing the radical term on one side of the equation by itself. Then, move all other terms to the other side of the equation. Look at the index of the radical symbol. Remember, if no number is given, then you have a square root. Raise both sides of the equation to the power equal to the index of the radical. Solve the equation as you would a normal polynomial equation. When you have found the roots, you must check them in the original problem to remove any remaining roots.

Systems of Equations

Systems of Equations are a set of simultaneous equations that all use the same variables. A solution to a system of equations must be true for each equation in the system. *Consistent Systems* are those with at least one solution. *Inconsistent Systems* are systems of equations that have no solution.

> ➤ **Review Video: Systems of Equations**
> *Visit **mometrix.com/academy** and enter Code:* **658153**

To solve a system of linear equations by *substitution*, start with the easier equation and solve for one of the variables. Express this variable in terms of the other variable. Substitute this expression in the other equation, and solve for the other variable. The solution should be expressed in the form (x, y). Substitute the values into both of the original equations to check your answer. Consider the following problem. Solve the system using substitution:

$$x + 6y = 15$$
$$3x - 12y = 18$$

$$x = 15 - 6y$$
$$3(15 - 6y) - 12y = 18$$
$$45 - 18y - 12y = 18$$
$$30y = 27$$
$$y = \frac{27}{30} = \frac{9}{10} = 0.9$$
$$x = 15 - 6(0.9) = 15 - 5.4 = 9.6$$

Now check both equations

$$9.6 + 6(0.9) = 9.6 + 5.4 = 15$$
$$3(9.6) - 12(0.9) = 28.8 - 10.8 = 18$$

Therefore, the solution is (9.6, 0.9).

To solve a system of equations using *elimination* or *addition*, begin by rewriting both equations in standard form $Ax + By = C$. Check to see if the coefficients of one pair of like variables add to zero. If not, multiply one or both of the equations by a non-zero number to make one set of like variables add to zero. Add the two equations to solve for one of the variables. Substitute this value into one of the original equations to solve for the other variable. Check your work by substituting into the other equation. Next we will solve the same problem as above, but using the addition method.

Solve the system using substitution:

$$x + 6y = 15$$
$$3x - 12y = 18$$

For practice we will multiply the first equation by 6 and the second equation by -2 to get rid of the x variables.

$$6x + 36y = 90$$
$$-6x + 24y = -36$$

Add the equations together to get $60y = 54$. Thus, $y = \frac{54}{60} = \frac{9}{10} = 0.9$.

Plug the value for y back in to either of the original equations to get the value for x.

$$x + 6(0.9) = 15$$
$$x = 15 - 5.4 = 9.6$$

Now check both equations

$$9.6 + 6(0.9) = 9.6 + 5.4 = 15$$
$$3(9.6) - 12(0.9) = 28.8 - 10.8 = 18$$

Therefore, the solution is $(9.6, 0.9)$.

> ➤ **Review Video: Linear Equations Basics**
> Visit *mometrix.com/academy* and enter *Code:* **793005**

> ➤ **Review Video: Linear Equations**
> Visit *mometrix.com/academy* and enter *Code:* **746745**

Functions

Function Notation

Equations use numbers to show the equality of two expressions. These equations use the variables x and y. Equation notation is written in "$y =$" form. With an equation, you can find values for x and y by putting in a value for x and solving for y. These values are given as ordered pairs in a table of values. Then, the ordered pairs can be used as coordinates to graph the equation. An equation is a function if there is a relationship between x and y. The relationship is that for every x-value, there is only one y-value. This can be decided from a graph using the vertical line test.

Function notation is written in the "$f(x)$" form. The notation y and $f(x)$ are basically the same. The y refers to an equation. The $f(x)$ refers to a function. Knowing that an equation is a function can give you more information about its graph. Functions use equations to show relationships between quantities. All functions have equations. However, not all equations are functions.

Determining a Function

You can decide if an equation is a function by putting in different values into the equation for x. These values are called input values. All possible input values are known as the domain. The result of putting these values into the equation is called the output or range. You can show and organize these numbers in a data table.

A data table has the values for x and y which you can list as coordinates. For a function to exist, the table cannot have any repeating x-values that go with different y-values. If each x-coordinate has one y-coordinate, the table has a function. However, there can be repeating y-values that go with different x-values. An example of this is when the function has an exponent. For example, $x^2 = y$. So, $2^2 = 4$, and $(-2)^2 = 4$.

For example, look at the following graphs.

The vertical line test is used to decide if a graph has a function. The test says that if you pass a vertical line anywhere along the graph, then the line will only pass through the graph at one point. If it passes through the graph at more than one point, it is not considered a function. The vertical line in the image on the left intersects the graph in three points. So, the graph on the left is *not* a function. On the right, it does not matter where you place the vertical line. The line will never intersect more than one point. So, the graph on the right is a function.

Finding the Domain of the Function
A function is given in the table below. How can you find the domain of the function?

x	0	3	2	1	8	10	6	7
$f(x)$	2	8	6	8	2	3	4	5

The *domain* of a function $f(x)$ is the set of all input values for a function. It is simple to find the domain of a function with this table. The reason is that every point in the function (i.e., every input-output pair) is given to you.

To find the domain, list all the *x* values. So, you have {0, 3, 2, 1, 8, 10, 6, 7}. Or, you can put them in ascending order: {0, 1, 2, 3, 6, 7, 8, 10}. You do not have to put the values in ascending order. However, this does make the set easier to read.

Note that you don't have to worry about an input value being repeated. By definition of a function, no input value can go with more than one output value.

> ➤ **Review Video: <u>Using a Graph</u>**
> *Visit **mometrix.com/academy** and enter **Code: 255891***

Finding the Domain of a Function from a Graph
The domain of a function can be seen from the graph by looking for the values of *x*. Basically, if a vertical line drawn through the graph at a *x* value intercepts the graph of the function, then the function is defined at that point. If a vertical line intercepts the function no matter where it is drawn, then the domain is all real numbers.

Special Cases
Sometimes the full graph of a function cannot be displayed. So, the vertical line test cannot always be used. An asymptote is a line that a curve is always moving towards. Yet the curve never meets the line. Usually, if a function has an asymptote, it will be displayed on the graph as a dashed line. A function is never defined at a vertical asymptote.

If $f(x)$ is limited at the endpoint of the interval, then the endpoint is drawn as a filled circle to show that it is part of the function. Or, there is an empty circle to show that is not part of the function. The graph on the left has a domain of $[-1, \infty)$. The graph on the right has a domain of $(-1, \infty)$.

Finding the Range of a Function
A function is given in the table below. How can you find the range of the function?

x	-1	4	2	1	0	3	8	6
$f(x)$	3	0	3	−1	−1	2	4	6

The *range* of a function $f(x)$ is the set of all possible output values of the function. In other words, it includes every possible value of $f(x)$ for all values of x in the function's domain. It's easy to find the range with the table above. The reason is that every point in the function (i.e., every input-output pair) is given to you.

To find the range, you can list all the values of $f(x)$. For this example, that would be {3, 0, 3, −1, −1, 2, 4, 6}. Some of these values come up more than once. This is allowed for a function.

Each value of x must be matched to one value of $f(x)$. However, the opposite is not true. So, you don't need to list each value more than once. Now, the range is {3, 0, −1, 2, 4, 6}. You do not have to put the values in increasing order. However, this does make the set easier to read.

Function and Relation
When expressing functional relationships, the variables x and y are used. These values are written as the coordinates (x, y). The x-value is the independent variable. The y-value is the dependent variable. A relation is a set of data where there is not one y-value for each x-value in the data set. This means that there can be two of the same x-values that go with different y-values.

A relation is simply a relationship between the x and y-values in each coordinate. This does not apply to the relationship between the values of x and y in the data set. A function is a relation where one quantity depends on the other. For example, the amount of money that you make depends on the number of hours that you work. In a function, each x-value in the data set has one y-value. The reason is that the y-value depends on the x-value.

Graphing a Function
To graph a function, make a table of values based on the equation from the problem. Choose *x*-values for the table. Then, put them into the equation to find the matching *y*-values. There need to be at least 2 x-values for linear functions and more for quadratic.

Use each *x* and *y* value as a coordinate pair. Then, put these points on the coordinate grid. Next, connect the points with a line. The graph of a function will show a relationship among the coordinates so there are no two *y*-values for each *x*-value. Also, use the vertical line test to decide if a graph has a function.

> ➢ **Review Video: Graphs of Functions**
> *Visit **mometrix.com/academy** and enter Code:* **492785**

Graphs of Linear and Quadratic Functions

Linear functions are in the form $y = x$. When they are graphed, they make a straight line. To graph a function, you need to find at least two points on the line. Choose values for x and put them into the equation. If $y = x$, then $0 = 0$, $1 = 1$, $2 = 2$, and so on. This means that the coordinates $(0, 0)$, $(1, 1)$, and $(2, 2)$ are on the line.

> **Review Video: Graphing Linear Equations**
> Visit *mometrix.com/academy* and enter *Code: 479576*

> **Review Video: Changing Constants in Graphs of Functions: Linear Functions**
> Visit *mometrix.com/academy* and enter *Code: 699478*

Quadratic functions are written as $y = x^2$. When graphed, they make a u-shaped parabola. Every x-value is squared (i.e., multiplied by itself). After multiplying, you will find that the coordinates $(-2, 4)$, $(1, 1)$, and $(2, 4)$ are on the parabola. The graphs go forever in both directions. So, they have an unending number of points. These graphs are called the parent functions of linear and quadratic equations. The reason is that they are the most basic in their family of functions. The equations do not have any coefficients or constants.

> **Review Video: Changing Constants in Graphs of Functions: Quadratic Equations**
> Visit *mometrix.com/academy* and enter *Code: 798319*

> **Review Video: Solutions of a Quadratic Equation on a Graph**
> Visit *mometrix.com/academy* and enter *Code: 328231*

Example

You drive 12 miles to school and keep a constant speed until you come to traffic at 7:40 am. When the traffic clears, you return to your original speed until you get to school. Explain what the graph of this function would look like.

First, think about the variables that are part of this situation. You are comparing the miles that you travel to school, and the time that it takes you to get there. On the graph, the line that is made by this relationship stands for the speed that you travel. The graph should have the correct labels and scales. So, the independent variable (e.g., the time) goes on the x-axis. The dependent variable (e.g., the distance) goes on the y-axis.

If you keep a constant speed, the graph would show a diagonal line increasing from zero. When you are stopped in traffic at 7:40 am, the distance is not increasing. However, the time is increasing. So, you would see the line going horizontally for an amount of time. When the traffic clears, the line would again increase diagonally. This would stand for the return of the speed. You can use the graph to look at trends in the data to predict future events.

Writing a Function Rule Using a Table

With a set of data, place the matching x and y-values into a table. Then, review the relationship between them. Think about what you can do to each x-value to have the matching y-value. Try adding or subtracting different numbers to and from x. Then, try multiplying or dividing different numbers to and from x.

If none of these operations give you the y-value, try combining the operations. When you find a rule that works for one pair, make sure to try it with each set of ordered pairs in the table. If the same operation or combination of operations takes care of each set of coordinates, then the table has a function. Then, the rule is used to write the equation of the function in "y =" form.

Example
What does the statement f(x) = x² + 1 mean?

This kind of statement defines a certain function. The statement tells how to match up each point in the domain with a point in the range. The possible values of x are part of the domain. Usually, this can be thought to have all real numbers unless you are told that it does not. Or, you are told that there are some points that make the expression on the right side of the equation undefined. Then, each value of x is matched with a value of $f(x)$ (or y) that may not be unique. All the values of $f(x)$ that are matched to values of x are part of the range.

The statement $f(x) = x^2 + 1$ defines a function where each real number x is matched to the number $x^2 + 1$. For example, $x = 0$ means that $f(0) = 0^2 + 1 = 1$. Also, $= 1 f(1) = 1^2 + 1 = 2$. Now, this will continue for each real number. Note that $f(x)$ in this example can never be less than 1. So, the range of this function is $[1, \infty)$.

Relative Maximum and Relative Minimum

A *relative maximum* of a function is a point where the function has a higher value than any other point that is near it. In other words, a relative maximum is a point (x, y). Let's say that we choose an acceptable small interval around x. Then, $f(x) > f(c)$ for any other point within the interval (c).

A relative minimum is just the opposite. This is a point where the function has a *lower* value than any other point that is near it. In other words, a point (x, y). Let's say that we choose an acceptable small interval around x. Then, $f(x) < f(c)$ for any other point within the interval (c).

A function may have many relative maxima* and relative minima*. However, it may have none. A linear function like $y = x$ has no relative maxima or minima. Now, $y = \sin(x)$ has an unending amount of relative maxima and minima.

*Note that *maxima* is plural for maximum. Also, *minima* is plural for minimum.

Finding a Relative Maximum or Minimum from a Graph
At a relative maximum, the graph goes from increasing to decreasing. This makes a "peak" on the graph. Also, at a relative minimum, the graph goes from decreasing to increasing. This makes a "trough". On the graph below, the points A and C are relative maxima. The point B is a relative minimum.

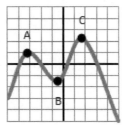

Note that point A is a relative maximum. However, this is not an absolute maximum. Also, this function has a higher value at point C. Now, point B is a relative minimum. However, this is not an absolute minimum. Also, the function has a lower value at the left and right ends of the graph than at point B. Point C is a relative and an absolute maximum. The reason is that at no place on the graph is there a function that has a higher value than at point C.

Periodic Functions

A function is *periodic* if there is a repetition of the same shape. In other words, a periodic function is unchanged if it is moved some distance left or right on the graph. The distance that it has to be moved is called the function's *period* (P). A function $f(x)$ is periodic if $f(x + P) = f(x)$ for all x. Note that if this is true for P, then it's also true for all multiples of P. However, the function's period is known as the smallest possible value of P that the relation holds.

Symmetrical Functions

A function is symmetrical if it does not change with certain kinds of transformations. There are many kinds of transformations and symmetries. For functions, the type of transformation that is considered is reflection. Two important pieces are reflections through the y-axis and reflections through the origin on a coordinate plane.

If the mirror image (i.e., reflection) of a function is the same through the y-axis, then the function is symmetrical. This can be written as $f(x) = f(-x)$. This function is known to be *even*. A function can be symmetrical with reflection through the origin. The function needs to stay the same when each point is reflected to the other side of the origin. This can be written as $f(x) = -f(-x)$. This function is known to be *odd*.

A periodic function is also symmetrical. This may not be with reflection. However, this can be done with *translation*. The function is unchanged when translated (i.e., moved) horizontally by a distance that is equal to the function's period.

Function's End Behavior

A function's *end behavior* is its tendency or activity at the extreme right and left sides of the graph. In other words, this is what happens to the function as x moves towards positive or negative ∞. There are three main possibilities.

First, $f(x)$ increases without limit (i.e., $f(x)$ goes to infinity). Second, $f(x)$ decreases without limit (i.e., $f(x)$ goes to negative infinity). Third, $f(x)$ tends toward some finite value (i.e., a horizontal asymptote). The behavior may be different at the two sides. For example, while $f(x) = x^2$ goes to ∞ on both sides, $g(x) = x^3$ goes to ∞ on the right side and to $-∞$ on the left. Also, $h(x) = e^{-x}$ goes to ∞ on the left and approaches the horizontal asymptote $y = 0$ on the right.

Comparing Properties of Functions

<u>Example 1</u>
One function is represented algebraically and one graphically. Which has the larger maximum?

You can compare two functions that are given in different ways by changing them to the same way of being presented. If one function is given algebraically and the other graphically, you can graph the first function on the same axis as the second. This allows you to see the comparison of their maxima. So, you can know which one goes farther in the positive y direction.

Also, you can compare their maxima without changing them to the same way of being presented. For example, you can find the maximum of each function and compare them. A function that be expressed algebraically is one that you can find the maximum analytically (e.g., a quadratic function). So, you can compare that value directly with the maximum estimated from the graphed function by looking at the y coordinate of its highest peak.

Example 2
One function is given algebraically and the other in a verbal description. How can you know which has the larger maximum?

You can compare two functions in different formats by changing the functions to the same format. One of the functions may be given in the form of a verbal description. So, you can write an algebraic expression to stand for the described relationship.

For example, you're told that a function is for the area of a rectangular field. Also, the total distance around three sides is 40 meters. So, you write $l + 2w = 40$.

Also, you can write the relationship between the area and the width in algebraic form as $A = l \cdot w = (40 - 2w)w$. Or, using the more familiar f and x, $f(x) = (40 - 2x)x = -2x^2 + 40x$. Now, completing the square gives you $f(x) = -2(x - 10)^2 + 200$. This function has a maximum when $x = 10$ where $f(x) = 200$. Also, you can find the maximum of the other function that is given in algebraic form. Now, we can compare the maxima directly.

Example 3
One function is given graphically and one in a table. How you can find which has the larger y intercept?

You can compare two functions in different formats by changing the functions to the same format. If one of the functions is given as a table, you can graph that function. Then, compare it to the graph. As another way, you can find the values of the graphed function at the x values given in the table. Then, you can give both functions in table format.

Sometimes you can compare properties of the functions without changing them to the same format. When you need to find the y intercept, then this isn't difficult. Note that this way assumes that the y intercept of the second function is given in the table.

Also, you can find the y intercept of the graphed function by finding where the graph crosses the y-axis. Then, find the y intercept of the table function. Look for which value of the function matches with a x value of 0. Then, compare these values.

Writing Recursively Defined Functions

A recursively defined function is generally a *sequence*; that is, its domain consists of a subset of the integers (usually, though not always, the positive integers). Furthermore, the value of the function for a given value of x must be defined in terms of its value for smaller values of x. Often this means

$f(x)$ is defined in terms of $f(x-1)$, though it may also be defined in terms of even smaller values. Finally, we need to have $f(x_0)$ explicitly defined for the smallest value or values of x_0 to give us a starting point.

For example, consider the following relationship: A pile of stones starts with three stones, and then every day its size is doubled and then one stone is removed. On day one, then, the size of the pile is $f(1) = 3$. On day x thereafter, we have the relationship $f(x) = 2f(x-1) - 1$. This is a valid recursive definition.

Situations Modeled by Arithmetic Sequences

An arithmetic sequence is a good model for any situation that involves a quantity that increases at equal intervals by a constant difference. That is, if the quantity is only defined relative to the positive integers (or technically at any other discrete, evenly spaced intervals), and the difference between the quantity corresponding to any two consecutive integers is the same, then it can be modeled by an arithmetic sequence.

Consider, for instance, the following situation: a large jar initially contains five marbles, and every day three more marbles are added to it. This fits the criteria described above: the quantity is defined relative to the positive integers (number of days), and the difference between the quantity corresponding to consecutive integers (the number of marbles on consecutive days) is constant (three). We can model this situation by the arithmetic sequence $f(n) = 5 + 3(n-1)$.

> ➤ **Review Video: <u>Arithmetic Sequence</u>**
> Visit **mometrix.com/academy** and enter **Code: 676885**

Situations Modeled by Geometric Sequences

A geometric sequence is a good model for any situation that involves a quantity that increases at fixed intervals by a fixed ratio. That is, if the quantity is only defined relative to the positive integers (or technically at any other discrete, evenly spaced intervals), and the ratio of the quantity corresponding to any two consecutive integers is the same, then it can be modeled by a geometric sequence.

Consider, for instance, the following situation: the score for completing level one of a video game is 100, and the score for completing each level afterward is double the score for the previous level. This fits the criteria described above: the quantity is defined relative to the positive integers (levels), and the ratio between the quantity corresponding to consecutive integers (the scores for completing two consecutive levels) is constant (two). We can model this situation by the geometric sequence $f(n) = 100 \cdot 2^{n-1}$.

Identifying the Zeros of Functions and Polynomial

<u>Linear Factors of a Quadratic Expression and the Zeros of a Related Function</u>
Example: (x – a) and (x – b)
If the linear factors of a quadratic expression are $(x - a)$ and $(x - b)$, then the quadratic function can be written as $y = k(x - a)(x - b)$, where k is a nonzero constant. The zeros of this function are the values of x for which $y = 0$. Direct substitution of a or b for x makes the value of y equal to 0, so $x = a$ and $x = b$ are zeros of the quadratic function. Note that the value of k may affect the shape or direction of the graph of the function, but not the x-intercepts (the zeros of the function).

Finding the Zeros of a Function

Example: $y = 4x^2 - 10x$

The zeros of the function $y = 4x^2 - 10x$ are the values of x for which $y = 0$. To find the zeros, factor the right side of the equation, and set $y = 0$:

$$y = 4x^2 - 10x$$
$$y = 2x(2x - 5)$$
$$0 = 2x(2x - 5)$$

Next, since a product is only equal to zero if at least one of the terms is zero, set the linear factors of the function $2x$ and $(2x - 5)$ equal to 0:

$$2x = 0 \qquad 2x - 5 = 0$$
$$x = 0 \qquad 2x = 5$$
$$x = \frac{5}{2}$$

The zeros of the function $y = 4x^2 - 10x$ are $x = 0$ and $x = \frac{5}{2}$.

Zeros of a Quadratic Function

Give an Example of a Quadratic Function with Zeros $x = 1$ and $x = -3$

If a is a zero of a quadratic function, then $(x - a)$ is a factor of the quadratic expression that defines the function. Therefore $(x - 1)$ and $(x + 3)$ are both factors of the quadratic function. Quadratic functions with these zeros therefore have the form $y = k(x - 1)(x + 3)$. The reason that this is just a form, and not a unique function, is because multiplying the two binomial factors by any nonzero constant results in another quadratic function with the same zeros. For example, the functions $y = -5(x - 1)(x + 3)$ and $y = 7(x - 1)(x + 3)$ have zeros $x = 1$ and $x = -3$.

Factor a Quadratic Expression to Find the Zeros of a Function

Example: Find the x-intercepts of $y = 9x^2 - 6x + 1$.

The x-intercepts of $y = 9x^2 - 6x + 1$ are the zeros of the function. These can be determined by first factoring the quadratic expression $9x^2 - 6x + 1$: $9x^2 - 6x + 1 = (3x - 1)(3x - 1) = (3x - 1)^2$

The expression is a perfect square trinomial. Because the two factors are the same, there is only one x-intercept of the function. Set the factor equal to 0:

$$3x - 1 = 0$$
$$3x = 1$$
$$x = \frac{1}{3}$$

The x-intercept of $y = 9x^2 - 6x + 1$ is therefore $x = \frac{1}{3}$.

Zeros of a Polynomial with Cubics and Higher Polynomials

We can find the zeros of a polynomial by factoring it. Cubics and higher polynomials can be difficult to factor, but there are special cases that can be readily factored. In the first sample polynomial here, for instance, $x^3 - 3x^2 - 4x$, it's clear that every term of the polynomial is divisible by x. We can therefore factor out the x to get $x(x^2 - 3x - 4)$. This now leaves a quadratic factor, which can be further factored to yield $x(x + 1)(x - 4)$. The zeros of the polynomial are therefore 0, –1, and 4.

Graphing a Polynomial

To graph a polynomial, like most other functions, there are a few key characteristics we can observe. First, we can observe the end behavior, which depends only on the largest order term. To find the y intercept, we evaluate the function at $x = 0$. To find the x intercepts, the points where the polynomial equals zero, is a little harder, but often we can factor the function and set each factor equal to zero. Depending on the polynomial, there may be other characteristics we can find, such as the local maxima and minima.

Example: $\frac{1}{4}x^4 - \frac{9}{4}x^2$

Since the highest order term has an even order and a positive coefficient, the polynomial goes to positive infinity at both ends. The y intercept is at $\frac{1}{4}(0^4) - \frac{9}{4}(0^2) = 0$. We can factor the polynomial as $\frac{1}{4}x^4 - \frac{9}{4}x^2 = \frac{1}{4}x^2(x^2 - 9) = \frac{1}{4}x^2(x + 3)(x - 3)$, so it has x intercepts at $x = 0, 3$, and -3. Its graph looks like this:

Rate of Change of a Function

Table

The function's average rate of change over the interval $[x_1, x_2]$ can be calculated as $\frac{f(x_2)-f(x_1)}{x_2-x_1}$. For the sample table, for instance, if we want to determine the function's rate of change during the entire interval represented in the table, then $x_1 = 0$ and $x_2 = 16$. By reference to the table, $f(x_1) = f(0) = -100$, and $f(x_2) = f(16) = 100$. Thus, the function's rate of change is equal to $\frac{100-(-100)}{16-0} = \frac{200}{16} = 12.5$.

x	0	2	4	6	8	10	12	14	16
$f(x)$	-100	-54	-26	-10	0	10	26	54	100

If on the other hand we only want to find the rate of change between 0 and 4, then $x_1 = 0, x_2 = 4$, $f(x_1) = f(0) = -100$, and $f(x_2) = f(4) = -26$. The rate of change is then $\frac{-26-(-100)}{4-0} = \frac{74}{4} = 18.5$. If we are asked for the rate of change in the interval $[6, 10]$, then $x_1 = 6, x_2 = 10, f(x_1) = f(6) = -10$, and $f(x_2) = f(10) = 10$. The rate of change is then $\frac{10-(-10)}{10-6} = \frac{20}{4} = 5$.

Algebraic

The function's average rate of change over the interval $[x_1, x_2]$ can be calculated as $\frac{f(x_2)-f(x_1)}{x_2-x_1}$. Example: $f(x) = x^2 + 1$. Find the function's average rate of change between 0 and 10. So, $x_1 = 0$ and $x_2 = 10$.

To find $f(x_1)$ and $f(x_2)$, we simply evaluate the function at these two points: $f(x_1) = f(0) = 0^2 + 1 = 1$, and $f(x_2) = f(10) = 10^2 + 1 = 101$. The function's average rate of change in this interval is therefore $\frac{101-1}{10-0} = \frac{100}{10} = 10$.

If we're asked to find the function's average rate of change over the interval [-4, 2], then $x_1 = -4$, $x_2 = 2$, $f(x_1) = f(-4) = (-4)^2 + 1 = 17$, and $f(x_2) = f(2) = 2^2 + 1 = 5$. The average rate of change is therefore $\frac{5-17}{2-(-4)} = \frac{-12}{6} = -2$. If we're asked to find the average rate of change over the interval [-5, 5], then $x_1 = -5$, $x_2 = 5$, $f(x_1) = f(-5) = (-5)^2 + 1 = 26$, and $f(x_2) = f(5) = 5^2 + 1 = 26$. The average rate of change is therefore $\frac{26-26}{5-(-5)} = \frac{0}{10} = 0$.

Estimate from a Graph

To estimate the average rate of change over an interval for a function given graphically, then, we have to estimate the coordinates of the endpoints of the desired interval and then put the appropriate values into that expression and carry out the calculation.

For example, consider the sample function over the entire interval shown on the graph, $[-5,5]$. At the left end is passes through the point $(-5, -5)$, and at the right end $(5,5)$; the average rate of change is therefore $\frac{f(5)-f(-5)}{5-(-5)} = \frac{5-(-5)}{10} = \frac{10}{10} = 1$. If we instead consider the interval $[-2,0]$, the left endpoint is about $(-2,1)$ and the right about $(0,-2)$; the average rate of change over the interval $[-2, 0]$ is then $\frac{f(0)-f(-2)}{0-(-2)} = \frac{-2-1}{2} = \frac{-3}{2} = -\frac{3}{2}$. The average rate of change over the interval $[-5, 0]$ is $\frac{f(0)-f(-5)}{0-(-5)} = \frac{-2-(-5)}{5} = \frac{3}{5}$.

Geometry

Lines and Planes

A point is a fixed location in space; has no size or dimensions; commonly represented by a dot.

A line is a set of points that extends infinitely in two opposite directions. It has length, but no width or depth. A line can be defined by any two distinct points that it contains. A line segment is a portion of a line that has definite endpoints. A ray is a portion of a line that extends from a single point on that line in one direction along the line. It has a definite beginning, but no ending.

A plane is a two-dimensional flat surface defined by three non-collinear points. A plane extends an infinite distance in all directions in those two dimensions. It contains an infinite number of points, parallel lines and segments, intersecting lines and segments, as well as parallel or intersecting rays. A plane will never contain a three-dimensional figure or skew lines. Two given planes will either be parallel or they will intersect to form a line. A plane may intersect a circular conic surface, such as a cone, to form conic sections, such as the parabola, hyperbola, circle or ellipse.

Perpendicular lines are lines that intersect at right angles. They are represented by the symbol $\perp$. The shortest distance from a line to a point not on the line is a perpendicular segment from the point to the line.

Parallel lines are lines in the same plane that have no points in common and never meet. It is possible for lines to be in different planes, have no points in common, and never meet, but they are not parallel because they are in different planes.

A bisector is a line or line segment that divides another line segment into two equal lengths. A perpendicular bisector of a line segment is composed of points that are equidistant from the endpoints of the segment it is dividing.

Intersecting lines are lines that have exactly one point in common. Concurrent lines are multiple lines that intersect at a single point.

A transversal is a line that intersects at least two other lines, which may or may not be parallel to one another. A transversal that intersects parallel lines is a common occurrence in geometry.

Coordinate Plane

When algebraic functions and equations are shown graphically, they are usually shown on a *Cartesian Coordinate Plane*. The Cartesian coordinate plane consists of two number lines placed perpendicular to each other, and intersecting at the zero point, also known as the origin. The horizontal number line is known as the *x*-axis, with positive values to the right of the origin, and negative values to the left of the origin. The vertical number line is known as the *y*-axis, with positive values above the origin, and negative values below the origin.

Any point on the plane can be identified by an ordered pair in the form (*x,y*), called coordinates. The *x*-value of the coordinate is called the abscissa, and the *y*-value of the coordinate is called the ordinate. The two number lines divide the plane into four quadrants: I, II, III, and IV.

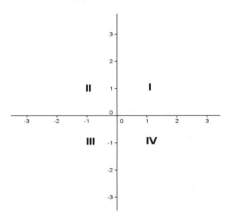

Before learning the different forms equations can be written in, it is important to understand some terminology. A ratio of the change in the vertical distance to the change in horizontal distance is called the *Slope*. On a graph with two points, (x_1, y_1) and (x_2, y_2), the slope is represented by the formula $= \frac{y_2 - y_1}{x_2 - x_1}$; $x_1 \neq x_2$. If the value of the slope is positive, the line slopes upward from left to right. If the value of the slope is negative, the line slopes downward from left to right. If the *y*-coordinates are the same for both points, the slope is 0 and the line is a *Horizontal Line*. If the *x*-coordinates are the same for both points, there is no slope and the line is a *Vertical Line*. Two or more lines that have equal slopes are *Parallel Lines*. *Perpendicular Lines* have slopes that are negative reciprocals of each other, such as $\frac{a}{b}$ and $\frac{-b}{a}$.

As mentioned previously, equations can be written many ways. Below is a list of the many forms equations can take.

- *Standard Form*: $Ax + By = C$; the slope is $\frac{-A}{B}$ and the *y*-intercept is $\frac{C}{B}$
- *Slope Intercept Form*: $y = mx + b$, where *m* is the slope and *b* is the *y*-intercept
- *Point-Slope Form*: $y - y_1 = m(x - x_1)$, where *m* is the slope and (x_1, y_1) is a point on the line
- *Two-Point Form*: $\frac{y - y_1}{x - x_1} = \frac{y_2 - y_1}{x_2 - x_1}$, where (x_1, y_1) and (x_2, y_2) are two points on the given line
- *Intercept Form*: $\frac{x}{x_1} + \frac{y}{y_1} = 1$, where $(x_1, 0)$ is the point at which a line intersects the *x*-axis, and $(0, y_1)$ is the point at which the same line intersects the *y*-axis

Calculations Using Points

Sometimes you need to perform calculations using only points on a graph as input data. Using points, you can determine what the midpoint and distance are. If you know the equation for a line you can calculate the distance between the line and the point.

To find the *Midpoint* of two points (x_1, y_1) and (x_2, y_2), average the x-coordinates to get the x-coordinate of the midpoint, and average the y-coordinates to get the y-coordinate of the midpoint. The formula is midpoint $= \left(\frac{x_1 + x_2}{2}, \frac{y_1 + y_2}{2} \right)$.

The *Distance* between two points is the same as the length of the hypotenuse of a right triangle with the two given points as endpoints, and the two sides of the right triangle parallel to the x-axis and y-axis, respectively. The length of the segment parallel to the x-axis is the difference between the x-coordinates of the two points. The length of the segment parallel to the y-axis is the difference between the y-coordinates of the two points. Use the Pythagorean Theorem $a^2 + b^2 = c^2$ or $c = \sqrt{a^2 + b^2}$ to find the distance. The formula is: distance $= \sqrt{(x_2 - x_1)^2 + (y_2 - y_1)^2}$.

When a line is in the format $Ax + By + C = 0$, where A, B, and C are coefficients, you can use a point (x_1, y_1) not on the line and apply the formula $d = \frac{|Ax_1 + By_1 + C|}{\sqrt{A^2 + B^2}}$ to find the distance between the line and the point (x_1, y_1).

> ➢ **Review Video: <u>Distance & Midpoint for Points on the Coordinate Plane</u>**
> *Visit **mometrix.com/academy** and enter **Code: 331768***

Transformation

- Rotation: An object is rotated, or turned, between 0 and 360 degrees, around a fixed point. The size and shape of the object are unchanged.
- Reflection: An object is reflected, or flipped, across a line, so that the original object and reflected object are the same distance from the line of reflection. The size and shape of the object are unchanged.
- Translation: An object is translated, or shifted, horizontally and/or vertically to a new location. The orientation, size, and shape of the object are unchanged.
- Dilation: An object is dilated, or proportionally stretched or shrunken, by a scale factor. The dilated image is the same shape and orientation as the original image but a different size. A polygon and its dilated image are similar.

Rotation
A line segment begins at (1, 4) and ends at (5, 4). Draw the line segment and rotate the line segment 90º about the point (3, 4).

The point about which the line segment is being rotated is on the line segment. This point should be on both the original and rotated line. The point (3, 4) is the center of the original line segment, and should still be the center of the rotated line segment. The dashed line is the rotated line segment.

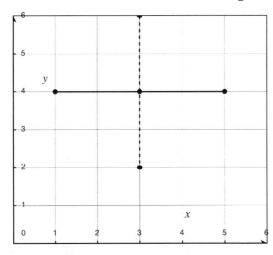

Reflection

Example 1: To create a congruent rectangle by reflecting, first draw a line of reflection. The line can be next to or on the figure. Then draw the image reflected across this line.

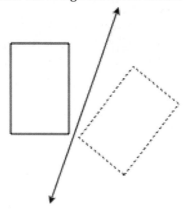

Example 2: A line segment begins at (1, 5) and ends at (5, 4). Draw the line segment, then reflect the line segment across the line $y = 3$.

To reflect a segment, consider folding a piece of paper at the line of reflection. The new image should line up exactly with the old image when the paper is folded. The dashed line is the reflected line se

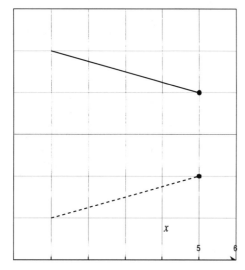

<u>Translation</u>
Example 1: A line segment on an x-y grid starts at (3, 2) and ends at (4, 1). Draw the line segment, and translate the segment up 2 units and left 2 units.

The solid line segment is the original line segment, and the dashed line is the translated line segment. The *y*-coordinate of each point has increased by 2, because the points moved two units away from 0. The *x*-coordinate of each point has decreased by 2, because the points moved two units closer to 0.

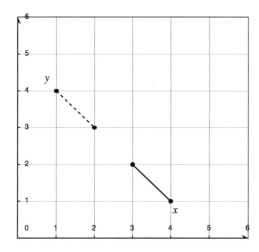

Example 2: Identify a transformation that could have been performed on the solid triangle to result in the dashed triangle.

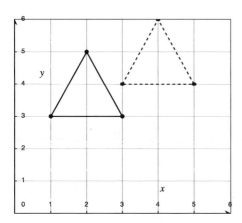

The transformed triangle has the same orientation as the original triangle. It has been shifted up one unit and two units to the right. Because the orientation of the figure has not changed, and its new position can be described using shifts up and to the right, the figure was translated.

<u>Dilation</u>

Example 1: Let $\Delta A'B'C'$ be the image of ΔABC after a dilation with center at the origin and a scale factor of $\frac{1}{3}$. Graph $\Delta A'B'C'$.

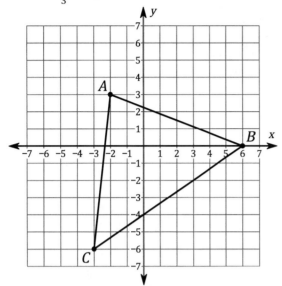

A dilation with center at the origin and a scale factor of k maps a point $P(x, y)$ onto $P'(kx, ky)$. First find the coordinates of the vertices of the given triangle. From the figure, they are: $A(-2, 3)$, $B(6, 0)$, and $C(-3, -6)$. Then use these values to calculate the coordinates of $\Delta A'B'C'$.

$$A(-2, 3) \rightarrow A'\left(-\frac{2}{3}, 1\right)$$
$$B(6, 0) \rightarrow B'(2, 0)$$
$$C(-3, -6) \rightarrow C'(-1, -2)$$

Finally, the triangle can be graphed:

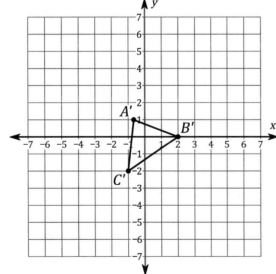

Example 2: In the coordinate plane, ΔDEF is the image of ΔABC after a sequence of transformations. What sequence of transformations can be used to go from ΔABC to ΔDEF?

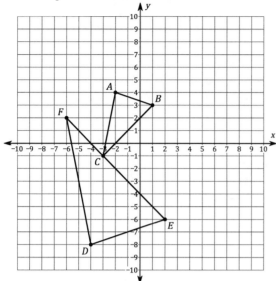

Notice that ΔDEF has the same shape as ΔABC, but it is twice as large. Thus, you need to perform a dilation with a center at the origin and a scale factor of 2. A dilation with center at the origin and a scale factor of k maps a point $P(x, y)$ onto $P'(kx, ky)$. Thus, the coordinates of $\Delta A'B'C'$ are:

$A(-2, 4) \rightarrow A'(-4, 8)$
$B(1, 3) \rightarrow B'(2, 6)$
$C(-3, -1) \rightarrow C'(-6, -2)$

Graph this triangle.

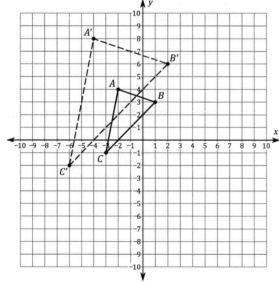

Angles

An angle is formed when two lines or line segments meet at a common point. It may be a common starting point for a pair of segments or rays, or it may be the intersection of lines. Angles are represented by the symbol ∠.

The vertex is the point at which two segments or rays meet to form an angle. If the angle is formed by intersecting rays, lines, and/or line segments, the vertex is the point at which four angles are formed. The pairs of angles opposite one another are called vertical angles, and their measures are equal.

An acute angle is an angle with a degree measure less than 90°.
A right angle is an angle with a degree measure of exactly 90°.
An obtuse angle is an angle with a degree measure greater than 90° but less than 180°.
A straight angle is an angle with a degree measure of exactly 180°. This is also a semicircle.
A reflex angle is an angle with a degree measure greater than 180° but less than 360°.
A full angle is an angle with a degree measure of exactly 360°.

> ➤ **Review Video: <u>Angles</u>**
> *Visit **mometrix.com/academy** and enter **Code: 264624***

Two angles whose sum is exactly 90° are said to be complementary. The two angles may or may not be adjacent. In a right triangle, the two acute angles are complementary.

Two angles whose sum is exactly 180° are said to be supplementary. The two angles may or may not be adjacent. Two intersecting lines always form two pairs of supplementary angles. Adjacent supplementary angles will always form a straight line.

Two angles that have the same vertex and share a side are said to be adjacent. Vertical angles are not adjacent because they share a vertex but no common side.

Adjacent
Share vertex and side

Not adjacent
Share part of side, but not vertex

When two parallel lines are cut by a transversal, the angles that are between the two parallel lines are interior angles. In the diagram below, angles 3, 4, 5, and 6 are interior angles.

When two parallel lines are cut by a transversal, the angles that are outside the parallel lines are exterior angles. In the diagram below, angles 1, 2, 7, and 8 are exterior angles.

When two parallel lines are cut by a transversal, the angles that are in the same position relative to the transversal and a parallel line are corresponding angles. The diagram below has four pairs of corresponding angles: angles 1 and 5; angles 2 and 6; angles 3 and 7; and angles 4 and 8. Corresponding angles formed by parallel lines are congruent.

When two parallel lines are cut by a transversal, the two interior angles that are on opposite sides of the transversal are called alternate interior angles. In the diagram below, there are two pairs of alternate interior angles: angles 3 and 6, and angles 4 and 5. Alternate interior angles formed by parallel lines are congruent.

When two parallel lines are cut by a transversal, the two exterior angles that are on opposite sides of the transversal are called alternate exterior angles. In the diagram below, there are two pairs of alternate exterior angles: angles 1 and 8, and angles 2 and 7. Alternate exterior angles formed by parallel lines are congruent.

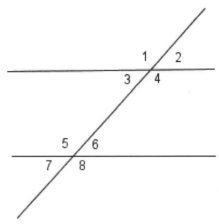

When two lines intersect, four angles are formed. The non-adjacent angles at this vertex are called vertical angles. Vertical angles are congruent. In the diagram, $\angle ABD \cong \angle CBE$ and $\angle ABC \cong \angle DBE$.

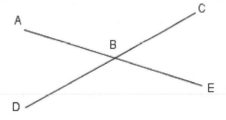

Triangles

An equilateral triangle is a triangle with three congruent sides. An equilateral triangle will also have three congruent angles, each 60°. All equilateral triangles are also acute triangles.

An isosceles triangle is a triangle with two congruent sides. An isosceles triangle will also have two congruent angles opposite the two congruent sides.

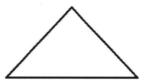

A scalene triangle is a triangle with no congruent sides. A scalene triangle will also have three angles of different measures. The angle with the largest measure is opposite the longest side, and the angle with the smallest measure is opposite the shortest side.

An acute triangle is a triangle whose three angles are all less than 90°. If two of the angles are equal, the acute triangle is also an isosceles triangle. If the three angles are all equal, the acute triangle is also an equilateral triangle.

A right triangle is a triangle with exactly one angle equal to 90°. All right triangles follow the Pythagorean Theorem. A right triangle can never be acute or obtuse.

An obtuse triangle is a triangle with exactly one angle greater than 90°. The other two angles may or may not be equal. If the two remaining angles are equal, the obtuse triangle is also an isosceles triangle.

> ➤ **Review Video:** <u>**Right Triangle Word Problem**</u>
> *Visit **mometrix.com/academy** and enter **Code: 612687***

Triangle Terminology

Altitude of a Triangle: A line segment drawn from one vertex perpendicular to the opposite side. In the diagram below, $\overline{BE}$, $\overline{AD}$, and $\overline{CF}$ are altitudes. The three altitudes in a triangle are always concurrent.

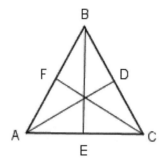

Height of a Triangle: The length of the altitude, although the two terms are often used interchangeably.

Orthocenter of a Triangle: The point of concurrency of the altitudes of a triangle. Note that in an obtuse triangle, the orthocenter will be outside the triangle, and in a right triangle, the orthocenter is the vertex of the right angle.

Median of a Triangle: A line segment drawn from one vertex to the midpoint of the opposite side. This is not the same as the altitude, except the altitude to the base of an isosceles triangle and all three altitudes of an equilateral triangle.

Centroid of a Triangle: The point of concurrency of the medians of a triangle. This is the same point as the orthocenter only in an equilateral triangle. Unlike the orthocenter, the centroid is always inside the triangle. The centroid can also be considered the exact center of the triangle. Any shape triangle can be perfectly balanced on a tip placed at the centroid. The centroid is also the point that is two-thirds the distance from the vertex to the opposite side.

> ➤ **Review Video: <u>Orthocenter and Centroid of a Triangle</u>**
> *Visit **mometrix.com/academy** and enter **Code: 598260***

Similarity and Congruence Rules

Similar triangles are triangles whose corresponding angles are equal and whose corresponding sides are proportional. Represented by AA. Similar triangles whose corresponding sides are congruent are also congruent triangles.

Three sides of one triangle are congruent to the three corresponding sides of the second triangle. Represented as SSS.

Two sides and the included angle (the angle formed by those two sides) of one triangle are congruent to the corresponding two sides and included angle of the second triangle. Represented by SAS.

Two angles and the included side (the side that joins the two angles) of one triangle are congruent to the corresponding two angles and included side of the second triangle. Represented by ASA.

Two angles and a non-included side of one triangle are congruent to the corresponding two angles and non-included side of the second triangle. Represented by AAS.

Note that AAA is not a form for congruent triangles. This would say that the three angles are congruent, but says nothing about the sides. This meets the requirements for similar triangles, but not congruent triangles.

> ➤ **Review Video: <u>Similar Triangles</u>**
> Visit *mometrix.com/academy* and enter *Code:* **398538**

> ➤ **Review Video: <u>Measurements for Similar Triangles</u>**
> Visit *mometrix.com/academy* and enter *Code:* **891859**

> ➤ **Review Video: <u>Measurements for Similar Triangles Continued</u>**
> Visit *mometrix.com/academy* and enter *Code:* **239422**

> ➤ **Review Video: <u>Measurements for Similar Triangles Continued II</u>**
> Visit *mometrix.com/academy* and enter *Code:* **604785**

General Rules for Triangles

The Triangle Inequality Theorem states that the sum of the measures of any two sides of a triangle is always greater than the measure of the third side. If the sum of the measures of two sides were equal to the third side, a triangle would be impossible because the two sides would lie flat across the third side and there would be no vertex. If the sum of the measures of two of the sides was less than the third side, a closed figure would be impossible because the two shortest sides would never meet.

The sum of the measures of the interior angles of a triangle is always 180°. Therefore, a triangle can never have more than one angle greater than or equal to 90°.

In any triangle, the angles opposite congruent sides are congruent, and the sides opposite congruent angles are congruent. The largest angle is always opposite the longest side, and the smallest angle is always opposite the shortest side.

The line segment that joins the midpoints of any two sides of a triangle is always parallel to the third side and exactly half the length of the third side.

> ➤ **Review Video: <u>Proof that a Triangle is 180 Degrees</u>**
> Visit *mometrix.com/academy* and enter *Code:* **687591**

Pythagorean Theorem

The side of a triangle opposite the right angle is called the hypotenuse. The other two sides are called the legs. The Pythagorean Theorem states a relationship among the legs and hypotenuse of a right triangle: $a^2 + b^2 = c^2$, where a and b are the lengths of the legs of a right triangle, and c is the length of the hypotenuse. Note that this formula will only work with right triangles.

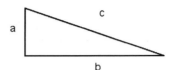

> ➤ **Review Video: Pythagorean Theorem**
> *Visit **mometrix.com/academy** and enter **Code: 906576***

Trigonometric Formulas

In the diagram below, angle C is the right angle, and side c is the hypotenuse. Side a is the side adjacent to angle B and side b is the side adjacent to angle A. These formulas will work for any acute angle in a right triangle. They will NOT work for any triangle that is not a right triangle. Also, they will not work for the right angle in a right triangle, since there are not distinct adjacent and opposite sides to differentiate from the hypotenuse.

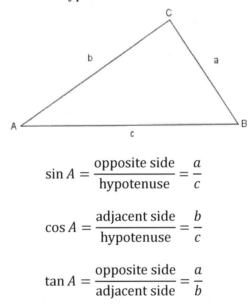

$$\sin A = \frac{\text{opposite side}}{\text{hypotenuse}} = \frac{a}{c}$$

$$\cos A = \frac{\text{adjacent side}}{\text{hypotenuse}} = \frac{b}{c}$$

$$\tan A = \frac{\text{opposite side}}{\text{adjacent side}} = \frac{a}{b}$$

Polygons

Each straight line segment of a polygon is called a side.

The point at which two sides of a polygon intersect is called the vertex. In a polygon, the number of sides is always equal to the number of vertices.

A polygon with all sides congruent and all angles equal is called a regular polygon.

A line segment from the center of a polygon perpendicular to a side of the polygon is called the apothem. In a regular polygon, the apothem can be used to find the area of the polygon using the formula $A = \frac{1}{2}ap$, where a is the apothem and p is the perimeter.

A line segment from the center of a polygon to a vertex of the polygon is called a radius. The radius of a regular polygon is also the radius of a circle that can be circumscribed about the polygon.

Triangle – 3 sides
Quadrilateral – 4 sides
Pentagon – 5 sides
Hexagon – 6 sides
Heptagon – 7 sides
Octagon – 8 sides
Nonagon – 9 sides
Decagon – 10 sides
Dodecagon – 12 sides

More generally, an *n*-gon is a polygon that has *n* angles and *n* sides.

The sum of the interior angles of an *n*-sided polygon is $(n - 2)180°$. For example, in a triangle n = 3, so the sum of the interior angles is $(3 - 2)180° = 180°$. In a quadrilateral, n = 4, and the sum of the angles is $(4 - 2)180° = 360°$. The sum of the interior angles of a polygon is equal to the sum of the interior angles of any other polygon with the same number of sides.

A diagonal is a line segment that joins two non-adjacent vertices of a polygon.
A convex polygon is a polygon whose diagonals all lie within the interior of the polygon.
A concave polygon is a polygon with a least one diagonal that lies outside the polygon. In the diagram below, quadrilateral *ABCD* is concave because diagonal $\overline{AC}$ lies outside the polygon.

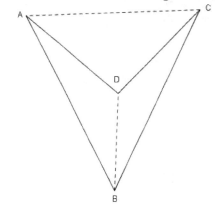

The number of diagonals a polygon has can be found by using the formula: number of diagonals $= \frac{n(n-3)}{2}$, where *n* is the number of sides in the polygon. This formula works for all polygons, not just regular polygons.

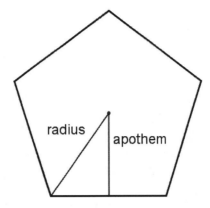

Congruent figures are geometric figures that have the same size and shape. All corresponding angles are equal, and all corresponding sides are equal. It is indicated by the symbol ≅.

Congruent polygons

Similar figures are geometric figures that have the same shape, but do not necessarily have the same size. All corresponding angles are equal, and all corresponding sides are proportional, but they do not have to be equal. It is indicated by the symbol ∼.

Similar polygons

Note that all congruent figures are also similar, but not all similar figures are congruent.

Line of Symmetry: The line that divides a figure or object into two symmetric parts. Each symmetric half is congruent to the other. An object may have no lines of symmetry, one line of symmetry, or more than one line of symmetry.

Lines of symmetry:

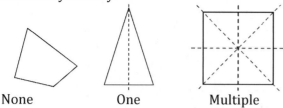

None   One   Multiple

Quadrilateral: A closed two-dimensional geometric figure composed of exactly four straight sides. The sum of the interior angles of any quadrilateral is 360°.

Parallelogram: A quadrilateral that has exactly two pairs of opposite parallel sides. The sides that are parallel are also congruent. The opposite interior angles are always congruent, and the consecutive interior angles are supplementary. The diagonals of a parallelogram bisect each other. Each diagonal divides the parallelogram into two congruent triangles.

Trapezoid: Traditionally, a quadrilateral that has exactly one pair of parallel sides. Some math texts define trapezoid as a quadrilateral that has at least one pair of parallel sides. Because there are no rules governing the second pair of sides, there are no rules that apply to the properties of the diagonals of a trapezoid.

Rectangles, rhombuses, and squares are all special forms of parallelograms.
Rectangle: A parallelogram with four right angles. All rectangles are parallelograms, but not all parallelograms are rectangles. The diagonals of a rectangle are congruent.

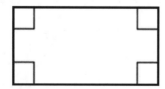

Rhombus: A parallelogram with four congruent sides. All rhombuses are parallelograms, but not all parallelograms are rhombuses. The diagonals of a rhombus are perpendicular to each other.

Square: A parallelogram with four right angles and four congruent sides. All squares are also parallelograms, rhombuses, and rectangles. The diagonals of a square are congruent and perpendicular to each other.

A quadrilateral whose diagonals bisect each other is a parallelogram. A quadrilateral whose opposite sides are parallel (2 pairs of parallel sides) is a parallelogram.

A quadrilateral whose diagonals are perpendicular bisectors of each other is a rhombus. A quadrilateral whose opposite sides (both pairs) are parallel and congruent is a rhombus.

A parallelogram that has a right angle is a rectangle. (Consecutive angles of a parallelogram are supplementary. Therefore if there is one right angle in a parallelogram, there are four right angles in that parallelogram.)

A rhombus with one right angle is a square. Because the rhombus is a special form of a parallelogram, the rules about the angles of a parallelogram also apply to the rhombus.

Circles

The center is the single point inside the circle that is equidistant from every point on the circle. (Point O in the diagram below.)

The radius is a line segment that joins the center of the circle and any one point on the circle. All radii of a circle are equal. (Segments OX, OY, and OZ in the diagram below.)

The diameter is a line segment that passes through the center of the circle and has both endpoints on the circle. The length of the diameter is exactly twice the length of the radius. (Segment XZ in the diagram below.)

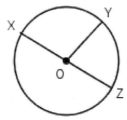

Area and Circumference of a Circle

The area of a circle is found by the formula $A = \pi r^2$, where r is the length of the radius. If the diameter of the circle is given, remember to divide it in half to get the length of the radius before proceeding.

Find the radius of a circle

You may have problems that give you the area of a circle. So, you are asked to find the radius. Example: The area of a circle is 30cm². Find the radius.

First: Set up the equation to set apart the radius.

The equation is $30 = \pi r^2$. Now, divide both sides by π: $\frac{30}{\pi} = \frac{\pi r^2}{\pi}$

Second: Take the square root of both sides: $\sqrt{9.55} = \sqrt{r^2}$.
So, you are left with: $3.09 = r$.

Note: You may have the area, and you are asked to find the diameter of the circle. So, follow the steps above to find the radius. Then, multiply the radius by 2 for the diameter.

> ➤ **Review Video: <u>Finding Measurements for Parts of a Circle</u>**
> *Visit **mometrix.com/academy** and enter **Code: 417932**

The circumference of a circle is found by the formula $C = 2\pi r$, where r is the radius. Again, remember to convert the diameter if you are given that measure rather than the radius.

Find the radius of a circle

You may have problems that give you the circumference of a circle. So, you are asked to find the radius. Example: The circumference is 20cm. Find the radius.

First: Set up the equation to set apart the radius.

The equation is $20 = 2\pi r$. Now divide both sides by 2: $\frac{20}{2} = \frac{2\pi r}{2}$.

Second: Divide both sides by π: $\frac{10}{\pi} = \frac{\pi r}{\pi}$. So, you are left with $3.18 = r$

Note: You may have the circumference, and you are asked to find the diameter of the circle. So, follow the steps above to find the radius. Then, multiply the radius by 2 for the diameter.

> ➤ **Review Video: <u>Area and Circumference of a Circle</u>**
> *Visit **mometrix.com/academy** and enter **Code: 243015**

An arc is a portion of a circle. Specifically, an arc is the set of points between and including two points on a circle. An arc does not contain any points inside the circle. When a segment is drawn from the endpoints of an arc to the center of the circle, a sector is formed.

A central angle is an angle whose vertex is the center of a circle and whose legs intercept an arc of the circle. Angle *XOY* in the diagram above is a central angle. A minor arc is an arc that has a measure less than 180°. The measure of a central angle is equal to the measure of the minor arc it intercepts. A major arc is an arc having a measure of at least 180°. The measure of the major arc can be found by subtracting the measure of the central angle from 360°. A semicircle is an arc whose endpoints are the endpoints of the diameter of a circle. A semicircle is exactly half of a circle.

An inscribed angle is an angle whose vertex lies on a circle and whose legs contain chords of that circle. The portion of the circle intercepted by the legs of the angle is called the intercepted arc. The measure of the intercepted arc is exactly twice the measure of the inscribed angle. In the diagram below, angle ABC is an inscribed angle. $\overset{\frown}{AC} = 2(m\angle ABC)$

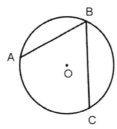

Any angle inscribed in a semicircle is a right angle. The intercepted arc is 180°, making the inscribed angle half that, or 90°. In the diagram below, angle ABC is inscribed in semicircle ABC, making angle ABC equal to 90°.

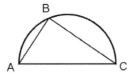

A chord is a line segment that has both endpoints on a circle. In the diagram below, $\overline{EB}$ is a chord. Secant: A line that passes through a circle and contains a chord of that circle. In the diagram below, $\overleftrightarrow{EB}$ is a secant and contains chord $\overline{EB}$.

A tangent is a line in the same plane as a circle that touches the circle in exactly one point. While a line segment can be tangent to a circle as part of a line that is tangent, it is improper to say a tangent can be simply a line segment that touches the circle in exactly one point. In the diagram below, $\overleftrightarrow{CD}$ is tangent to circle A. Notice that $\overline{FB}$ is not tangent to the circle. $\overline{FB}$ is a line segment that touches the circle in exactly one point, but if the segment were extended, it would touch the circle in a second point. The point at which a tangent touches a circle is called the point of tangency. In the diagram below, point B is the point of tangency.

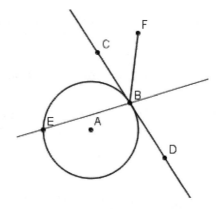

A secant is a line that intersects a circle in two points. Two secants may intersect inside the circle, on the circle, or outside the circle. When the two secants intersect on the circle, an inscribed angle is formed.

When two secants intersect inside a circle, the measure of each of two vertical angles is equal to half the sum of the two intercepted arcs. In the diagram below, $m\angle AEB = \frac{1}{2}(\overarc{AB} + \overarc{CD})$ and $m\angle BEC = \frac{1}{2}(\overarc{BC} + \overarc{AD})$.

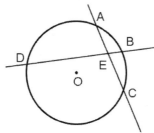

When two secants intersect outside a circle, the measure of the angle formed is equal to half the difference of the two arcs that lie between the two secants. In the diagram below, $m\angle E = \frac{1}{2}(\overarc{AB} - \overarc{CD})$.

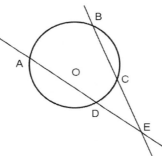

The arc length is the length of that portion of the circumference between two points on the circle. The formula for arc length is $s = \frac{\pi r\theta}{180°}$ where s is the arc length, r is the length of the radius, and θ is the angular measure of the arc in degrees, or $s = r\theta$, where θ is the angular measure of the arc in radians (2π radians = 360 degrees).

A sector is the portion of a circle formed by two radii and their intercepted arc. While the arc length is exclusively the points that are also on the circumference of the circle, the sector is the entire area bounded by the arc and the two radii.

The area of a sector of a circle is found by the formula, $A = \frac{\theta r^2}{2}$, where A is the area, θ is the measure of the central angle in radians, and r is the radius. To find the area when the central angle is in degrees, use the formula, $A = \frac{\theta \pi r^2}{360}$, where θ is the measure of the central angle in degrees and r is the radius.

Other Conic Sections

An ellipse is the set of all points in a plane, whose total distance from two fixed points called the foci (singular: focus) is constant, and whose center is the midpoint between the foci.

The standard equation of an ellipse that is taller than it is wide is $\frac{(y-k)^2}{a^2} + \frac{(x-h)^2}{b^2} = 1$, where a and b are coefficients. The center is the point (h, k) and the foci are the points $(h, k + c)$ and $(h, k - c)$, where $c^2 = a^2 - b^2$ and $a^2 > b^2$.

The major axis has length $2a$, and the minor axis has length $2b$. Eccentricity (e) is a measure of how elongated an ellipse is, and is the ratio of the distance between the foci to the length of the major axis. Eccentricity will have a value between 0 and 1. The closer to 1 the eccentricity is, the closer the ellipse is to being a circle. The formula for eccentricity is $= \frac{c}{a}$.

Parabola: The set of all points in a plane that are equidistant from a fixed line, called the directrix, and a fixed point not on the line, called the focus. Axis: The line perpendicular to the directrix that passes through the focus.

For parabolas that open up or down, the standard equation is $(x - h)^2 = 4c(y - k)$, where h, c, and k are coefficients. If c is positive, the parabola opens up. If c is negative, the parabola opens down. The vertex is the point (h, k). The directrix is the line having the equation $y = -c + k$, and the focus is the point $(h, c + k)$. For parabolas that open left or right, the standard equation is $(y - k)^2 = 4c(x - h)$, where k, c, and h are coefficients. If c is positive, the parabola opens to the right. If c is negative, the parabola opens to the left. The vertex is the point (h, k). The directrix is the line having the equation $x = -c + h$, and the focus is the point $(c + h, k)$.

A hyperbola is the set of all points in a plane, whose distance from two fixed points, called foci, has a constant difference.

The standard equation of a horizontal hyperbola is $\frac{(x-h)^2}{a^2} - \frac{(y-k)^2}{b^2} = 1$, where a, b, h, and k are real numbers. The center is the point (h, k), the vertices are the points $(h + a, k)$ and $(h - a, k)$, and the foci are the points that every point on one of the parabolic curves is equidistant from and are found using the formulas $(h + c, k)$ and $(h - c, k)$, where $c^2 = a^2 + b^2$. The asymptotes are two lines the graph of the hyperbola approaches but never reaches, and are given by the equations $y = \left(\frac{b}{a}\right)(x - h) + k$ and $y = -\left(\frac{b}{a}\right)(x - h) + k$.

A vertical hyperbola is formed when a plane makes a vertical cut through two cones that are stacked vertex-to-vertex.

The standard equation of a vertical hyperbola is $\frac{(y-k)^2}{a^2} - \frac{(x-h)^2}{b^2} = 1$, where a, b, k, and h are real numbers. The center is the point (h, k), the vertices are the points $(h, k + a)$ and $(h, k - a)$, and the foci are the points that every point on one of the parabolic curves is equidistant from and are found using the formulas $(h, k + c)$ and $(h, k - c)$, where $c^2 = a^2 + b^2$. The asymptotes are two lines the graph of the hyperbola approaches but never reach, and are given by the equations $y = \left(\frac{a}{b}\right)(x - h) + k$ and $y = -\left(\frac{a}{b}\right)(x - h) + k$.

Area and Perimeter Formulas: Polygons

<u>Triangle</u>
The perimeter of any triangle is found by summing the three side lengths; $P = a + b + c$. For an equilateral triangle, this is the same as $P = 3s$, where s is any side length, since all three sides are the same length.

Find the side of a triangle
You may have problems that give you the perimeter of a triangle. So, you are asked to find one of the sides.

Example: The perimeter of a triangle is 35 cm. One side length is 10 cm. Another side length is 20cm. Find the length of the missing side.

    First: Set up the equation to set apart a side length.
           Now, the equation is $35 = 10 + 20 + c$. So, you are left with $35 = 30 + c$.

    Second: Subtract 30 from both sides: $35 - 30 = 30 - 30 + c$
           Then, you are left with $5 = c$

The area of any triangle can be found by taking half the product of one side length (base or b) and the perpendicular distance from that side to the opposite vertex (height or h). In equation form, $A = \frac{1}{2}bh$. For many triangles, it may be difficult to calculate h, so using one of the other formulas given here may be easier.

Find the height or the area of the base
You may have problems that give you the area of a triangle. So, you are asked to find the height or the base.

Example: The area of a triangle is 70 cm², and the height is 10. Find the base.
    First: Set up the equation to set apart the base.
           The equation is $70 = \frac{1}{2}10b$.
           Now, multiply both sides by 2: $70 \times 2 = \frac{1}{2}10b \times 2$.
           So, you are left with: $140 = 10b$.

    Second: Divide both sides by 10 to get the base: $\frac{140}{10} = \frac{10b}{10}$
           Then, you have $14 = b$.

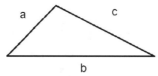

> ➤ **Review Video:** <u>**Area and Perimeter of a Triangle**</u>
> *Visit **mometrix.com/academy** and enter **Code: 817385**

Another formula that works for any triangle is $A = \sqrt{s(s-a)(s-b)(s-c)}$, where A is the area, s is the semiperimeter $s = \frac{a+b+c}{2}$, and a, b, and c are the lengths of the three sides.

The area of an equilateral triangle can found by the formula $A = \frac{\sqrt{3}}{4}s^2$, where A is the area and s is the length of a side. You could use the $30° - 60° - 90°$ ratios to find the height of the triangle and then use the standard triangle area formula, but this is faster.

The area of an isosceles triangle can found by the formula, $A = \frac{1}{2}b\sqrt{a^2 - \frac{b^2}{4}}$, where A is the area, b is the base (the unique side), and a is the length of one of the two congruent sides. If you do not remember this formula, you can use the Pythagorean Theorem to find the height so you can use the standard formula for the area of a triangle.

Square
The area of a square is found by using the formula $A = s^2$, where and s is the length of one side.

Find the side of a square
You may have problems that give you the area of a square. So, you are asked to find the side.
Example: The area of a square is 9 cm². Find the side.

    First: Set up the equation to set apart s.
             The equation is $9 = s^2$.

    Second: Now, you can take the square root of both sides: $\sqrt{9} = \sqrt{s^2}$.
              So, you are left with: $3 = s$

The perimeter of a square is found by using the formula $P = 4s$, where s is the length of one side. Because all four sides are equal in a square, it is faster to multiply the length of one side by 4 than to add the same number four times. You could use the formulas for rectangles and get the same answer.

Find the side of a square
You may have problems that give you the perimeter of a square. So, you are asked to find the side.
Example: The perimeter of a square is 60 cm. Find the side.

    First: Set up the equation to set apart s.
             The equation is $60 = 4s$.

    Second: Now, you can divide both sides by 4: $\frac{60}{4} = \frac{4s}{4}$. You are left with $15 = s$

> ➤ **Review Video: <u>Area and Perimeter of a Square</u>**
> *Visit **mometrix.com/academy** and enter **Code: 620902***

<u>Rectangle</u>
The area of a rectangle is found by the formula $A = lw$, where A is the area of the rectangle, l is the length (usually considered to be the longer side) and w is the width (usually considered to be the shorter side). The numbers for l and w are interchangeable.

Find the width or length of a rectangle
You may have problems that give you the area of a rectangle. So, you are asked to find the width.
Example: The area of a rectangle is 150cm², and the length is 10cm. Find the width.
>   First: Set up the equation to set apart width. The equation is $150 = 10w$.

>   Second: Divide both sides by 10: $\frac{150}{10} = \frac{10w}{10}$. You are left with $15 = w$

Note: When you need to find the length, you can follow the steps above to find it.

The perimeter of a rectangle is found by the formula $P = 2l + 2w$ or $P = 2(l + w)$, where l is the length, and w is the width. It may be easier to add the length and width first and then double the result, as in the second formula.

Find the width or length of a rectangle
You may have problems that give you the perimeter of a rectangle. So, you are asked to find the width.
Example: The perimeter of a rectangle is 100cm, and the length is 20cm. Find the width.
>   First: Set up the equation to set apart the width. The equation is $100 = 2(20 + w)$

>   Second: Distribute the 2 across $(20 + w)$: $100 = 40 + 2w$
>   Then, subtract 40 from both sides: $100 - 40 = 40 + 2w - 40$
>   So, you are left with: $60 = 2w$. Then, divide both sides by 2: $\frac{60}{2} = \frac{2w}{2}$.
>   Now, you have $30 = w$.

Note: When you need to find the length, you can follow the steps above to find it.

> ➢ **Review Video: <u>Area and Perimeter of a Rectangle</u>**
> *Visit **mometrix.com/academy** and enter **Code: 933707***

<u>Parallelogram</u>
The area of a parallelogram is found by the formula $A = bh$, where b is the length of the base, and h is the height. Note that the base and height correspond to the length and width in a rectangle, so this formula would apply to rectangles as well. Do not confuse the height of a parallelogram with the length of the second side. The two are only the same measure in the case of a rectangle.

Find the length of the base or the height of a parallelogram
You may have problems that give you the area of a parallelogram. So, you are asked to find the area of the base or the height.
Example: The area of the parallelogram is 84 cm². The base is 7cm. Find the height.
>   Set up the equation to set apart the height.
>   So, you have $84 = 7h$. Now, divide both sides by 7: $\frac{84}{7} = \frac{7h}{7}$.
>   Then, you are left with $12 = h$

The perimeter of a parallelogram is found by the formula $P = 2a + 2b$ or $P = 2(a + b)$, where a and b are the lengths of the two sides.

Find the missing side of a parallelogram
You may have problems that give you the perimeter of a parallelogram. So, you are asked to find one of the sides. Example: The perimeter of a parallelogram is 100cm, and one side is 20cm. Find the other side.

First: Set up the equation to set apart one of the side lengths.
The equation is $100 = 2(20 + b)$

Second: Distribute the 2 across $(20 + b)$: $100 = 40 + 2b$
Then, subtract 40 from both sides: $100 - 40 = 40 + 2b - 40$
So, you are left with: $60 = 2b$. Then, divide both sides by 2: $\frac{60}{2} = \frac{2b}{2}$
Now, you have $30 = b$.

> ➢ **Review Video: <u>Area and Perimeter of a Parallelogram</u>**
> *Visit **mometrix.com/academy** and enter **Code: 718313***

Trepezoid
The area of a trapezoid is found by the formula $A = \frac{1}{2}h(b_1 + b_2)$, where h is the height (segment joining and perpendicular to the parallel bases), and b_1 and b_2 are the two parallel sides (bases). Do not use one of the other two sides as the height unless that side is also perpendicular to the parallel bases.

Find the height of a trapezoid
You may have problems that give you the area of a trapezoid. So, you are asked to find the height. Example: The area of a trapezoid is 30cm². B_1 is 3cm, and B_2 is 9cm. Find the height.

First: Set up the equation to set apart the height. The equation is $30 = \frac{1}{2}h(3 + 9)$.

Second: Now, multiply both sides by 2: $30 \times 2 = \frac{1}{2}(12)h \times 2$.
So, you are left with: $60 = (12)h$.

Third: Divide both sides by 12: $\frac{60}{12} = \frac{(12)h}{12}$. Now, you have $5 = h$

Find a base of a trapezoid
You may have problems that give you the area of a trapezoid and the height. So, you are asked to find one of the bases.
Example: The area of a trapezoid is 90cm². b_1 is 5cm, and the height is 12cm. Find b_2.

First: Set up the equation to set apart b_2.
The equation is $90 = \frac{1}{2}12(5 + b_2)$.

Second: Now, multiply the height by $\frac{1}{2}$: $90 = 6(5 + b_2)$.
So, you can distribute the 6 across $(5 + b_2)$: $90 = 30 + 6b_2$

Third: Subtract 30 from both sides $90 - 30 = 30 + 6b_2 - 30$.
Now, you have $60 = 6b_2$.
Then, divide both sides by 6: $\frac{60}{6} = \frac{6b_2}{6}$. So, $b_2 = 10$.

The perimeter of a trapezoid is found by the formula $P = a + b_1 + c + b_2$, where a, b_1, c, and b_2 are the four sides of the trapezoid.

Find the missing side of a trapezoid
Example: The perimeter of a trapezoid is 50cm. B_1 is 20cm, B_2 is 10cm, and a is 5cm. Find the length of side c.

      First: Set up the equation to set apart the missing side.
      The equation is $50 = 5 + 20 + c + 10$. So, you have $50 = 35 + c$

      Second: Subtract 35 from both sides: $50 - 35 = 35 + c - 35$.
      So, you are left with $15 = c$

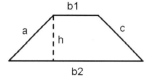

> ➤ **Review Video: <u>Area and Perimeter of a Trapezoid</u>**
> *Visit **mometrix.com/academy** and enter **Code: 587523***

Volume and Surface Area

The surface area of a solid object is the area of all sides or exterior surfaces. For objects such as prisms and pyramids, a further distinction is made between base surface area (B) and lateral surface area (LA). For a prism, the total surface area (SA) is $SA = LA + 2B$. For a pyramid or cone, the total surface area is $SA = LA + B$.

<u>Sphere</u>

The **surface area of a sphere** can be found with the formula $SA = 4\pi r^2$, where r is the radius.

Find the radius of a sphere
You may have problems that give you the surface area of a sphere. So, you are asked to find the radius.
Example: The surface area of a sphere is 100 cm². Find the radius.
      First: Set up the equation to set apart the radius.
      You begin with: $SA = 4\pi r^2$. Then, you move 4π to the other side of the equal sign and cancel
      out the 4π on the right side of the formula: $\frac{SA}{4\pi} = r^2$.
      Next, you square both sides to set apart the radius:
      $\sqrt{\frac{SA}{4\pi}} = \sqrt{r^2}$. So, you are left with $r = \sqrt{\frac{SA}{4\pi}}$

      Second: Solve the equation.
      $\sqrt{\frac{100}{4\pi}} = \sqrt{\frac{100}{12.57}} = 2.82$. So, the radius equals 2.82 cm.

The **volume of a sphere** can be found with the formula $V = \frac{4}{3}\pi r^3$, where r is the radius. Sometimes, you may be asked to give the volume of a sphere in terms of π. For example, the volume of the sphere is 30π.

Find the radius of a sphere
You may have problems that give you the volume of a sphere. So, you are asked to find the radius.
Example: The volume of a sphere is 100 cm³. Find the radius.

First: Set up the equation and cancel out the fraction.
$\frac{3}{4} \times \frac{4}{3}\pi r^3 = 100 \times \frac{3}{4}$. So, you are left with: $\pi r^3 = 75$

Second: Cancel out π.
$\frac{\pi r^3}{\pi} = \frac{75}{\pi}$. So, you are left with: $r^3 = \frac{75}{\pi} = 23.87$

Third: Take the cubed root of r³ and 23.87 to solve for the radius.
$\sqrt[3]{r^3} = \sqrt[3]{23.87}$. So, you have the result of r= 2.88

> ➤ **Review Video: <u>Volume and Surface Area of a Sphere</u>**
> *Visit **mometrix.com/academy** and enter **Code: 786928***

<u>Rectangular Prism</u>

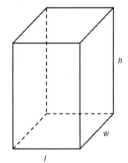

For a rectangular prism, the volume can be found by the formula $V = lwh$, where V is the volume, l is the length, w is the width, and h is the height.

Find the length, width, or height of a rectangular prism
You may have problems that give you the volume of a rectangular prism. So, you are asked to find the length, width, or height.
Example: The volume of the rectangular prism is 200 cm³. The width is 10cm, and the height is 10cm. Find the length.

First: Set up the equation to set apart the length.
So, you have $200 = l(10)(10)$ that becomes $200 = (100)l$.

Second: Divide both sides by 100.
Now, you have $\frac{200}{100} = \frac{(100)l}{100}$. So, you are left with $2 = l$.

Note: When you need to find the width or height, you can follow the steps above to solve for either.

The surface area can be calculated as $SA = 2lw + 2hl + 2wh$ or $SA = 2(lw + hl + wh)$.

Find the length, width, or height of a rectangular prism
You may have problems that give you the surface area of a rectangular prism. So, you are asked to find the length, width, or height.
Example: The surface area of the rectangular prism is 200 cm². The width is 15cm, and the height is 5cm. Find the length.

First: Set up the equation to set apart the length.
         So, you have $200 = 2(15)l + 2(5)l + 2(15)(5)$ that becomes: $200 = (40)l + 150$.

Second: Subtract 150 from both sides.
         So, $200 - 150 = (40)l + 150 - 150$ becomes $50 = (40)l$.
         Then, divide both sides by 40 to set apart l: $\frac{50}{40} = \frac{(40)l}{40}$.
         You are left with $1.25 = l$.

Note: When you need to find the width or height, you can follow the steps above to solve for either.

> ➤ **Review Video: 3D Geometric Shapes**
> *Visit **mometrix.com/academy** and enter **Code: 738045***

Cube
The volume of a cube can be found by the formula $V = s^3$, where s is the length of a side.

Find the side of a cube
You may have problems that give you the volume of a cube. So, you are asked to find the side.
Example: The volume of a cube is 20 cm³. Find the side.

First: Set up the equation to set apart the side length. Then, take the cube root of both sides. So, $20 = s^3$ becomes $\sqrt[3]{20} = \sqrt[3]{s^3}$ Then, you are left with $\sqrt[3]{20} = s$

Second: Solve for the side length.
         $\sqrt[3]{20} = 2.71$. So, s equals 2.71.

> ➤ **Review Video: Volume and Surface Area of a Cube**
> *Visit **mometrix.com/academy** and enter **Code: 664455***

The surface area of a cube is calculated as $SA = 6s^2$, where SA is the total surface area and s is the length of a side. These formulas are the same as the ones used for the volume and surface area of a rectangular prism, but simplified since all three quantities (length, width, and height) are the same.

Find the side of a cube
You may have problems that give you the surface area of a cube. So, you are asked to find the side.
Example: The surface area of a cube is 60 cm². Find the side.

First: Set up the equation to set apart the side length.
So, $60 = 6s^2$ becomes $\frac{60}{6} = \frac{6s^2}{6}$. Then, you are left with $10 = s^2$

Second: Take the square root of both sides to set apart the *s*.
So, $10 = s^2$ becomes $\sqrt{10} = \sqrt{s^2}$.
Then, you are left with $3.16 = s$

➢ **Review Video: <u>Volume and Surface Area of a Rectangular Solid</u>**
*Visit **mometrix.com/academy** and enter **Code: 386780***

<u>Cylinder</u>

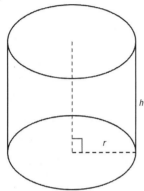

The volume of a cylinder can be calculated by the formula $V = \pi r^2 h$, where *r* is the radius, and *h* is the height.

Find the height of a cylinder
You may have problems that give you the volume of a cylinder. So, you are asked to find the height.
Example: The volume of a cylinder is 300 cm³ and the radius is 5 cm. Find the height.

First: Set up the equation and put in the known numbers.
You begin with $300 = \pi 5^2 h$. Now, $\pi 5^2 h = 78.5h$.
So, you have $300 = 78.5h$

Second: Set apart h to solve for the height.
$\frac{300}{78.5} = \frac{78.5h}{78.5}$. So, you are left with: $\frac{300}{78.5} = h$

Solve: $\frac{300}{78.5} = 3.82$cm is the height.

Find the radius of a cylinder
You may have problems that give you the volume of a cylinder. So, you are asked to find the radius.
Example: The volume of a cylinder is 200 cm³ and the radius is 15cm. Find the radius.

First: Set up the equation to set apart the radius.
You begin with $200 = \pi(15)r^2$. Now, you move π and (15) to both sides of the equation: $\frac{200}{\pi(15)} = \frac{\pi(15)r^2}{\pi(15)}$. Then, you are left with: $\frac{200}{\pi(15)} = r^2$.

Second: Take the square root of both sides to solve for the radius: $\sqrt{\frac{200}{\pi(15)}} = \sqrt{r^2}$.

Then, you have $\sqrt{4.25} = r$. So, the radius is equal to 2.06.

The surface area of a cylinder can be found by the formula $SA = 2\pi r^2 + 2\pi rh$. The first term is the base area multiplied by two, and the second term is the perimeter of the base multiplied by the height.

Find the height of a cylinder
You may have problems that give you the surface area of a cylinder. So, you are asked to find the height. Example: The surface area of a cylinder is 150 cm² and the radius is 2 cm. Find the height.

First: Set up the equation and put in the known numbers.
You begin with $150 = 2\pi 2^2 + 2\pi(2)h$.
So, you have $150 = 25.12 + 12.56h$.

Second: Subtract 25.12 from both sides of the equation.
So, $150 - 25.12 = 25.12 + 12.56h - 25.12$ becomes $124.85 = 12.56h$.
Then, divide both sides by 12.56.
Now, you are left with $9.94 = h$.

Find the radius of a cylinder
You may have problems that give you the surface area of a cylinder. So, you are asked to find the radius. Example: The surface area of a cylinder is 327 cm², and the height is 12cm. Find the radius.

First: Set up the equation and put in the known numbers.
You begin with $327 = 2\pi r^2 + 2\pi 12(r)$. So, you have $327 = 2\pi r^2 + 75.36r$.

Second: Set up the quadratic formula.
So, you now have $6.28r^2 + 75.36r - 327 = 0$

Third: Solve the equation using the quadratic formula steps.
Now, radius $= \frac{-75.36 \pm \sqrt{(75.36)^2 - 4(6.28)(-327)}}{2(6.28)}$
So, the radius equals a positive 3.39.

> ➤ **Review Video: <u>Volume and Surface Area of a Right Circular Cylinder</u>**
> *Visit **mometrix.com/academy** and enter **Code: 226463***

Pyramid

The **volume of a pyramid** is found with the formula $V = \frac{1}{3}Bh$, where B is the area of the base, and h is the height. The perpendicular distance from the vertex to the base is the height. This formula is the same as $\frac{1}{3}$ times the volume of a prism. Like a prism, the base of a pyramid can be any shape.

Find the area of the base or the height of a pyramid
You may have problems that give you the volume of a pyramid. So, you are asked to find the area of the base or the height.
Example: The volume of the pyramid is 100 cm³. The area of the base is 5cm². Find the height.

First: Set up the equation to set apart the height.
The equation is $100 = \frac{1}{3}5h$.

Now, you start by multiplying both sides by 3: $100 \times 3 = \frac{1}{3}5h \times 3$.

Second: You have $300 = 5h$. Now, divide both sides by 5: $\frac{300}{5} = \frac{5h}{5}$.
So, you have found that the height is 60.

Note: When you need to find the area of the base, you can follow the steps above to find it.

A right pyramid means that the base is a regular polygon. Also, the vertex is directly over the center of that polygon. If the pyramid is a right pyramid, the **surface area** can be calculated as $SA = B + \frac{1}{2}Ph_s$, where P is the perimeter of the base, and h_s is the slant height. The distance from the vertex to the midpoint of one side of the base is the slant height.

If the pyramid is irregular, the area of each triangle side must be calculated one at a time. Then, take the sum of the areas and the base to have the surface area.

Find the area of the base, the perimeter of the base, or the height
You may have problems that give you the surface area of a pyramid. So, you are asked to find the area of the base, the perimeter of the base, or the height.
Example: The surface area of the pyramid is 100 cm². The area of the base is 40cm², and the height is 12cm.

First: Set up the equation to set apart the perimeter of the base.
The equation is $100 = 40 + \frac{1}{2}12P$
Now, you can multiply the height by $\frac{1}{2}$.
So, you have: $100 = 40 + 6P$

Second: Subtract both sides of the equation by 40: $100 - 40 = 40 + 6P - 40$.

So, you have: $60 = 6P$
Now, divide both sides by 6: $\frac{60}{6} = \frac{6P}{6}$. So, you are left with: P=10cm.

Note: When you need to find the area of the base or the height, you can follow the steps above.

> ➤ **Review Video: <u>Volume and Surface Area of a Pyramid</u>**
> *Visit **mometrix.com/academy** and enter **Code: 621932***

Cone

The **volume of a cone** is found with the formula $V = \frac{1}{3}\pi r^2 h$, where r is the radius, and h is the height. This formula is the same as $\frac{1}{3}$ times the volume of a cylinder.

Find the radius or height of a cone
You may have problems that give you the volume of a cone. So, you are asked to find the radius or the height.
Example: The volume of the cone is 47.12 cm³. The height is 5cm. Find the radius.

First: Set up the equation to set apart the radius.

The equation is $47.12 = \frac{1}{3}\pi 5 r^2$

Now, you can multiply both sides by 3: $47.12 \times 3 = \frac{1}{3}\pi 5 r^2 \times 3$

So, you have $141.36 = \pi 5 r^2$.

Second: Divide both sides by 5: $\frac{141.36}{5} = \frac{\pi 5 r^2}{5}$.

Now, you have: $28.27 = \pi r^2$

You can divide both sides by π: $\frac{28.27}{\pi} = \frac{\pi r^2}{\pi}$.

So, you have $9 = \pi r^2$.

Third: Take the square root of both sides: $\sqrt{9} = \sqrt{r^2}$.

Now, you have $3 = r$

Note: When you need to find the height, you can follow the steps above to find it.

The **surface area of a cone** can be found with the formula $SA = \pi r^2 + \pi rs$, where s is the slant height. The slant height can be found with the Pythagorean Theorem to be $\sqrt{r^2 + h^2}$. So, the surface area formula for a cone can also be written as $SA = \pi r^2 + \pi r\sqrt{r^2 + h^2}$.

Find the radius of a cone
You may have problems that give you the surface area of a cone. So, you are asked to find the radius.
Example: The surface area of the cone is 43.96 cm². The slant height is 5cm. Find the radius.

First: Set up the equation to set apart the radius.
The equation is $43.96 = \pi r^2 + 5\pi r$
Then, you can factor out the π: $43.96 = \pi(r^2 + 5r)$

Second: Now, you can divide both sides by π: $\frac{43.96}{\pi} = \frac{\pi(r^2+5r)}{\pi}$
So, you have: $14 = r^2 + 5r$. Then, subtract 14 from both sides, and you have: $x = r^2 + 5r - 14$

Third: Use the quadratic formula

$$x = \frac{-5 \pm \sqrt{5^2 - 4(1)(-14)}}{2(1)}$$

So, the radius equals a positive 2.

Find the slant height of a cone
You may have problems that give you the surface area of a cone. So, you are asked to find the slant height.

Example: The surface area of the cone is 37.68 cm². The radius is 2cm. Find the slant height.

First: Set up the equation to set apart the slant height.

The equation is $37.68 = \pi 2^2 + \pi 2s$

Now, calculate both sides: $37.68 = 12.56 + 6.28s$

Second: Divide 6.28 across all three terms: $\frac{37.68}{6.28} = \frac{12.56}{6.28} + \frac{6.28s}{6.28}$

Then, you have $6 = 2 + s$. Now, subtract 2 from both sides: $6 - 2 = 2 + s - 2$

So, you are left with $4 = s$

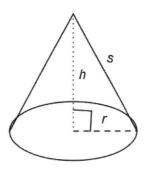

> ➤ **Review Video: <u>Volume and Surface Area of a Right Circular Cone</u>**
> *Visit **mometrix.com/academy** and enter **Code: 573574***

Geometry Modeling

Example 1

The following table lists the four states with the largest populations in 2010 and the area (in square miles) of each state. Find the population density of each and list the states from highest to lowest population density.

State	2010 Population	Area (square miles)
California	37,253,956	158,648
Texas	25,145,561	266,874
New York	19,378,102	49,112
Florida	18,801,310	58,681

California:

$$\frac{37,253,956}{158,648} \approx 235 \text{ people/sq. mi}$$

Texas:

$$\frac{25,145,561}{266,874} \approx 94 \text{ people/sq. mi}$$

New York:

$$\frac{19,378,102}{49,112} \approx 395 \text{ people/sq. mi}$$

Florida:

$$\frac{18,801,310}{58,681} \approx 320 \text{ people/sq. mi}$$

Highest population density: New York, Florida, California.
Lowest population density: Texas.

Example 2

A factory cuts large sheets of cardstock (100 in by 102 in) into cards (3 in by 5 in). Determine the maximum number of cards the factory can cut and which side of the cards should be cut from the 100 in side of the sheets.

Area of the large sheet:
$$A_{sheet} = l \cdot w = 100 \cdot 102 = 10200 \text{ square inches}$$

Area of one card:
$$A_{card} = l \cdot w = 3 \cdot 5 = 15 \text{ square inches}$$

Number of cards made:
$$\frac{10200}{15} = 680$$

Option 1: 3 *in* side cut from 100 *in* side

$\frac{100}{3} = 33.3333 \rightarrow 99$ *in* used and 33 cards per side

$\frac{102}{5} = 20.4 \rightarrow 100$ *in* used and 20 cards per side

$33 \cdot 20 = 660$ cards total

Option 2: 5 *in* side cut from the 100 *in* side

$\frac{100}{5} = 20 \rightarrow 100$ *in* used and 20 cards per side

$\frac{102}{3} = 34 \rightarrow 102$ *in* used and 34 cards per side

$34 \cdot 20 = 680$ cards total

Option 2 should be used to achieve the maximum number of cards made and avoid any wasted material.

Example 3

A display box is designed to hold a single baseball so the ball touches all six faces of the box. If the diameter of a baseball is 2.9 in, how much empty space is in the box around the ball?

$$V_{box} = s^3 = 2.9^3 = 24.389$$

$$V_{ball} = \frac{4}{3} \cdot \pi r^3 = \frac{4}{3} \cdot \pi \cdot (1.45)^3 = 12.77$$

$$V_{space} = V_{box} - V_{ball} = 24.389 - 12.77 = 11.619$$

The box has 11.619 cubic inches of space around the baseball.

Data Analysis, Probability, and Statistics

Statistics

Statistics is the branch of mathematics that deals with collecting, recording, interpreting, illustrating, and analyzing large amounts of data. The following terms are often used in the discussion of data and statistics:

Data – the collective name for pieces of information (singular is datum).

Quantitative data – measurements (such as length, mass, and speed) that provide information about quantities in numbers

Qualitative data – information (such as colors, scents, tastes, and shapes) that cannot be measured using numbers

Discrete data – information that can be expressed only by a specific value, such as whole or half numbers; For example, since people can be counted only in whole numbers, a population count would be discrete data.

Continuous data – information (such as time and temperature) that can be expressed by any value within a given range

Primary data – information that has been collected directly from a survey, investigation, or experiment, such as a questionnaire or the recording of daily temperatures; Primary data that has not yet been organized or analyzed is called raw data.

Secondary data – information that has been collected, sorted, and processed by the researcher

Ordinal data – information that can be placed in numerical order, such as age or weight

Nominal data – information that cannot be placed in numerical order, such as names or places

Measures of Central Tendency

The quantities of mean, median, and mode are all referred to as measures of central tendency. They can each give a picture of what the whole set of data looks like with just a single number. Knowing what each of these values represents is vital to making use of the information they provide.

The mean, also known as the arithmetic mean or average, of a data set is calculated by summing all of the values in the set and dividing that sum by the number of values. For example, if a data set has 6 numbers and the sum of those 6 numbers is 30, the mean is calculated as 30/6 = 5.

The median is the middle value of a data set. The median can be found by putting the data set in numerical order, and locating the middle value. In the data set (1, 2, 3, 4, 5), the median is 3. If there is an even number of values in the set, the median is calculated by taking the average of the two middle values. In the data set, (1, 2, 3, 4, 5, 6), the median would be (3 + 4)/2 = 3.5.

The mode is the value that appears most frequently in the data set. In the data set (1, 2, 3, 4, 5, 5, 5), the mode would be 5 since the value 5 appears three times. If multiple values appear the same number of times, there are multiple values for the mode. If the data set were (1, 2, 2, 3, 4, 4, 5, 5), the modes would be 2, 4, and 5. If no value appears more than any other value in the data set, then there is no mode.

Measures of Dispersion

The standard deviation expresses how spread out the values of a distribution are from the mean. Standard deviation is given in the same units as the original data and is represented by a lower case sigma (σ). A high standard deviation means that the values are very spread out. A low standard deviation means that the values are close together.

If every value in a distribution is increased or decreased by the same amount, the mean, median, and mode are increased or decreased by that amount, but the standard deviation stays the same. If every value in a distribution is multiplied or divided by the same number, the mean, median, mode, and standard deviation will all be multiplied or divided by that number.

The range of a distribution is the difference between the highest and lowest values in the distribution. For example, in the data set (1, 3, 5, 7, 9, 11), the highest and lowest values are 11 and 1, respectively. The range then would be calculated as $11 - 1 = 10$.

The three quartiles are the three values that divide a data set into four equal parts. Quartiles are generally only calculated for data sets with a large number of values. As a simple example, for the data set consisting of the numbers 1 through 99, the first quartile (Q1) would be 25, the second quartile (Q2), always equal to the median, would be 50, and the third quartile (Q3) would be 75. The difference between Q1 and Q3 is known as the interquartile range.

Probability

Probability is a branch of statistics that deals with the likelihood of something taking place. One classic example is a coin toss. There are only two possible results: heads or tails. The likelihood, or probability, that the coin will land as heads is 1 out of 2 (1/2, 0.5, 50%). Tails has the same probability. Another common example is a 6-sided die roll. There are six possible results from rolling a single die, each with an equal chance of happening, so the probability of any given number coming up is 1 out of 6.

> ➤ **Review Video: <u>Simple Probability</u>**
> *Visit **mometrix.com/academy** and enter **Code:** 212374*

Terms frequently used in probability:
Event – a situation that produces results of some sort (a coin toss)

Compound event – event that involves two or more items (rolling a pair of dice; taking the sum)

Outcome – a possible result in an experiment or event (heads, tails)

Desired outcome (or success) – an outcome that meets a particular set of criteria (a roll of 1 or 2 if we are looking for numbers less than 3)

Independent events – two or more events whose outcomes do not affect one another (two coins tossed at the same time)

Dependent events – two or more events whose outcomes affect one another (two cards drawn consecutively from the same deck)

Certain outcome – probability of outcome is 100% or 1

Impossible outcome – probability of outcome is 0% or 0

Mutually exclusive outcomes – two or more outcomes whose criteria cannot all be satisfied in a single outcome (a coin coming up heads and tails on the same toss)

Theoretical probability is the likelihood of a certain outcome occurring for a given event. It can be determined without actually performing the event. It is calculated as P (probability of success) = (desired outcomes)/(total outcomes).
Example:
There are 20 marbles in a bag and 5 are red. The theoretical probability of randomly selecting a red marble is 5 out of 20, (5/20 = 1/4, 0.25, or 25%).

Most of the time, when we talk about probability, we mean theoretical probability. Experimental probability, or relative frequency, is the number of times an outcome occurs in a particular experiment or a certain number of observed events.

While theoretical probability is based on what *should* happen, experimental probability is based on what *has* happened. Experimental probability is calculated in the same way as theoretical, except that actual outcomes are used instead of possible outcomes.

> **Review Video: Theoretical and Experimental Probability**
> *Visit mometrix.com/academy and enter Code:* **444349**

Conditional Probability
Given two events A and B, the conditional probability P(A|B) is the probability that event B will occur, given that event A has occurred. For instance, suppose you have a jar containing two red marbles and two blue marbles, and you draw two marbles at random. Note. The first drawn marble is not replaced. Consider event A being the event that the first marble drawn is red, and event B being the event that the second marble drawn is blue. With no conditions set, both P(A) and P(B) are equal to $\frac{1}{2}$. However, if we know that the first marble drawn was red—that is, that event A occurred—then that leaves one red marble and two blue marbles in the jar. In that case, the probability that the second marble is blue given that the first marble was red—that is, P(A|B)—is equal to $\frac{2}{3}$.

		Size			
		Small	Medium	Large	Total
Color	Blue	25	40	35	100
	White	27	25	22	74
	Black	8	23	15	26
	Total	60	88	72	220

Common Charts and Graphs

Charts and *Tables* are ways of organizing information into separate rows and columns. These rows and columns are labeled to find and to explain the information in them. Some charts and tables are organized horizontally with rows giving the details about the labeled information. Other charts and tables are organized vertically with columns giving the details about the labeled information.

Frequency Tables show how many times each value comes up within the set. A *Relative Frequency Table* shows the proportions of each value compared to the entire set. Relative frequencies are given as percents. However, the total percent for a relative frequency table may not equal 100 percent because of rounding.

This is an example of a frequency table with relative frequencies:

Favorite Color	Frequency	Relative Frequency
Blue	4	13%
Red	7	22%
Purple	3	9%
Green	6	19%
Cyan	12	38%

> ➤ **Review Video: <u>Proportions and Percents</u>**
> *Visit **mometrix.com/academy** and enter **Code: 941388***

A *Bar Graph* is one of the few graphs that can be drawn correctly in two ways: horizontally and vertically. A bar graph is similar to a line plot because of how the data is organized on the graph. Both axes must have their categories defined for the graph to be useful. A thick line is drawn from zero to the exact value of the data. This line can be used for a number, a percentage, or other numerical value. Longer bar lengths point to greater data values. To understand a bar graph, read the labels for the axes to know the units being reported. Then look where the bars end and match this to the scale on the other axis. This will show you the connection between the axes. This bar graph shows the responses from a survey about the favorite colors of a group.

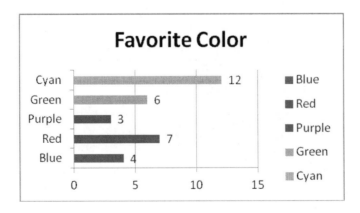

Line Graphs have one or more lines of different styles (e.g., solid or broken). These lines show the different values for a data set. Each point on the graph is shown as an ordered pair. This is similar to a Cartesian plane. In this case, the *x*- and *y*- axes are given certain units (e.g., dollars or time). Each point that is for one measurement is joined by line segments. Then, these lines show what the values are doing.

The lines may be increasing (i.e., line sloping upward), decreasing (i.e., line sloping downward), or staying the same (i.e., horizontal line). More than one set of data can be put on the same line graph. This is done to compare more than one piece of data. An example of this would be graphing test scores for different groups of students over the same stretch of time. This allows you to see which group had the greatest increase or decrease in performance over a certain amount of years. This example is shown in the graph below.

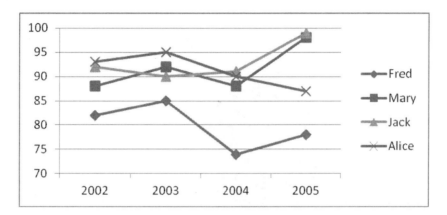

A *Line Plot*, or a *Dot Plot*, has plotted points that are NOT connected by line segments. In this graph, the horizontal axis lists the different possible values for the data. The vertical axis lists how many times one value happens. A single dot is graphed for each value. The dots in a line plot are connected. If the dots are connected, then this will not correctly represent the data.

The *5-Number Summary* of a set of data gives a very informative picture of the set. The five numbers in the summary are the minimum value, maximum value, and the three quartiles. This information gives you the range and the median of the set. Also, this information hints at how the data is spread across the median.

A *Box-and-Whiskers Plot* shows the 5-number summary on a graph. To draw a box-and-whiskers plot, place the points of the 5-number summary on a number line. Draw a box whose ends come through the points for the first and third quartiles. This is called the interquartile range. Draw a vertical line in the box that comes through the median and divides the box in half. Then, draw a line segment from the first quartile point to the minimum value. Also, draw a point from the third quartile point to the maximum value.

A *Pictograph* is a graph that is given in the horizontal format. This graph uses pictures or symbols to show the data. Each pictograph must have a key that defines the picture or symbol. Also, this key should give the number that stands for each picture or symbol. The pictures or symbols on a pictograph are not always shown as whole elements.

In this case, the fraction of the picture or symbol stands for the same fraction of the quantity that a whole picture or symbol represents. For example, there is a row in the pictograph with $3\frac{1}{2}$ ears of corn. Each ear of corn represents 100 stalks of corn in a field. So, this would equal $3\frac{1}{2} \times 100 = 350$ stalks of corn in the field.

Circle Graphs, or *Pie Charts*, show the relationship of each type of data compared to the whole set of data. The circle graph is divided into sections by drawing radii (i.e., plural for radius) to make central angles. These angles stand for a percentage of the circle. Each 1% of data is equal to 3.6° in the graph. So, data that stands for a 90° section of the circle graph makes up 25% of the whole. The pie chart below shows the data from the frequency table where people were asked about their favorite color.

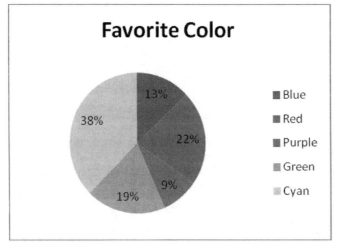

At first glance, a *Histogram* looks like a vertical bar graph. The difference is that a bar graph has a separate bar for each piece of data. A histogram has one bar for each stretch of data. For example, a histogram may have one bar for the stretch of 0–9 and one bar for the stretch of 10–19. A bar graph has numerical values on one axis.

A histogram has numbers on both axes. Each range is of equal size, and they are ordered left to right from lowest to highest. The height of each column on a histogram stands for the number of data values within that range. Like a stem and leaf plot, a histogram makes it easy to look at the graph and find which range has the greatest number of values. Below is an example of a histogram.

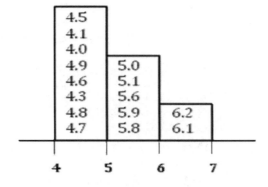

A *Stem and Leaf Plot* can outline groups of data that fall into a range of values. Each piece of data is split into two parts: the first, or left, part is called the stem. The second, or right, part is called the leaf. Each stem is listed in a column from smallest to largest. Each leaf that has the common stem is listed in that stem's row from smallest to largest.

For example, in a set of two-digit numbers, the digit in the tens place is the stem. So, the digit in the ones place is the leaf. With a stem and leaf plot, you can see which subset of numbers (10s, 20s, 30s, etc.) is the largest. This information can be found by looking at a histogram. However, a stem and leaf plot also lets you look closer and see which values fall in that range. Using all of the test scores from the line graph, we can put together a stem and leaf plot:

Test Scores								
7	4	8						
8	2	5	7	8	8			
9	0	0	1	2	2	3	5	8	9

Again, a stem-and-leaf plot is similar to histograms and frequency plots. However, a stem-and-leaf plot keeps all of the original data. In this example, you can see that almost half of the students scored in the 80s. Also, all of the data has been maintained. These plots can be used for larger numbers as well. However, they work better for small sets of data.

Bivariate Data is data from two different variables. The prefix *bi-* means *two*. In a *Scatter Plot*, each value in the set of data is put on a grid. This is similar to the Cartesian plane where each axis represents one of the two variables. When you look at the pattern made by the points on the grid, you may know if there is a relationship between the two variables. Also, you may know what that relationship is and if it exists.

The variables may be directly proportionate, inversely proportionate, or show no proportion. Also, you may be able to see if the data is linear. If the data is linear, you can find an equation to show the two variables. The following scatter plot shows the relationship between preference for brand "A" and the age of the consumers surveyed.

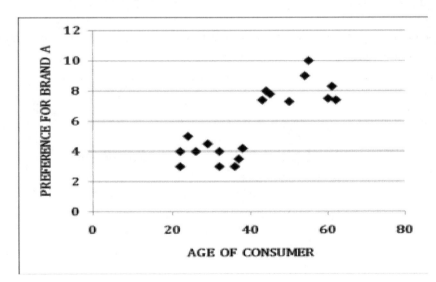

Scatter Plots are useful for knowing the types of functions that are given with the data. Also, they are helpful for finding the simple regression. A regression is a chart that is used to predict future events. Linear scatter plots may be positive or negative. Many nonlinear scatter plots are exponential or quadratic. Below are some common types of scatter plots:

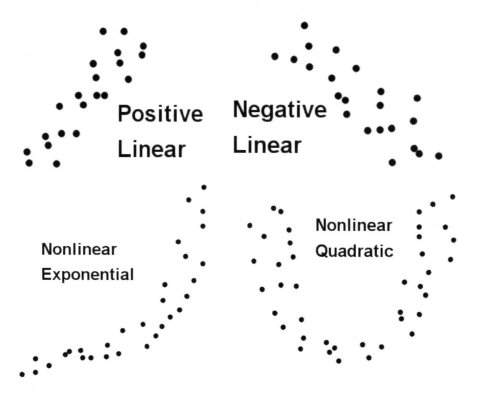

In statistics, *Simple Regression* is using an equation to represent a relation between an independent and dependent variables. The independent variable is also referred to as the explanatory variable or the predictor, and is generally represented by the variable x in the equation. The dependent variable, usually represented by the variable y, is also referred to as the response variable. The equation may be any type of function – linear, quadratic, exponential, etc. The best way to handle this task is to use the regression feature of your graphing calculator. This will easily give you the curve of best fit and provide you with the coefficients and other information you need to derive an equation.

In a scatter plot, the *Line of Best Fit* is the line that best shows the trends of the data. The line of best fit is given by the equation $\hat{y} = ax + b$, where a and b are the regression coefficients. The regression coefficient a is also the slope of the line of best fit, and b is also the *y*-coordinate of the point at which the line of best fit crosses the *x*-axis. Not every point on the scatter plot will be on the line of best fit. The differences between the y-values of the points in the scatter plot and the corresponding y-values according to the equation of the line of best fit are the residuals. The line of best fit is also called the least-squares regression line because it is also the line that has the lowest sum of the squares of the residuals.

Shape of Data Distribution

Symmetry and Skewness
Symmetry is a characteristic of the shape of the plotted data. Specifically, it refers to how well the data on one side of the median mirrors the data on the other side.

A skewed data set is one that has a distinctly longer or fatter tail on one side of the peak or the other. A data set that is skewed left has more of its values to the left of the peak, while a set that is skewed right has more of its values to the right of the peak. When actually looking at the graph, these names may seem counterintuitive since, in a left-skewed data set, the bulk of the values seem to be on the right side of the graph, and vice versa. However, if the graph is viewed strictly in relation to the peak, the direction of skewness makes more sense.

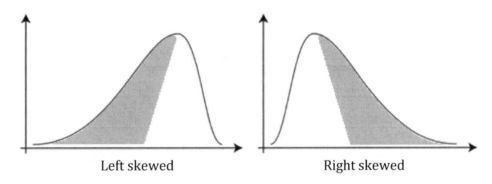

Left skewed   Right skewed

Unimodal vs. Bimodal
If a distribution has a single peak, it would be considered unimodal. If it has two discernible peaks it would be considered bimodal. Bimodal distributions may be an indication that the set of data being considered is actually the combination of two sets of data with significant differences.

Uniformity
A uniform distribution is a distribution in which there is no distinct peak or variation in the data. No values or ranges are particularly more common than any other values or ranges.

Outlier

An outlier is an extremely high or extremely low value in the data set. It may be the result of measurement error, in which case, the outlier is not a valid member of the data set. However, it may also be a valid member of the distribution. Unless a measurement error is identified, the experimenter cannot know for certain if an outlier is or is not a member of the distribution. There are arbitrary methods that can be employed to designate an extreme value as an outlier. One method designates an outlier (or possible outlier) to be any value less than $Q_1 - 1.5(IQR)$ or any value greater than $Q_3 + 1.5(IQR)$, where Q_1 and Q_3 are the first and third quartiles and IQR is the interquartile range. For instance, in the data set {42, 71, 22, 500, 33, 38, 62, 44, 58, 37, 61, 25}, the point 500 may be considered an outlier, since 500 is greater than 101.25 (61.5 + 1.5(26.5) = 101.25).

The Reading Test

The 35 minute ACT Reading Test consists of four reading selections each followed by 10 questions. One of the four selections is drawn from the humanities, one from social studies, one from the natural sciences, and one from prose fiction.

Key Ideas and Details

Summarizing a Complex Text

<u>Summarize</u>
A helpful tool is the ability to summarize the information that you have read in a paragraph or passage format. This process is similar to creating an effective outline. First, a summary should accurately define the main idea of the passage though the summary does not need to explain this main idea in exhaustive detail. The summary should continue by laying out the most important supporting details or arguments from the passage. All of the significant supporting details should be included, and none of the details included should be irrelevant or insignificant. Also, the summary should accurately report all of these details. Too often, the desire for brevity in a summary leads to the sacrifice of clarity or accuracy. Summaries are often difficult to read because they omit all of the graceful language, digressions, and asides that distinguish great writing. However, an effective summary should contain much the same message as the original text.

<u>Paraphrase</u>
Paraphrasing is another method that the reader can use to aid in comprehension. When paraphrasing, one puts what they have read into their words by rephrasing what the author has written, or one "translates" all of what the author shared into their words by including as many details as they can.

Identifying the Logical Conclusion

Identifying a logical conclusion can help you determine whether you agree with the writer or not. Coming to this conclusion is much like making an inference: the approach requires you to combine the information given by the text with what you already know in order to make a logical conclusion. If the author intended the reader to draw a certain conclusion, then you can expect the author's argumentation and detail to be leading in that direction. One way to approach the task of drawing conclusions is to make brief notes of all the points made by the author. When the notes are arranged on paper, they may clarify the logical conclusion. Another way to approach conclusions is to consider whether the reasoning of the author raises any pertinent questions. Sometimes you will be able to draw several conclusions from a passage. On occasion these will be conclusions that were never imagined by the author. Therefore, be aware that these conclusions must be supported directly by the text.

> ➤ **Review Video:** <u>Identifying a Logical Conclusion</u>
> *Visit* **mometrix.com/academy** *and enter* **Code: 157215**

Directly Stated Information

A reader should always be drawing conclusions from the text. Sometimes conclusions are implied from written information, and other times the information is **stated directly** within the passage. One should always aim to draw conclusions from information stated within a passage, rather than to draw them from mere implications. At times an author may provide some information and then describe a counterargument. Readers should be alert for direct statements that are subsequently rejected or weakened by the author. Furthermore, you should always read through the entire passage before drawing conclusions. Many readers are trained to expect the author's conclusions at either the beginning or the end of the passage, but many texts do not adhere to this format.

> ➤ **Review Video: <u>Conclusions that are Stated Directly</u>**
> *Visit **mometrix.com/academy** and enter **Code: 851825***

Inferences

Readers are often required to understand a text that claims and suggests ideas without stating them directly. An **inference** is a piece of information that is implied but not written outright by the author. For instance, consider the following sentence: *After the final out of the inning, the fans were filled with joy and rushed the field*. From this sentence, a reader can infer that the fans were watching a baseball game and their team won the game. Readers should take great care to avoid using information beyond the provided passage before making inferences. As you practice with drawing inferences, you will find that they require concentration and attention.

> ➤ **Review Video: <u>Inference</u>**
> *Visit **mometrix.com/academy** and enter **Code: 379203***

Test-taking tip: While being tested on your ability to make correct inferences, you must look for contextual clues. An answer can be *true* but not *correct*. The contextual clues will help you find the answer that is the best answer out of the given choices. Be careful in your reading to understand the context in which a phrase is stated. When asked for the implied meaning of a statement made in the passage, you should immediately locate the statement and read the context in which the statement was made. Also, look for an answer choice that has a similar phrase to the statement in question.

Implications

Drawing conclusions from information implied within a passage requires confidence on the part of the reader. **Implications** are things that the author does not state directly, but readers can assume based on what the author does say. Consider the following passage: *I stepped outside and opened my umbrella. By the time I got to work, the cuffs of my pants were soaked*. The author never states that it is raining, but this fact is clearly implied. Conclusions based on implication must be well supported by the text. In order to draw a solid conclusion, readers should have multiple pieces of evidence. If readers have only one piece, they must be assured that there is no other possible explanation than their conclusion. A good reader will be able to draw many conclusions from information implied by the text which will be a great help in the exam.

Topics, Main Ideas, and Supporting Details

Topics and Main Ideas

One of the most important skills in reading comprehension is the identification of **topics** and **main ideas.** There is a subtle difference between these two features. The topic is the subject of a text (i.e., what the text is all about). The main idea, on the other hand, is the most important point being made by the author. The topic is usually expressed in a few words at the most while the main idea often needs a full sentence to be completely defined. As an example, a short passage might have the topic of penguins and the main idea could be written as *Penguins are different from other birds in many ways.* In most nonfiction writing, the topic and the main idea will be stated directly and often appear in a sentence at the very beginning or end of the text. When being tested on an understanding of the author's topic, you may be able to skim the passage for the general idea, by reading only the first sentence of each paragraph. A body paragraph's first sentence is often—but not always—the main topic sentence which gives you a summary of the content in the paragraph.

However, there are cases in which the reader must figure out an unstated topic or main idea. In these instances, you must read every sentence of the text and try to come up with an overarching idea that is supported by each of those sentences.

> **Review Video:** <u>Topics and Main Ideas</u>
> *Visit **mometrix.com/academy** and enter **Code: 407801***

Supporting Details
Supporting details provide evidence and backing for the main point. In order to show that a main idea is correct, or valid, authors add details that prove their point. All texts contain details, but they are only classified as supporting details when they serve to reinforce some larger point. Supporting details are most commonly found in informative and persuasive texts. In some cases, they will be clearly indicated with terms like *for example* or *for instance*, or they will be enumerated with terms like *first*, *second*, and *last*. However, you need to be prepared for texts that do not contain those indicators. As a reader, you should consider whether the author's supporting details really back up his or her main point. Supporting details can be factual and correct, yet they may not be relevant to the author's point. Conversely, supporting details can seem pertinent, but they can be ineffective because they are based on opinion or assertions that cannot be proven.

> **Review Video:** <u>Supporting Details</u>
> *Visit **mometrix.com/academy** and enter **Code: 396297***

Topic and Summary Sentences
Topic and summary sentences are a convenient way to encapsulate the main idea of a text. In some textbooks and academic articles, the author will place a topic or summary sentence at the beginning of each section as a means of preparing the reader for what is to come. Research suggests that the brain is more receptive to new information when it has been prepared by the presentation of the main idea or some key words. The phenomenon is somewhat akin to the primer coat of paint that allows subsequent coats of paint to absorb more easily. A good topic sentence will be clear and not contain any jargon. When topic or summary sentences are not provided, good readers can jot down their own so that they can find their place in a text and refresh their memory.

Events in a Sequence

Readers must be able to identify a text's **sequence**, or the order in which things happen. Often, when the sequence is very important to the author, the text is indicated with signal words like *first*, *then*, *next*, and *last*. However, a sequence can be merely implied and must be noted by the reader. Consider the sentence *He walked through the garden and gave water and fertilizer to the plants.* Clearly, the man did not walk through the garden before he collected water and fertilizer for the plants. So, the implied sequence is that he first collected water, then he collected fertilizer, next he walked through the garden, and last he gave water or fertilizer as necessary to the plants. Texts do not always proceed in an orderly sequence from first to last. Sometimes they begin at the end and start over at the beginning. As a reader, you can enhance your understanding of the passage by taking brief notes to clarify the sequence.

> ➤ **Review Video: <u>Sequence</u>**
> *Visit **mometrix.com/academy** and enter **Code: 489027***

Cause and Effect

In **cause and effect**, an author presents one thing that makes something else happen. For example, if one were to go to bed very late and awake very early, then they would be tired in the morning. The cause is lack of sleep, with the effect of being tired the next day.

Identifying the cause-and-effect relationships in a text can be tricky, but there are a few ways to approach this task. Often, these relationships are signaled with certain terms. When an author uses words like *because*, *since*, *in order*, and *so*, he or she is likely describing a cause-and-effect relationship. Consider the sentence: *He called her because he needed the homework.* This is a simple causal relationship in which the cause was his need for the homework, and the effect was his phone call. Yet, not all cause-and-effect relationships are marked in this way. Consider the sentences: *He called her. He needed the homework.* When the cause-and-effect relationship is not indicated with a keyword, the relationship can be discovered by asking why something happened. He called her: why? The answer is in the next sentence: He needed the homework.

> ➤ **Review Video: <u>When There's No Keyword</u>**
> *Visit **mometrix.com/academy** and enter **Code: 312791***

Persuasive essays, in which an author tries to make a convincing argument and change the minds of readers, usually include cause-and-effect relationships. However, these relationships should not always be taken at face value. Frequently, an author will assume a cause or take an effect for granted. To read a persuasive essay effectively, readers need to judge the cause-and-effect relationships that the author is presenting. For instance, imagine an author wrote the following: *The parking deck has been unprofitable because people would prefer to ride their bikes.* The relationship is clear: the cause is that people prefer to ride their bikes, and the effect is that the parking deck has been unprofitable. However, readers should consider whether this argument is conclusive. Perhaps there are other reasons for the failure of the parking deck: a down economy, excessive fees, etc. Too often, authors present causal relationships as if they are fact rather than opinion. Readers should be on the alert for these dubious claims.

Comparing Ideas

Many texts follow the **compare-and-contrast** model in which the similarities and differences between two ideas or things are explored. Analysis of the similarities between ideas is called comparison. In an ideal comparison, the author places ideas or things in an equivalent structure (i.e., the author presents the ideas in the same way). If an author wants to show the similarities between cricket and baseball, then he or she may do so by summarizing the equipment and rules for each game. Be mindful of the similarities as they appear in the passage and take note of any differences that are mentioned. Often, these small differences will only reinforce the more general similarity.

Contrasting Ideas

Thinking critically about ideas and conclusions can seem like a daunting task. One way to ease this task is to understand the basic elements of ideas and writing techniques. Looking at the way different ideas relate to each other can be a good way for readers to begin their analysis. For instance, sometimes authors will write about two ideas that are in opposition to each other. Or one author will provide his or her ideas on a topic, and another author may respond in opposition. The analysis of these opposing ideas is known as **contrast**. Contrast is often marred by the author's obvious partiality to one of the ideas. A discerning reader will be put off by an author who does not engage in a fair fight. In an analysis of opposing ideas, both ideas should be presented in clear and reasonable terms. If the author does prefer a side, you need to read carefully to determine the areas where the author shows or avoids this preference. In an analysis of opposing ideas, you should proceed through the passage by marking the major differences point by point with an eye that is looking for an explanation of each side's view. For instance, in an analysis of capitalism and communism, there is an importance in outlining each side's view on labor, markets, prices, personal responsibility, etc. Additionally, as you read through the passages, you should note whether the opposing views present each side in a similar manner.

> ➢ **Review Video:** <u>Compare and Contrast</u>
> Visit **mometrix.com/academy** and enter **Code: 798319**

Themes in Print and Other Sources

Themes are seldom expressed directly in a text and can be difficult to identify. A theme is an issue, an idea, or a question raised by the text. For instance, a theme of *Cinderella* (the Charles Perrault version) is perseverance as the title character serves her step-sisters and step-mother, and the prince seeks to find the girl with the missing slipper. A passage may have many themes, and you, as a dedicated reader, must take care to identify only themes that you are asked to find. One common characteristic of themes is that they raise more questions than they answer. In a good piece of fiction, authors are trying to elevate the reader's perspective and encourage him or her to consider the themes in a deeper way. In the process of reading, one can identify themes by constantly asking about the general issues that the text is addressing. A good way to evaluate an author's approach to a theme is to begin reading with a question in mind (e.g., How does this text approach the theme of love?) and to look for evidence in the text that addresses that question.

> ➢ **Review Video:** <u>Theme</u>
> Visit **mometrix.com/academy** and enter **Code: 732074**

<u>Similar Themes across Cultures</u>
A brief study of world literature suggests that writers from vastly different cultures address similar themes. For instance, works like the *Odyssey* and *Hamlet* both consider the individual's battle for self-control and independence. In most cultures, authors address themes of personal growth and the struggle for maturity. Another universal theme is the conflict between the individual and society. Works that are as culturally disparate as *Native Son*, the *Aeneid*, and *1984* dramatize how people struggle to maintain their personalities and dignity in large (sometimes) oppressive groups. Finally, many cultures have versions of the hero's or heroine's journey in which an adventurous

person must overcome many obstacles in order to gain greater knowledge, power, and perspective. Some famous works that treat this theme are the *Epic of Gilgamesh*, Dante's *Divine Comedy*, and Cervantes' *Don Quixote*.

Differences in Addressing Themes in Various Cultures and Genres

Authors from different genres and cultures may address similar themes, but they do so in different ways. For instance, poets are likely to address subject matter indirectly through the use of images and allusions. In a play, the author is more likely to dramatize themes by using characters to express opposing viewpoints; this disparity is known as a dialectical approach. In a passage, the author does not need to express themes directly; indeed, they can be expressed through events and actions. In some regional literatures, such as Greece or England, authors use more irony: their works have characters that express views and make decisions that are clearly disapproved of by the author. In Latin America, there is a great tradition of using supernatural events to illustrate themes about real life. Chinese and Japanese authors frequently use well-established regional forms (e.g., haiku poetry in Japan) to organize their treatment of universal themes.

Craft and Structure

Word Meaning from Context

One of the benefits of reading is the expansion of one's vocabulary. In order to obtain this benefit, however, one needs to know how to identify the definition of a word from its context. This means defining a word based on the words around it and the way it is used in a sentence. Consider the following sentence: *The elderly scholar spent his evenings hunched over arcane texts that few other people even knew existed.* The adjective *arcane* is uncommon, but you can obtain significant information about it based on its use in the sentence. The fact that few other people know of their existence allows you to assume that "arcane texts" must be rare and be of interest to a few people. Also, the texts are being read by an elderly scholar. So, you can assume that they focus on difficult academic subjects. Sometimes, words can be defined by what they are not. Consider the following sentence: *Ron's fealty to his parents was not shared by Karen, who disobeyed their every command.* Someone who disobeys is not demonstrating *fealty*. So, you can infer that the word means something like *obedience* or *respect*.

Figurative Language
There are many types of language devices that authors use to convey their meaning in a descriptive way. Understanding these concepts will help you understand what you read. These types of devices are called *figurative language* – language that goes beyond the literal meaning of a word or phrase. **Descriptive language** that evokes imagery in the reader's mind is one type of figurative language. **Exaggeration** is another type of figurative language. Also, when you compare two things, you are using figurative language. **Similes** and **metaphors** are ways of comparing things, and both are types of figurative language commonly found in poetry. An example of figurative language (a simile in this case): *The child howled like a coyote when her mother told her to pick up the toys.* In this example, the child's howling is compared to that of a coyote and helps the reader understand the sound being made by the child.

> ➤ **Review Video: Idiom**
> Visit ***mometrix.com/academy*** *and enter* **Code: 355353**

Metaphor
A **metaphor** is a type of figurative language in which the writer equates one thing with a different thing. For instance: *The bird was an arrow arcing through the sky.* In this sentence, the arrow is serving as a metaphor for the bird. The point of a metaphor is to encourage the reader to consider the item being described in a different way. Let's continue with this metaphor for a bird: you are asked to envision the bird's flight as being similar to the arc of an arrow. So, you imagine the flight to be swift and bending. Metaphors are a way for the author to describe an item without being direct and obvious. This literary device is a lyrical and suggestive way of providing information. Note that the reference for a metaphor will not always be mentioned explicitly by the author. Consider the following description of a forest in winter: *Swaying skeletons reached for the sky and groaned as the wind blew through them.* In this example, the author is using *skeletons* as a metaphor for leafless trees. This metaphor creates a spooky tone while inspiring the reader's imagination.

> ➤ **Review Video: Metaphor**
> Visit ***mometrix.com/academy*** *and enter* **Code: 133295**

Simile

A **simile** is a figurative expression that is similar to a metaphor, yet the expression requires the use of the distancing words *like* or *as*. Some examples: *The sun was like an orange, eager as a beaver*, and *nimble as a mountain goat*. Because a simile includes *like* or a*s*, the device creates a space between the description and the thing being described. If an author says that *a house was like a shoebox*, then the tone is different than the author saying that the house *was* a shoebox. In a simile, authors explicitly indicate that the description is not the same thing as the thing being described. In a metaphor, there is no such distinction. The decision of which device to use will be made based on the authors' intended tone.

> ➤ **Review Video: <u>Simile</u>**
> *Visit **mometrix.com/academy** and enter **Code: 642949***

Personification

Another type of figurative language is **personification.** This is the description of a nonhuman thing as if the item were human. Literally, the word means the process of making something into a person. The general intent of personification is to describe things in a manner that will be comprehensible to readers. When an author states that a tree *groans* in the wind, he or she does not mean that the tree is emitting a low, pained sound from a mouth. Instead, the author means that the tree is making a noise similar to a human groan. Of course, this personification establishes a tone of sadness or suffering. A different tone would be established if the author said that the tree was *swaying* or *dancing*.

> ➤ **Review Video: <u>Personification</u>**
> *Visit **mometrix.com/academy** and enter **Code: 260066***

Denotative Meaning of Words

The **denotative** meaning of a word is the literal meaning of the word. The **connotative** meaning goes beyond the denotative meaning to include the emotional reaction that a word may invoke. The connotative meaning often takes the denotative meaning a step further due to associations which the reader makes with the denotative meaning. Readers can differentiate between the denotative and connotative meanings by first recognizing how authors use each meaning. Most non-fiction, for example, is fact-based and authors do not use flowery, figurative language. The reader can assume that the writer is using the denotative meaning of words. In fiction, the author may use the connotative meaning. Readers can determine whether the author is using the denotative or connotative meaning of a word by implementing context clues.

> ➤ **Review Video: <u>Denotative and Connotative Meanings</u>**
> *Visit **mometrix.com/academy** and enter **Code: 736707***

Structure of Texts

Problem-Solution Text Structure

Some nonfiction texts are organized to present a problem followed by a solution. For this type of text, the problem is often explained before the solution is offered. In some cases, as when the problem is well known, the solution may be introduced briefly at the beginning. Other passages may focus on the solution, and the problem will be referenced only occasionally. Some texts will outline multiple solutions to a problem, leaving readers to choose among them. If the author has an interest or an allegiance to one solution, he or she may fail to mention or describe accurately some of the other solutions. Readers should be careful of the author's agenda when reading a problem-solution text. Only by understanding the author's perspective and interests can one develop a proper judgment of the proposed solution.

> **Review Video:** <u>Text Structure</u>
> *Visit **mometrix.com/academy** and enter **Code:** **656503***

Descriptive Text

In a sense, almost all writing is descriptive, insofar as an author seeks to describe events, ideas, or people to the reader. Some texts, however, are primarily concerned with **description**. A descriptive text focuses on a particular subject and attempts to depict the subject in a way that will be clear to readers. Descriptive texts contain many adjectives and adverbs (i.e., words that give shades of meaning and create a more detailed mental picture for the reader). A descriptive text fails when it is unclear to the reader. A descriptive text will certainly be informative, and the passage may be persuasive and entertaining as well.

> **Review Video:** <u>Descriptive Text</u>
> *Visit **mometrix.com/academy** and enter **Code:** **174903***

> **Review Video:** <u>Rhetorical Strategy of Description</u>
> *Visit **mometrix.com/academy** and enter **Code:** **175865***

Comparison and Contrast

Authors will use different stylistic and writing devices to make their meaning clear for readers. One of those devices is comparison and contrast. As mentioned previously, when an author describes the ways in which two things are alike, he or she is comparing them. When the author describes the ways in which two things are different, he or she is contrasting them. The "compare and contrast" essay is one of the most common forms in nonfiction. These passages are often signaled with certain words: a comparison may have indicating terms such as *both*, *same*, *like*, *too*, and *as well*; while a contrast may have terms like *but*, *however*, *on the other hand*, *instead*, and *yet*. Of course, comparisons and contrasts may be implicit without using any such signaling language. A single sentence may both compare and contrast. Consider the sentence *Brian and Sheila love ice cream, but Brian prefers vanilla and Sheila prefers strawberry*. In one sentence, the author has described both a similarity (love of ice cream) and a difference (favorite flavor).

> **Review Video:** <u>Rhetorical Strategy of Comparing and Contrasting</u>
> *Visit **mometrix.com/academy** and enter **Code:** **438042***

Cause and Effect

One of the most common text structures is cause and effect. A cause is an act or event that makes something happen, and an effect is the thing that happens as a result of the cause. A cause-and-effect relationship is not always explicit, but there are some terms in English that signal causes, such as *since*, *because*, and *due to*. Furthermore, terms that signal effects include *consequently*, *therefore*, *this lead(s) to*. As an example, consider this sentence: *Because the sky was clear, Ron did not bring an umbrella*. The cause is the clear sky, and the effect is that Ron did not bring an umbrella. However, readers may find that sometimes the cause-and-effect relationship will not be clearly noted. For instance, the sentence *He was late and missed the meeting* does not contain any signaling words, but the sentence still contains a cause (he was late) and an effect (he missed the meeting).

> ➢ **Review Video: Rhetorical Strategy of Cause and Effect Analysis**
> *Visit mometrix.com/academy and enter Code: 725944*

Types of Passages

Narrative Passage

A **narrative** passage is a story that can be fiction or nonfiction. However, there are a few elements that a text must have in order to be classified as a narrative. First, the text must have a plot (i.e., a series of events). Narratives often proceed in a clear sequence, but this is not a requirement. If the narrative is good, then these events will be interesting to readers. Second, a narrative has characters. These characters could be people, animals, or even inanimate objects—so long as they participate in the plot. Third, a narrative passage often contains figurative language which is meant to stimulate the imagination of readers by making comparisons and observations. For instance, a metaphor, a common piece of figurative language, is a description of one thing in terms of another. *The moon was a frosty snowball* is an example of a metaphor. In the literal sense this is obviously untrue, but the comparison suggests a certain mood for the reader.

> ➢ **Review Video: Style, Tone, and Mood**
> *Visit mometrix.com/academy and enter Code: 234852*

Expository Passage

An **expository** passage aims to inform and enlighten readers. The passage is nonfiction and usually centers around a simple, easily defined topic. Since the goal of exposition is to teach, such a passage should be as clear as possible. Often, an expository passage contains helpful organizing words, like *first*, *next*, *for example*, and *therefore*. These words keep the reader oriented in the text. Although expository passages do not need to feature colorful language and artful writing, they are often more effective with these features. For a reader, the challenge of expository passages is to maintain steady attention. Expository passages are not always about subjects that will naturally interest a reader, so the writer is often more concerned with clarity and comprehensibility than with engaging the reader. By reading actively, you will ensure a good habit of focus when reading an expository passage.

> ➢ **Review Video: Interpretation of Expository or Literary Text**
> *Visit mometrix.com/academy and enter Code: 860442*

Technical Passage

A **technical** passage is written to describe a complex object or process. Technical writing is common in medical and technological fields, in which complex ideas of mathematics, science, and engineering need to be explained simply and clearly. To ease comprehension, a technical passage usually proceeds in a very logical order. Technical passages often have clear headings and subheadings, which are used to keep the reader oriented in the text. Additionally, you will find that these passages divide sections up with numbers or letters. Many technical passages look more like an outline than a piece of prose. The amount of jargon or difficult vocabulary will vary in a technical passage depending on the intended audience. As much as possible, technical passages try to avoid language that the reader will have to research in order to understand the message, yet readers will find that jargon cannot always be avoided.

> **Review Video: Word Choice and Intended Audience**
> Visit *mometrix.com/academy* and enter *Code: 505088*

Persuasive Passage

A **persuasive** passage is meant to change the mind of readers and lead them into agreement with the author. The persuasive intent may be very obvious or quite difficult to discern. In some cases, a persuasive passage will be indistinguishable from one that is informative. Both passages make an assertion and offer supporting details. However, a persuasive passage is more likely to appeal to the reader's emotions and to make claims based on opinion. Persuasive passages may not describe alternate positions, but when they do, they often display significant bias. Readers may find that a persuasive passage is giving the author's viewpoint, or the passage may adopt a seemingly objective tone. A persuasive passage is successful if it can make a convincing argument and win the trust of the reader.

> **Review Video: Persuasive Techniques**
> Visit *mometrix.com/academy* and enter *Code: 577997*

> **Review Video: Persuasive Text and Bias**
> Visit *mometrix.com/academy* and enter *Code: 479856*

Identifying an Author's Position

In order to be an effective reader, one must pay attention to the author's **position** and purpose. Even those texts that seem objective and impartial, like textbooks, have a position and bias. Readers need to take these positions into account when considering the author's message. When an author uses emotional language or clearly favors one side of an argument, his or her position is clear. However, the author's position may be evident not only in what he or she writes, but also in what he or she doesn't write. In a normal setting, a reader would want to review some other texts on the same topic in order to develop a view of the author's position. If this was not possible, then you would want to acquire some background about the author. However, since you are in the middle of an exam and the only source of information is the text, you should look for language and argumentation that seems to indicate a particular stance on the subject.

> **Review Video: Author's Position**
> Visit *mometrix.com/academy* and enter *Code: 827954*

> **Review Video: Different Perspectives from Different Authors**
> Visit *mometrix.com/academy* and enter *Code: 615727*

Purpose

Usually, identifying the **purpose** of an author is easier than identifying his or her position. In most cases, the author has no interest in hiding his or her purpose. A text that is meant to entertain, for instance, should be written to please the reader. Most narratives, or stories, are written to entertain, though they may also inform or persuade. Informative texts are easy to identify, while the most difficult purpose of a text to identify is persuasion because the author has an interest in making this purpose hard to detect. When a reader discovers that the author is trying to persuade, he or she should be skeptical of the argument. For this reason persuasive texts often try to establish an entertaining tone and hope to amuse the reader into agreement. On the other hand, an informative tone may be implemented to create an appearance of authority and objectivity.

> ➤ **Review Video: Purpose**
> *Visit mometrix.com/academy and enter Code:* **511819**

An author's purpose is evident often in the organization of the text (e.g., section headings in bold font points to an informative text). However, you may not have such organization available to you in your exam. Instead, if the author makes his or her main idea clear from the beginning, then the likely purpose of the text is to inform. If the author begins by making a claim and provides various arguments to support that claim, then the purpose is probably to persuade. If the author tells a story or seems to want the attention of the reader more than to push a particular point or deliver information, then his or her purpose is most likely to entertain. As a reader, you must judge authors on how well they accomplish their purpose. In other words, you need to consider the type of passage (e.g., technical, persuasive, etc.) that the author has written and if the author has followed the requirements of the passage type.

> ➤ **Review Video: Purpose of the Author**
> *Visit mometrix.com/academy and enter Code:* **497555**

> ➤ **Review Video: Organization in a Paper**
> *Visit mometrix.com/academy and enter Code:* **479120**

Persuasive Writing

In a persuasive essay, the author is attempting to change the reader's mind or convince him or her of something that he or she did not believe previously. There are several identifying characteristics of persuasive writing. One is opinion presented as fact. When authors attempt to persuade readers, they often present their opinions as if they were fact. Readers must be on guard for statements that sound factual but which cannot be subjected to research, observation, or experiment. Another characteristic of persuasive writing is emotional language. An author will often try to play on the emotions of readers by appealing to their sympathy or sense of morality. When an author uses colorful or evocative language with the intent of arousing the reader's passions, then the author may be attempting to persuade. Finally, in many cases, a persuasive text will give an unfair explanation of opposing positions, if these positions are mentioned at all.

> ➤ **Review Video: Rhetorical Strategy of Persuasion**
> *Visit mometrix.com/academy and enter Code:* **302658**

Informative Texts

An informative text is written to educate and enlighten readers. Informative texts are almost always nonfiction and are rarely structured as a story. The intention of an informative text is to deliver information in the most comprehensible way. So, look for the structure of the text to be very clear. In an informative text, the thesis statement is one or sometimes two sentences that normally appear at the end of the first paragraph. The author may use some colorful language, but he or she is likely to put more emphasis on clarity and precision. Informative essays do not typically appeal to the emotions. They often contain facts and figures and rarely include the opinion of the author; however, readers should remain aware of the possibility for a bias as those facts are presented. Sometimes a persuasive essay can resemble an informative essay, especially if the author maintains an even tone and presents his or her views as if they were established fact.

> **Review Video: Informative Text**
Visit **mometrix.com/academy** and enter **Code: 924964**

Entertaining Texts

The success or failure of an author's intent to **entertain** is determined by those who read the author's work. Entertaining texts may be either fiction or nonfiction, and they may describe real or imagined people, places, and events. Entertaining texts are often narratives or poems. A text that is written to entertain is likely to contain colorful language that engages the imagination and the emotions. Such writing often features a great deal of figurative language, which typically enlivens the subject matter with images and analogies.

Though an entertaining text is not usually written to persuade or inform, authors may accomplish both of these tasks in their work. An entertaining text may appeal to the reader's emotions and cause him or her to think differently about a particular subject. In any case, entertaining texts tend to showcase the personality of the author more than other types of writing.

> **Review Video: Figurative Language**
Visit **mometrix.com/academy** and enter **Code: 584902**

Expression of Feelings

When an author intends to **express feelings,** he or she may use expressive and bold language. An author may write with emotion for any number of reasons. Sometimes, authors will express feelings because they are describing a personal situation of great pain or happiness. In other situations, authors will attempt to persuade the reader and will use emotion to stir up the passions. This kind of expression is easy to identify when the writer uses phrases like *I felt* and *I sense*. However, readers may find that the author will simply describe feelings without introducing them. As a reader, you must know the importance of recognizing when an author is expressing emotion and not to become overwhelmed by sympathy or passion. Readers should maintain some detachment so that they can still evaluate the strength of the author's argument or the quality of the writing.

Point of View

Another element that impacts a text is the author's point-of-view. The **point of view** of a text is the perspective from which a passage is told. An author will always have a point of view about a story before he or she draws up a plot line. The author will know what events they want to take place, how they want the characters to interact, and how they want the story to resolve. An author will also have an opinion on the topic or series of events which is presented in the story that is based on their prior experience and beliefs.

> ➢ **Review Video:** <u>Plotline</u>
> *Visit **mometrix.com/academy** and enter **Code:** 944011*

The two main points of view that authors use--especially in a work of fiction--are first person and third person. If the narrator of the story is also the main character, or *protagonist*, the text is written in first-person point of view. In first person, the author writes from the perspective of *I*. Third-person point of view is probably the most common that authors use in their passages. Using third person, authors refer to each character by using *he* or *she*. In third-person omniscient, the narrator is not a character in the story and tells the story of all of the characters at the same time.

> ➢ **Review Video:** <u>Point of View</u>
> *Visit **mometrix.com/academy** and enter **Code:** 383336*

Integration of Knowledge and Ideas

Fact and Opinion

Readers must always be conscious of the distinction between fact and opinion. A fact can be subjected to analysis and can be either proved or disproved. An opinion, on the other hand, is the author's personal thoughts or feelings which may not be alterable by research or evidence. If the author writes that the distance from New York to Boston is about two hundred miles, then he or she is stating a fact. If an author writes that New York is too crowded, then he or she is giving an opinion because there is no objective standard for overpopulation.

An opinion may be indicated by words like *believe*, *think*, or *feel*. Readers must be aware that an opinion may be supported by facts. For instance, the author might give the population density of New York as a reason for an overcrowded population. An opinion supported by fact tends to be more convincing. On the other hand, when authors support their opinions with other opinions, readers should not be persuaded by the argument to any degree.

> ➢ **Review Video:** <u>Fact or Opinion</u>
> *Visit **mometrix.com/academy** and enter **Code: 870899***

Biases and Stereotypes

Every author has a point-of-view, but authors demonstrate a bias when they ignore reasonable counterarguments or distort opposing viewpoints. A bias is evident whenever the author is unfair or inaccurate in his or her presentation. Bias may be intentional or unintentional, and readers should be skeptical of the author's argument. Remember that a biased author may still be correct; however, the author will be correct in spite of his or her bias, not because of the bias. A stereotype is like a bias, yet a stereotype is applied specifically to a group or place. Stereotyping is considered to be particularly abhorrent because the practice promotes negative generalizations about people. Readers should be very cautious of authors who stereotype in their writing. These faulty assumptions typically reveal the author's ignorance and lack of curiosity.

> ➢ **Review Video:** <u>Bias</u>
> *Visit **mometrix.com/academy** and enter **Code: 456336***

Evaluating an Argument

Argumentative and persuasive passages take a stand on a debatable issue, seek to explore all sides of the issue, and find the best possible solution. Argumentative and persuasive passages should not be combative or abusive. The word *argument* may remind you of two or more people shouting at each other and walking away in anger. However, an argumentative or persuasive passage should be a calm and reasonable presentation of an author's ideas for others to consider. When an author writes reasonable arguments, his or her goal is not to win or have the last word. Instead, authors want to reveal current understanding of the question at hand and suggest a solution to a problem. The purpose of argument and persuasion in a free society is to reach the best solution.

Evidence

The term **text evidence** refers to information that supports a main point or minor points and can help lead the reader to a conclusion. Information used as text evidence is precise, descriptive, and factual. A main point is often followed by supporting details that provide evidence to back up a claim. For example, a passage may include the claim that winter occurs during opposite months in the Northern and Southern hemispheres. Text evidence based on this claim may include countries where winter occurs in opposite months along with reasons that winter occurs at different times of the year in separate hemispheres (due to the tilt of the Earth as it rotates around the sun).

> **Review Video: Text Evidence**
> Visit *mometrix.com/academy* and enter *Code:* **486236**

Evidence needs to be provided that supports the thesis and additional arguments. Most arguments must be supported by facts or statistics. Facts are something that is known with certainty and have been verified by several independent individuals. Examples and illustrations add an emotional component to arguments. With this component, you persuade readers in ways that facts and statistics cannot. The emotional component is effective when used with objective information that can be confirmed.

Credibility
The text used to support an argument can be the argument's downfall if the text is not credible. A text is **credible**, or believable, when the author is knowledgeable and objective, or unbiased. The author's motivations for writing the text play a critical role in determining the credibility of the text and must be evaluated when assessing that credibility. Reports written about the ozone layer by an environmental scientist and a hairdresser will have a different level of credibility.

Appeal to Emotion
Sometimes, authors will appeal to the reader's emotion in an attempt to persuade or to distract the reader from the weakness of the argument. For instance, the author may try to inspire the pity of the reader by delivering a heart-rending story. An author also might use the bandwagon approach, in which he suggests that his opinion is correct because it is held by the majority. Some authors resort to name-calling, in which insults and harsh words are delivered to the opponent in an attempt to distract. In advertising, a common appeal is the celebrity testimonial, in which a famous person endorses a product. Of course, the fact that a famous person likes something should not really mean anything to the reader. These and other emotional appeals are usually evidence of poor reasoning and a weak argument.

> **Review Video: Appeal to Readers Emotions**
> Visit *mometrix.com/academy* and enter *Code:* **163442**

Counter Arguments
When authors give both sides to the argument, they build trust with their readers. As a reader, you should start with an undecided or neutral position. If an author presents only his or her side to the argument, then you will need to be concerned at best.

Building common ground with neutral or opposed readers can be appealing to skeptical readers. Sharing values with undecided readers can allow people to switch positions without giving up what they feel is important. For people who may oppose a position, they need to feel that they can change their minds without betraying who they are as a person. This appeal to having an open mind can be a powerful tool in arguing a position without antagonizing other views. Objections can be countered on a point-by-point basis or in a summary paragraph. Be mindful of how an author points out flaws in counter arguments. If they are unfair to the other side of the argument, then you should lose trust with the author.

Primary Sources and Internet Sources

Primary Sources

When conducting research, it is important to depend on reputable primary sources. A primary source is the documentary evidence closest to the subject being studied. For instance, the primary sources for an essay about penguins would be photographs and recordings of the birds, as well as accounts of people who have studied penguins in person. A secondary source would be a review of a movie about penguins or a book outlining the observations made by others. A primary source should be credible and, if it is on a subject that is still being explored, recent. One way to assess the credibility of a work is to see how often it is mentioned in other books and articles on the same subject. Just by reading the works cited and bibliographies of other books, one can get a sense of what the reliable sources authorities in the field are.

Internet Sources

The Internet was once considered a poor place to find sources for an essay or article, but its credibility has improved greatly over the years. Still, students need to exercise caution when performing research online. The best sources are those affiliated with established institutions, such as universities, public libraries, and think tanks. Most newspapers are available online, and many of them allow the public to browse their archives. Magazines frequently offer similar services. When obtaining information from an unknown website, however, one must exercise considerably more caution. A website can be considered trustworthy if it is referenced by other sites that are known to be reputable. Also, credible sites tend to be properly maintained and frequently updated. A site is easier to trust when the author provides some information about himself, including some credentials that indicate expertise in the subject matter.

Making Predictions and Drawing Conclusions

Predictions

A prediction is a guess about what will happen next. Readers constantly make predictions based on what they have read and what they already know. Consider the following sentence: *Staring at the computer screen in shock, Kim blindly reached over for the brimming glass of water on the shelf to her side.* The sentence suggests that Kim is agitated, and that she is not looking at the glass that she is going to pick up. So, a reader might predict that Kim is going to knock over the glass. Of course, not every prediction will be accurate: perhaps Kim will pick the glass up cleanly. Nevertheless, the author has certainly created the expectation that the water might be spilled. Predictions are always subject to revision as the reader acquires more information.

> ➢ **Review Video:** <u>**Predictions**</u>
> Visit ***mometrix.com/academy*** *and enter* ***Code:*** **437248**

Foreshadowing

Foreshadowing uses hints in a narrative to let the audience anticipate future events in the plot. Foreshadowing can be indicated by a number of literary devices and figures of speech, as well as through dialogue between characters.

> **Review Video: <u>Textual Evidence for Predictions</u>**
> *Visit **mometrix.com/academy** and enter **Code: 261070***

Drawing Conclusions

In addition to inference and prediction, readers must often **draw conclusions** about the information they have read. When asked for a *conclusion* that may be drawn, look for critical "hedge" phrases, such as *likely, may, can, will often*, among many others. When you are being tested on this knowledge, remember the question that writers insert into these hedge phrases to cover every possibility. Often an answer will be wrong simply because there is no room for exception. Extreme positive or negative answers (such as always or never) are usually not correct. The reader <u>should not</u> use any outside knowledge that is not gathered from the passage to answer the related questions. Correct answers can be derived straight from the passage.

The Science Test

The Science test may scare you. For even the most accomplished student, many of the terms will be unfamiliar. General test-taking skill will help the most. Make sure you don't run out of time: move quickly and use the easy pacing methods we outline in the test-taking tactics section.

The most important thing you can do is to ignore your fears and jump into the test immediately. Don't be overwhelmed by all of the strange-sounding terms. You have to jump into the test like jumping into a pool; all at once is the easiest way. Once you get past the jargon, you'll find that the Science Reasoning test is in some ways easier than even the Reading Test. Unfortunately, most students don't finish this test. This is why managing your time on this test is at least as important as on the Math test.

The test lasts 35 minutes, 5 minutes per section.

The first thing to do is to read the passage. Use 2 minutes to do this. Really try to understand what's going on, treating all of the scientific terms as you would characters in a novel; just accept their names as they are, and follow the story. Use another 3 minutes to answer as many questions as you can. It's important to answer all of the easy questions.

Overall, the Science Reasoning is the test that is the hardest to study for and has the lowest test average for all test-takers, even lower than the Math. If science is a subject you take because you have to, and not because you want to, your primary goal on Science Reasoning is damage control; you want to prevent it from dragging down your higher scores when ACT averages your test scores to get the composite.

In addition, the Science Reasoning test is probably unlike any other science test you've ever taken in high school. It's vital that you work a few practice Science Reasoning tests before the test day. Familiarity alone will boost your score by 1-2 points.

Life Science

Functions for Life and Energy

Cellular Respiration

Cellular respiration is a set of metabolic reactions. These reactions change chemical bonds into energy that is stored in the form of ATP. Respiration has many oxidation and reduction reactions. This happens with the electron transport system inside the cell.

Oxidation is a loss of electrons. Reduction is a gain of electrons. Electrons in C-H (carbon/hydrogen) and C-C (carbon/carbon) bonds are given to oxygen atoms. Some systems in cellular respiration are glycolysis, the Krebs cycle, and the electron transport chain.

The two forms of respiration are aerobic and anaerobic. Aerobic respiration is very common. With aerobic respiration, oxygen is the final electron acceptor. In anaerobic respiration, the final electron acceptor is not oxygen. Aerobic respiration causes more ATP than anaerobic respiration.

Photosynthesis

Photosynthesis changes sunlight into energy in plant cells. This can also happen in some types of bacteria and protists. Carbon dioxide and water are changed into glucose during photosynthesis. Light is needed in this process. Cyanobacteria are thought to come from the first organisms to use photosynthesis about 3.5 billion years ago.

Photosynthesis is a form of cellular respiration. It happens in chloroplasts that use thylakoids. These thylakoids are structures in the membrane that have light reaction chemicals. Chlorophyll is a pigment that takes in light. During the process, water is used, and oxygen is released.

The equation for the chemical reaction that happens during photosynthesis:
$6H_2O + 6CO_2 \rightarrow C_6H_{12}O_6 + 6O_2$.

During photosynthesis, six molecules of water and six molecules of carbon dioxide react. So, one molecule of sugar and six molecules of oxygen are the products.

> ➢ **Review Video: Photosynthesis**
> Visit **mometrix.com/academy** and enter **Code: 227035**

Homeostasis

Homeostasis is when an organism, cell, or body makes changes to stay balanced. A human body can maintain homeostasis with the release of hormones. Some hormones work in pairs. When a condition reaches an upper limit, a hormone is released to correct the condition. When a condition reaches the lower limit, another hormone is released. Hormones that work in this way are known as antagonistic. Insulin and glucagon are a pair of antagonistic hormones that help to manage the level of glucagon in the blood. Positive feedback loops can unbalance systems by increasing changes. A negative feedback loop acts to make a system more stable by handling changes.

Cell Structure

<u>Nuclear Parts of a Cell</u>
All eukaryotic cells have a nucleus. The nucleus is a small structure that holds the chromosomes. Also, the nucleus manages the DNA of a cell. The nucleus is the defining structure of eukaryotic cells. The nucleus is responsible for passing on genetic traits between generations. The nucleus has a nuclear envelope, nucleoplasm, a nucleolus, nuclear pores, chromatin, and ribosomes.

Chromosomes: These are tight, threadlike rods of DNA (deoxyribonucleic acid). DNA is the genetic material that stores information about the plant or animal.

Chromatin: This is made of DNA and protein that makes up chromosomes.

Nucleolus (or nucleole): This structure inside the nucleus is made of protein. The nucleolus is small and round. It does not have a membrane. This piece works in protein synthesis. Also, it combines and stores RNA (ribonucleic acid).

Nuclear envelope: This surrounds the structures of the nucleus. It has inner and outer membranes that are made of lipids.

Nuclear pores: These help in the trade of material between the nucleus and the cytoplasm.

Nucleoplasm: This is the liquid inside the nucleus. It is similar to cytoplasm.

<u>Other Parts of a Cell</u>
Ribosomes: Ribosomes help to put together proteins from amino acids. There are many in one cell. They make up about one fourth of the cell. Some cells have thousands of ribosome. Some are free to move. Others are tied down in the rough endoplasmic reticulum.

Golgi complex (i.e., Golgi apparatus): This helps to put together materials. An example is proteins that are moved out of the cell. It is near the nucleus and has layers of membranes.

Vacuoles: These are sacs used for storage, digestion, and waste removal. There is one large vacuole in plant cells. Animal cells have small vacuoles. Sometimes animal cells have many vacuoles.

Vesicle: This is a small organelle inside a cell. It has a membrane and has many roles. One role is moving materials inside a cell.

Cytoskeleton: This has microtubules that help to shape and to support the cell.

Microtubules: These are part of the cytoskeleton and help support the cell. They are made of protein.

Cytosol: This is the liquid material in the cell. The liquid is mostly water. However, it also has some floating molecules.

Cytoplasm: This is a general term for the cytosol and the substructures (i.e., organelles) inside the plasma membrane. This is not for the parts in the nucleus.

Cell membrane (or plasma membrane): This is a barrier for the cell. It keeps cytoplasm in and substances not inside the cell are kept out of the cell. It decides what can enter and exit the cell.

Endoplasmic reticulum: There are two types of endoplasmic reticulum. One is rough that has ribosomes on the surface. The other is smooth and does not have ribosomes on the surface. It is a network of tubes that is the transport system of a cell. It is tied to the nuclear membrane. Also, it goes through the cytoplasm to the cell membrane.

Mitochondrion (plural: mitochondria): These cell structures can be different in their size and how many are in a cell. Some cells may have one mitochondrion. Other cells may have thousands. The mitochondrion has many roles. One important role is to make ATP. The mitochondrion also helps with cell growth and death. Mitochondria have their own DNA. This DNA is separate from what is in the nucleus.

Cell Cycle

A cell cycle is when a cell reproduces. This includes cell growth, the copy of genetic material, and cell division. Complex organisms with many cells use the cell cycle. The cell cycle replaces cells as they wear out. The entire cell cycle in animal cells can take 24 hours. The time needed is different for different cell types. An example is human skin cells. They are always reproducing. Other cells rarely divide.

When neurons are mature, they do not grow or divide. The two ways that cells can make more cells are through meiosis and mitosis. When cells make copies through mitosis, the "daughter cell" is an exact copy of the parent cell. When cells divide through meiosis, the daughter cells have different genetic coding than the parent cell. Meiosis only happens in special reproductive cells called gametes.

Cell Division
Cell division happens in organisms so they can grow and replace cells that are old, worn out, or damaged.

Chromatids: During cell division, the DNA is copied. So, the chromatids are the two exact copies of chromosomes that are joined at the centromere to make a "X."

Gametes: These are cells used by organisms to reproduce sexually. Gametes in humans are haploid. This means that they have 23 chromosomes. This is half of the organism's genetic information. Other human cells have all 46 chromosomes.

Haploid/diploid: Haploid means there is one set of chromosomes. Diploid means there are two sets of chromosomes. There is one set from each parent.

Mitosis
The following are the stages of mitosis:

Interphase: The cell gets ready for division by making copies of its genetic and cytoplasmic material. This step can be further divided into G_1, S, and G_2.

Prophase: The chromatin thickens into chromosomes. Then, the nuclear membrane begins to break down. Pairs of centrioles move to opposite sides of the cell. Then, spindle fibers are made. The mitotic spindle is made from cytoskeleton parts. This spindle moves chromosomes inside the cell.

Metaphase: The spindle moves to the center of the cell. Then, chromosome pairs line up along the center of the spindle structure.

Anaphase: The pairs of chromosomes are called sisters. In this stage, these pairs begin to pull apart and can bend. When they are pulled apart, they are called daughter chromosomes. In the cell membrane, grooves can be seen.

Telophase: In this stage, the spindle breaks down. Then, the nuclear membranes are made again. Then, the chromosomes return to chromatin. In animal cells, the membrane is divided. In plant cells, a new cell wall is made.

Cytokinesis: This is the physical splitting of the cell into two cells. Some think that this happens after telophase. Others say that it happens from anaphase through telophase.

> **Review Video: Mitosis**
> Visit **mometrix.com/academy** and enter **Code: 849894**

Meiosis
Meiosis has the same phases as mitosis. However, these stages happen twice. Also, different events happen during some phases of meiosis than mitosis. The events that happen in the first phase of meiosis are interphase (I), prophase (I), metaphase (I), anaphase (I), telophase (I), and cytokinesis (I).

In this first phase of meiosis, chromosomes cross over and genetic material is traded. Also, tetrads (i.e., four) of four chromatids are made. The nuclear membrane dissolves. Homologous pairs of chromatids are separated. Then, they move to different poles. At this point, one cell has been divided to make two cells.

Next, each cell goes through a second cell division. The stages are prophase (II), metaphase (II), anaphase (II), telophase (II), and cytokinesis (II). This makes four daughter cells with different sets of chromosomes. The daughter cells are haploid. This means that they have half the genetic material of the parent cell.

> **Review Video: Meiosis**
> Visit **mometrix.com/academy** and enter **Code: 247334**

Important Vocabulary

Meiosis: This is when the cell divides and the number of chromosomes in the parent cell is halved to make four gamete cells.

Mitosis: This is when the cell nucleus separates and the parent cell divides into two daughter cells.

Organelle: A general term for an organ or smaller structure inside a cell. Membrane-bound organelles are in eukaryotic cells.

RNA: Ribonucleic acid is a type of molecule that has a long chain (i.e., polymer) of nucleotide units.

Polymer: This is a compound of large molecules made by repeating monomers.

Monomer: A monomer is a small molecule. It is a single compound that makes chemical bonds with other monomers to make a polymer.

Nucleotides: These are molecules that combine to make DNA and RNA.

Nucleoid: This is the nucleus-like mass of DNA that has the chromatin in a prokaryotic cell.

Gene expression: This is the use of information in a gene. Usually, this is done in the processes of transcription and translation and ends in a protein product.

Transcription: This is the putting together of RNA. The information for this event comes from DNA.

Translation: This is the decoding of mRNA (i.e., messenger RNA) that is used in the building of protein. It happens after transcription.

Cellular differentiation: This is the event where a less specialized cell becomes a more specialized cell.

Genetics

DNA

Chromosomes are made of genes. A gene is a single unit of genetic information. Genes are made of deoxyribonucleic acid. DNA is a nucleic acid in the cell nucleus. DNA is also in the mitochondria. DNA makes copies of itself to pass on genetic information. The DNA in almost all cells is the same. It is also part of the biosynthesis of proteins.

The model of DNA is known as a double helix. A helix is a curve. So, a double helix is two congruent curves that are connected by horizontal pieces. The model can be compared to a spiral staircase.

The British scientist Rosalind Elsie Franklin is the one who took the x-ray diffraction image in 1952. This image was used by Francis Crick and James Watson to put together the double-helix model of DNA. With this information, they were able to think about its important role in carrying and moving genetic information.

DNA Structure

DNA has the shape of a double helix. This shape looks like a twisted ladder. It is made of nucleotides. Nucleotides have a five-carbon sugar (i.e., pentose), a phosphate group, and a nitrogenous base. Two bases pair up to make the bars of the ladder. The "side rails" or backbone is made of the covalently bonded sugar and phosphate. The bases are connected to each other with hydrogen bonds. These bonds can be easily separated for replication to happen.

There are four types of nitrogenous bases: adenine (A), guanine (G), cytosine (C), and thymine (T). Adenine (A) pairs with thymine (T). Cytosine (C) pairs with guanine (G). There are about 3 billion bases in human DNA. The bases are almost the same in everybody. However, their order is different. The order of these bases makes diversity in people.

Mendelian Genetics

Mendel's Laws

Mendel's laws are the law of segregation (the first law) and the law of independent assortment (the second law). The law of segregation says that there are two alleles and half of the total number of alleles comes from each parent organism. The law of independent assortment says that traits are passed on randomly. They are not influenced by other traits. The exception is linked traits.

A Punnett square can show how alleles combine from the donating genes to make different phenotypes. One set of a parent's genes are put in columns. The genes from the other parent are placed in rows. The allele combinations are shown in each cell. When two different alleles come in a pair, the dominant one is expressed. A Punnett square can be used to predict the outcome of crosses.

Non-Mendelian Terms

Polygenic inheritance: This goes past Mendel's idea that one gene affects one trait. This idea says that traits are affected by more than one gene. Also, environmental influences on development are important with this idea. An example is an individual who inherits genes that help decide height. However, if the person does not have the needed nutrients, then they may not reach their full height.

Genetic disposition: This is an increased chance of a certain disease that is genetically inherited. However, it may not carry out in a person. For example, people with certain skin types are more likely to have skin cancer. If they limit their time in the Sun, then they may not experience skin cancer.

Multiple alleles: Only two alleles make up a gene. When there are three or more possible alleles, it is known as a multiple allele. A gene where only two alleles are possible is called polymorphic.

Complete dominance: This is when a homozygous pair of dominant alleles (AA) and a heterozygous pair of alleles (Aa) carries out the same phenotype. Dominant genes have the following characteristics:
- they are expressed in each generation
- they are passed on to about half the offspring
- a parent that does not express the trait cannot pass it on to offspring.

Mendel's idea for complete dominance says that one gene that has two alleles is the only piece in the creation of a phenotype. However, most traits are more complex.

Evolution

Three Types of Evolution
Three types of evolution are divergent, convergent, and parallel.

Divergent evolution is when two species become different over time. This can be caused by one of the species changing to a different environment.

Convergent evolution is when two species start out fairly different. However, they evolve to share many similar traits.

Parallel evolution is when species do not become more or less similar over time. Also, this is for species that are not similar.

Mechanisms of evolution are descent (i.e., the passing on of genetic information), mutation, migration, natural selection, and genetic variation and drift. The biological definition of species is a group of individuals that can mate and reproduce. Speciation is the evolution of a new biological species. The biological species concept (BSC) says that a species is a community of individuals that can reproduce and have a clear role in nature.

Theories of Evolution

Natural Selection

Natural selection: This theory says that the traits that give a species a better chance of survival are passed on to future generations. Members of a species that do not have the trait die before they reproduce. Charles Darwin's four principles are:

- From generation to generation, there are different members in a species
- Genes decide differences
- More members are born than will survive to a mature stage
- Certain genes help an organism to survive

Gradualism

Gradualism: This is the idea that evolution goes at a steady pace. Also, it does not have sudden additions of new species or features from one generation to the next. This can be contrasted with punctuated equilibrium.

Punctuated Equilibrium

Punctuated equilibrium: This idea says that evolution has very long stretches of time with no change (i.e., stasis). Then, this stasis is followed by smaller amounts of time (e.g., hundreds of thousands of years) of fast change. This can be contrasted with gradualism.

Chemistry

Matter is a substance that has mass and takes up space (i.e., volume). Solid, liquid, and gas are the three states of matter. These states come from the differences in the distances and angles between molecules or atoms. This causes differences in the energy that keeps them together.

States of Matter

In the past, there were three states of matter. Solid states are rigid or nearly rigid and have strong bonds. The molecules or atoms in liquids move around and have weak bonds. However, these bonds are not weak enough to break. Molecules or atoms of gases move almost independently of each other. They are far apart and do not make bonds.

Today, matter has four states. The fourth is plasma. This is an ionized gas that has some electrons. These electrons are described as free. The reason is that they are not tied to an atom or molecule.

The Atom

All matter is made of atoms. These atoms are made of a nucleus and electrons. The nucleus has protons and neutrons. They have mass and an electrical charge. The nucleus has a positive charge because of protons. Neutrons are the uncharged atomic particles that are in the nucleus. Electrons have a negative charge, and they orbit the nucleus. The nucleus has much more mass than the surrounding electrons.

The number of protons in the nucleus is the atomic number of an element. Carbon atoms have six protons. So, the atomic number of carbon is 6. The nucleon is the combination of neutrons and protons.

> ➤ **Review Video: Structure of Atoms**
> *Visit **mometrix.com/academy** and enter **Code: 905932***

Atoms can bond together to make molecules. Atoms that have an equal number of protons and electrons are electrically neutral. The number of protons and electrons in an atom may not be equal. In this case, the atom has a positive or negative charge and is an ion. The number of protons minus the number of electrons gives the charge of an atom.

Atomic Number and Atomic Mass

The atomic number of an element is the number of protons in the nucleus of an atom. Atoms with a neutral charge have an atomic number that is equal to the number of electrons.

Atomic mass is also known as the mass number. The atomic mass (A) is equal to the number of protons (Z) plus the number of neutrons (N). This can be seen in the equation $A = Z + N$. The mass of electrons in an atom is not counted because it is so small.

Atomic mass unit (amu) is the smallest unit of mass. This is equal to 1/12 of the mass of the carbon isotope carbon-12. A mole (mol) is a measurement of molecular weight. This measurement is equal to the molecule's amu in grams. As an example, carbon has an amu of 12. So, a mole of carbon weighs 12 grams. One mole is equal to about 6.02×10^{23} atoms or molecules. This amount is also known as the Avogadro constant or Avogadro's number (NA). Another way to say this is that one mole of a substance is the same as one Avogadro's number of that substance. As an example, one mole of chlorine is 6.02×10^{23} chlorine atoms.

Electrons

Electrons orbit the nucleus at different levels. These levels are known as layers, shells, or clouds. An electron will move to the lowest energy level that it can. An atom has a stable layout of electrons when an atom has all its electrons in the lowest available positions.

The outermost electron shell of an atom in its uncombined state is known as the valence shell. The electrons there are called valence electrons. Their number decides their bonding behavior. Atoms will act to fill or to empty their valence shells. Electrons can absorb or release energy. This can change the location of their orbit. Also, this can allow them to break free from the atom. The valence layer can have or share eight electrons.

Chemical bonds have a negative-positive attraction between an electron or electrons and the nucleus of an atom or nuclei of more than one atom. The attraction keeps the atom connected. Also, it helps to make bonds with other atoms and molecules.

Physical and Chemical Properties

Chemical properties cannot be seen or measured without chemical reactions. Physical properties can be seen or measured without chemical reactions. These properties are color, elasticity, mass, volume, and temperature.

Mass measures how much of a substance is in an object.

Weight measures the gravitational pull of the Earth on an object.

Density is a measure of the amount of mass per unit volume.
The formula to find density is mass divided by volume (D=m/V). It is expressed in terms of mass per cubic unit (e.g., grams per cubic centimeter (g/cm^3)).

Volume measures the amount of space taken up.
The volume of an irregular shape can be known by finding out how much water it displaces.

Specific gravity measures the ratio of a substance's density to the density of water.

Physical changes and chemical reactions are everyday events. Physical changes do not bring about different substances. An example is when water becomes ice. It has gone through a physical change, not a chemical change. It has changed its state, not what it is made of. In other words, it is still H_2O.

Chemical properties deal with the particles that make up the structure of a substance. Chemical properties can be seen when chemical changes happen. The chemical properties of a substance are influenced by its electron configuration. This is decided somewhat by the number of protons in the nucleus (i.e., the atomic number). An example is carbon that has 6 protons and 6 electrons. The outermost valence electrons of an element mainly decide its chemical properties. Chemical reactions may give or take energy.

Properties of Water

The important properties of water (H_2O) are high polarity, hydrogen bonding, cohesiveness, adhesiveness, high specific heat, high latent heat, and high heat of vaporization. Water is vital to life as we know it. The reason is that water is one of the main parts of many living things.

Water is a liquid at room temperature. The high specific heat of water means that it does not easily break its hydrogen bonds. Also, it resists heat and motion. This is why it has a high boiling point and high vaporization point.

Most substances are denser in their solid forms. However, water is different because its solid state floats in its liquid state. Water is cohesive. This means that it is drawn to itself. It is also adhesive. This means that it draws in other molecules. If water will attach to another substance, the substance is said to be hydrophilic. Water makes a good solvent. Substances with polar ions and molecules easily dissolve in water.

Vocabulary

Elements — these are substances that are made of only one type of atom.

Compounds — these are substances that have two or more elements. Compounds are made from chemical reactions. Often, they have different properties than the original elements. Compounds are broken down by a chemical reaction. They are not separated by a physical reaction.

Solutions — these are homogeneous mixtures. They are made of two or more substances that have become one.

Mixtures — Two or more substances that are combined. However, they have not reacted chemically with each other. Mixtures can be separated with physical methods and compounds cannot.

Heat — This is the transfer of energy from a body or system from thermal contact. Heat is made of random motion and the vibration of atoms, molecules, and ions. Higher temperatures cause more motion with atoms or molecules.

Energy — the capacity to do work.

Work —the amount of energy that must be transferred to overcome a force. An example of work is lifting an object in the air. The opposing force that must be overcome is gravity. Work is measured in joules (J). The rate that work is done is known as power.

Earth and Space Science

Astronomy

Astronomy studies the positions, movements, and structures of celestial objects. Celestial is something that is in the sky or outer space. Objects are the Sun, the Moon, planets, asteroids, meteors, comets, stars, galaxies, the universe, and other space objects. The term astronomy has its roots in the Greek words "astro" and "nomos," which means "laws of the stars."

> ➤ **Review Video: Astronomy**
> *Visit **mometrix.com/academy** and enter **Code: 640556***

Galaxies

Galaxies are made of stars and dark matter. Dwarf galaxies can have as few as 10 million stars. Giant galaxies can have as many as 1 trillion stars. Galaxies are gravitationally bound. This means that the stars, star systems, gases, and dust spin around the galaxy's center. The Earth is in the Milky Way galaxy. The nearest galaxy to the Milky Way is the Andromeda galaxy.

Galaxies can be labeled by their visual shape. Examples are the elliptical, spiral, irregular, and starburst galaxies. It is estimated that there are more than 100 billion galaxies in the universe. The space between two galaxies is a gas that has an average density of less than one atom per cubic meter. Galaxies are organized into clusters which make superclusters. Up to 90% of the mass of galaxies may be dark mark. Today, dark matter is not understood very well.

Stars

There are different life cycles for stars after they begin and enter into the main sequence stage. Small, somewhat cold red dwarfs with low masses burn hydrogen slowly. They will remain in the main sequence for hundreds of billions of years. Large, hot supergiants will leave the main sequence after just a few million years. Hydrogen--in its plasma state--is the most common chemical element in stars' main sequences.

A nuclear fusion reaction is when multiple atomic nuclei collide to make a new nucleus. If nuclear fusion of hydrogen into helium begins, a star is born. The "main sequence" of a star's life has nuclear fusion reactions. During this time, the star shrinks over billions of years to make up for the lost heat and light energy. As the star shrinks, the temperature, density, and pressure rise at the star's core. So, the cycle continues.

The Sun is a mid-sized star that may be in the main sequence for 10 billion years. After the main sequence, the star will grow to become a red giant. Depending on the original mass of the star, it can become a black dwarf. Then, it will become a small, cooling white dwarf. Massive stars become red supergiants and sometimes blue supergiants. Then, they explode in a supernova and become neutron stars. The largest stars can become black holes.

Solar System

A solar system has a star and other objects that move in or around it. The start to the solar system began with the collapse of a cloud of interstellar gas and dust. This collapse made the solar nebula. The reason for the collapse is that the cloud was disturbed. As it collapsed, it heated up and compressed at the center. This made a flat protoplanetary disk with a protostar at the center. A protoplanetary disk is spinning disk of gas that is around a new star. Planets were made from the growth of the disk.

Then, gas cooled and condensed into small pieces of rock, metal, and ice. These pieces collided and made larger pieces. Then, the pieces became the size of small asteroids. Eventually, some became large enough to have enough gravity to affect objects around it.

Objects move around and are tied by gravity to a star called the Sun. These objects include: planets, dwarf planets, moons, asteroids, meteoroids, cosmic dust, and comets. The definition of planets has changed. At one time, there were nine planets in the solar system. There are now eight. Planetary objects in the solar system include four inner planets: Mercury, Venus, Earth, and Mars. These planets are small, dense, and rocky. They do not have rings, and they have few or no moons.

The four outer planets are Jupiter, Saturn, Uranus, and Neptune. These planets are large and have low densities, and they have rings and moons. They are also known as gas giants. The asteroid belt comes between the inner and outer planets. Beyond Neptune is the Kuiper belt. Inside this belt are five dwarf planets: Ceres, Pluto, Haumea, Makemake, and Eris.

Earth's Atmosphere

The atmosphere is made of 78% nitrogen, 21% oxygen, and 1% argon. Other pieces are water vapor, carbon dioxide, dust particles, and chemicals from Earth. The air in the atmosphere becomes thinner at higher levels above the Earth's surface. At about 3 km above sea level, you will have difficulty breathing. As you go higher, the atmosphere begins to fade into space.

> ➤ **Review Video: <u>Earth's Atmosphere</u>**
> *Visit **mometrix.com/academy** and enter **Code: 417614***

<u>Atmospheric Layers</u>
Earth's atmosphere has five main layers. From lowest to highest, these are the troposphere, the stratosphere, the mesosphere, the thermosphere, and the exosphere. A transition layer is between each pair of layers. This layer is known as a pause.

The lowest layer of the atmosphere is called the *troposphere*. Its thickness is different at the poles and the equator. The thickness at the poles is about 7 km. The thickness at the equator is about 17 km. Most weather events happen at this layer. As you go higher in this layer, the temperature decreases. The troposphere has the tropopause which is the transitional layer of the stratosphere.

The *stratosphere* is the next level. This layer goes to a height of about 51 km. In the stratosphere, the temperature is reversed. In other words, the temperature increases as you go higher in this layer. The stratosphere includes the ozone layer. The ozone layer helps to block ultraviolet light from the Sun. The stratopause is the transitional layer to the mesosphere.

The *mesosphere* goes from the stratosphere to a height of about 81 km. In this layer, meteors are likely to burn. This is the coldest layer. So, as you go higher in this layer, the temperature drops. This layer is thought of as the coldest place on Earth. The average temperature is -85 degrees Celsius.

The next layer is the *thermosphere*. This is where the International Space Station orbits. Temperature increases as you go higher in the thermosphere. The transitional layer to the exosphere is known as the thermopause.

Just past the thermosphere is the exobase. This is the base layer of the *exosphere*. The exosphere is the outermost layer that goes to 10,000 km. This layer is mostly made of hydrogen and helium.

Beyond the five main layers are the ionosphere, homosphere, heterosphere, and magnetosphere.

Layers of Earth
The Earth has many layers. Each has its own traits:
- Crust is the outermost layer of the Earth. It has the continents and the ocean basins. There are different thicknesses in different areas. For example, it is 35-70 km in the continents. Ocean basins can be about 5-10 km in thickness. Also, it is made of aluminosilicates.
- Mantle is about 2900 km thick. It is made of ferro-magnesium silicates. The mantle is divided into an upper and lower mantle. Most of the internal heat of the Earth is in the mantle. Large convective cells circulate heat. So, this may cause plate tectonic movement.
- Core is separated into the liquid outer core and the solid inner core. The outer core is 2300 km thick. This is made of nickel-iron alloy. The inner core is almost entirely iron. It is 12 km thick. The Earth's magnetic field is thought to be controlled by the liquid outer core.

Geology

Water Cycle
The water cycle is the movement of water on the Earth. Water can be in any of its three states for different parts of the cycle. The three states of water are liquid water, frozen ice, and water vapor. The parts of the water cycle are precipitation, canopy interception, snow melt, runoff, infiltration, subsurface flow, evaporation, sublimation, advection, condensation, and transpiration.

> ➤ **Review Video:** Hydrologic (Water) Cycle
> Visit ***mometrix.com/academy*** *and enter* ***Code:*** **426578**

Human Affairs and the Environment

With the industrial revolution, science and technology have made a great influence on humans. There have been more discoveries in many fields. Many discoveries have led to better things for many people. These discoveries have led to longer life because of better nutrition, better medical care, and better workplaces. These changes have helped the lives of many humans. However, they have brought changes to the environment. Not every problem has been solved. Many still exist in one way or another. For example, there are ways to recycle. Yet, not everyone recycles because of the cost.

Ecosystems

Human influences on ecosystems have many forms and causes. These changes have an influence on plants and animals in many biomes and ecosystems. So, the changes can be seen in widespread areas and small areas. Humans take many natural resources to have food or to make energy. This changes their environment to make food, energy, and shelter. Changes come from:
- use or overuse of pesticides
- the invasion of a habitat
- over hunting and over fishing
- bringing plant and animal species into non-native ecosystems
- people refusing to recycle
- people bringing dangerous wastes into the environment

These actions have many effects. Some are acid rain, decrease of ozone, destruction of forests, and loss of more species. Other effects are genetic flaws and harm to animals.

Greenhouse Effect

The greenhouse effect is a natural and important event. Greenhouse gases (e.g., ozone, carbon dioxide, water vapor, and methane) trap infrared radiation that is reflected to the atmosphere. So, warm air is trapped as well. Without the greenhouse effect, temperatures on Earth would be 30 degrees less on average. Some human activity puts out more greenhouse gas than necessary. These events put more greenhouse gases into the air:
- burning natural gas and oil
- farming actions that release methane and nitrous oxide
- factory actions that make gases
- destroying forests put more greenhouse gases into the air

So, those events decrease the amount of oxygen available to balance out greenhouse gases. Now, too many greenhouse gases trap infrared radiation. So, this increases the temperature at the Earth's surface.

Global Warming

Rising temperatures may lead to:
- higher sea levels as polar ice melts
- lower amounts of fresh water as coastal areas flood
- species extinction from changes in habitat
- increases in certain diseases
- lower standard of living for humans

Less fresh water and loss of habitat can lead to less agricultural production and food supply. Global warming brings drier and warmer weather. When dry areas become very arid, this upsets habitats for humans and other species. Increases in damaging weather (e.g., hurricanes or snowstorms) may be seen at unlikely latitudes. There may be more moisture in the atmosphere from evaporation. Global warming may cause the loss of glaciers and permafrost. Also, there is a greater chance for air pollution and acid rain.

Physics

Newton's Laws

First Law

An object at rest or in motion will stay at rest or in motion. This will continue until an outside force acts on the object. When a body stays in its present state of motion, the object is in a state known as inertia.

> ➢ **Review Video:** Newton's First Law of Motion
> *Visit* ***mometrix.com/academy*** *and enter* ***Code: 590367***

Second Law

An object's acceleration depends on two things. One is the net force that acts on the object. The other is the mass of the object. This can be seen with the formula: $F = ma$. F is the net force acting on a body, m is the mass of the body, and a is its acceleration. Note that the mass is always a positive quantity. So, the acceleration is always in the same direction as the force.

> ➢ **Review Video:** Newton's Second Law of Motion
> *Visit* ***mometrix.com/academy*** *and enter* ***Code: 737975***

Third Law

This law says that for every action, there is an equal and opposite reaction. An example is a hammer that strikes a nail. In this event, the nail hits the hammer just as hard. Think about two objects: A and B. Now, you can show the contact between these two bodies with the equation $F_{AB} = -F_{BA}$. In the equation, the order of the subscripts shows which body is applying the force.

At first glance, you may think that this law does not allow any movement. Every force is being countered with an equal and opposite force. However, these equal and opposite forces are acting on different objects with different masses. So, they will not cancel out each other.

> ➢ **Review Video:** Newton's Third Law of Motion
> *Visit* ***mometrix.com/academy*** *and enter* ***Code: 838401***

Gravitational Force

Gravitational force is a universal force. This causes every object to apply a force on every other object. The gravitational force between two objects can be seen with the formula, $F = Gm_1m_2/r^2$. In this example, m_1 and m_2 are the masses of two objects, r is the distance between them, and G is the gravitational constant, $G = 6.672 \times 10^{-11}$ N-m^2/kg^2.

For this force to have an effect that can be noticed, one or both of the objects must be extremely large. So, the equation is used only in problems that deal with objects in space. Problems that deal with objects on Earth are affected by Earth's gravitational pull. So, the force of gravity is calculated as $F = mg$. In this formula, g is 9.81 m/s^2 toward the ground.

Work

Work is the amount of energy that comes from finishing a set goal. A basic equation for mechanical work (W) is $W = Fd$. In the equation, F is the force put on the object, and d is the displacement of the object. This equation needs the force to be applied in the same direction as the displacement. If force and displacement have the same direction, then work is positive. If they are in opposite directions, then work is negative. If they are perpendicular, the work done is zero.

An example is a man who pushes a block horizontally across a surface. He uses a constant force of 10 N for a distance of 20 m. So, the work done by the man is 200 N-m or 200 J.

Another example is that the block is sliding, and the man tries to slow it down by pushing against it. So, his work done is -200 J. The reason is that he is pushing in the opposite direction of the block.

Now, let's say that the man pushes down on the block while it slides. In this example, his work done is zero. The reason is that his force vector is perpendicular to the displacement vector of the block.

> **Review Video: Work**
*Visit **mometrix.com/academy** and enter **Code: 681834***

Machines

Simple machines are the inclined plane, lever, wheel and axle, and pulley. These simple machines have no source of energy inside them. More complex or compound machines can be made from simple machines. Simple machines give a force that is known as a mechanical advantage. This advantage makes it easier to finish a task.

Simple Machines
Inclined plane: helps a force that is less than the object's weight to push an object to a greater height.

Lever: helps to multiply a force.

Wheel and axle: allows for movement with less resistance.

Single or double pulleys allows for easier direction of force.

Wedge: turns a small force that is working over a greater distance into a larger force.

Screw: this is an inclined plane that is wrapped around a shaft.

A certain amount of work is needed to move an object. The amount cannot be reduced. However, you can change the way the work is done. So, a mechanical advantage can be gained. A certain amount of work can be done to raise an object to a given height. By getting to the given height at an angle, the effort needed is reduced. However, the distance that is needed to reach a given height is increased. An example of this is walking up a hill.

A lever has a bar (i.e., plank) and a pivot point (i.e., fulcrum). Work is done with the bar. This bar moves at the pivot point to change the direction of the force. There are three types of levers: first, second, and third class. Examples of a first-class lever are balances, see-saws, and nail removers.

In a second-class lever, the fulcrum is placed at one end of the bar. So, the work is done at the other end. The weight or load to be moved is in between. When the weight is closer to the fulcrum, then the weight is easier to move. Force can be increased, but the distance that it is moved is decreased. Examples are pry bars, bottle openers, nutcrackers, and wheelbarrows.

In a third-class lever, the fulcrum is at one end. So, the positions of the weight and the location where the work is done are reversed. Examples are fishing rods, hammers, and tweezers.

> ➤ **Review Video: Levers**
> *Visit mometrix.com/academy and enter Code:* **994753**

The center of a wheel and axle can be compared to a fulcrum on a rotating lever. As it turns, the wheel moves a greater distance than the axle but with less force. However, this type of simple machine can be used to apply a greater force. An example is a person who can turn the handles of a winch. They can apply a greater force at the turning axle to move an object.

A clear example of the wheel and axle is the wheels of a car. Other examples are steering wheels, wrenches, faucets, waterwheels, windmills, gears, and belts. The four basic types of gears are spur, rack and pinion, bevel, and worm gears. Gears work together to change a force. The larger gear turns slower than the smaller. However, this larger gear applies a greater force. Gears at angles can be used to change the direction of forces.

A single pulley has a rope or line that is placed around a wheel. This allows force to go in a downward motion to lift an object. The force that is needed is not decreased. Instead, the force just changes its direction. The load is moved the same distance as the rope pulling it.

A combination pulley (e.g., a double pulley) moves the weight half the distance of the rope. In this way, the work effort is doubled. Pulleys are never 100% efficient because of friction. Examples of pulleys are cranes, chain hoists, block and tackles, and elevators.

> ➤ **Review Video: Pulleys**
> *Visit mometrix.com/academy and enter Code:* **495865**

Thermodynamics

Thermodynamics is a branch of physics that studies the conversion of energy into work and heat. It is especially concerned with variables such as temperature, volume, and pressure. Thermodynamic equilibrium refers to objects that have the same temperature because heat is transferred between them to reach equilibrium. Thermodynamics takes places within three different types of systems; open, isolated, and closed systems. Open systems are capable of interacting with a surrounding environment and can exchange heat, work (energy), and matter outside their system boundaries. A closed system can exchange heat and work, but not matter. An isolated system cannot exchange heat, work, or matter with its surroundings. Its total energy and mass stay the same. In physics, surrounding environment refers to everything outside a thermodynamic system (system). The terms "surroundings" and "environment" are also used. The term "boundary" refers to the division between the system and its surroundings.

The laws of thermodynamics are generalized principles dealing with energy and heat.
- The zeroth law of thermodynamics states that two objects in thermodynamic equilibrium with a third object are also in equilibrium with each other. Being in thermodynamic equilibrium basically means that different objects are at the same temperature.
- The first law deals with conservation of energy. It states that neither mass nor energy can be destroyed; only converted from one form to another.

- The second law states that the entropy (the amount of energy in a system that is no longer available for work or the amount of disorder in a system) of an isolated system can only increase. The second law also states that heat is not transferred from a lower-temperature system to a higher-temperature one unless additional work is done.
- The third law of thermodynamics states that as temperature approaches absolute zero, entropy approaches a constant minimum. It also states that a system cannot be cooled to absolute zero.

Thermal contact refers to energy transferred to a body by a means other than work. A system in thermal contact with another can exchange energy with it through the process of heat transfer. Thermal contact does not necessarily involve direct physical contact. Heat is energy that can be transferred from one body or system to another without work being done. Everything tends to become less organized and less useful over time (entropy). In all energy transfers, therefore, the overall result is that the heat is spread out so that objects are in thermodynamic equilibrium and the heat can no longer be transferred without additional work.

Electricity and Magnetism

Electric Charge
Much like gravity, electricity is an everyday observable phenomenon which is very complex, but may be understood as a set of behaviors. As the gravitational force exists between objects with mass, the electric force exists between objects with electrical charge. In all atoms, the protons have a positive charge, while the electrons have a negative charge. An imbalance of electrons and protons in an object results in a net charge. Unlike gravity, which only pulls, electrical forces can push objects apart as well as pulling them together. Similar electric charges repel each other. Opposite charges attract each other.

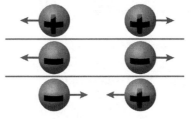

Current
The term for the rate at which the charge flows through a conductive material is current. Because each electron carries a specific charge, current can be thought of as the number of electrons passing a point in a length of time. Current is measured in Amperes (A).

Voltage

Voltage is the potential for electric work. Voltage is the push behind electrical work. Voltage is similar to gravitational potential energy.

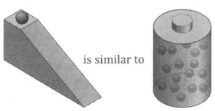

is similar to

Anything used to generate a voltage, such as a battery or a generator, is called a voltage source. Voltage is conveniently measured in Volts (V).

Magnetism

Magnetism is an attraction between opposite poles of magnetic materials and a repulsion between similar poles of magnetic materials. Magnetism can be natural or induced with the use of electric currents. Magnets almost always exist with two polar sides: north and south. A magnetic force exists between two poles on objects. Different poles attract each other. Like poles repel each other.

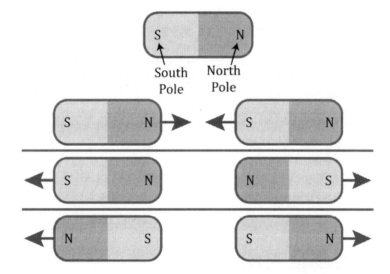

Interpretation of Data

Metric System

Using the metric system is generally accepted as the preferred method for taking measurements. Having a universal standard allows individuals to interpret measurements more easily, regardless of where they are located.

The basic units of measurement are: the meter, which measures length; the liter, which measures volume; and the gram, which measures mass. The metric system starts with a base unit and increases or decreases in units of 10. The prefix and the base unit combined are used to indicate an amount.

For example, deka is 10 times the base unit. A dekameter is 10 meters; a dekaliter is 10 liters; and a dekagram is 10 grams. The prefix hecto refers to 100 times the base amount; kilo is 1,000 times the base amount. The prefixes that indicate a fraction of the base unit are deci, which is 1/10 of the base unit; centi, which is 1/100 of the base unit; and milli, which is 1/1000 of the base unit.

S.I. Units of Measurement

SI uses second(s) to measure time. Fractions of seconds are usually measured in metric terms using prefixes such as millisecond (1/1,000 of a second) or nanosecond (1/1,000,000,000 of a second). Increments of time larger than a second are measured in minutes and hours, which are multiples of 60 and 24. An example of this is a swimmer's time in the 800-meter freestyle being described as 7:32.67, meaning 7 minutes, 32 seconds, and 67 one-hundredths of a second. One second is equal to 1/60 of a minute, 1/3,600 of an hour, and 1/86,400 of a day.

Other SI base units are the ampere (A) (used to measure electric current), the kelvin (K) (used to measure thermodynamic temperature), the candela (cd) (used to measure luminous intensity), and the mole (mol) (used to measure the amount of a substance at a molecular level). Meter (m) is used to measure length and kilogram (kg) is used to measure mass.

Metric Prefixes for Multiples and Subdivisions

The prefixes for multiples are as follows:
   deka (da), 10^1 (deka is the American spelling, but deca is also used)
   hecto (h), 10^2
   kilo (k), 10^3
   mega (M), 10^6
   giga (G), 10^9
   tera (T), 10^{12}

The prefixes for subdivisions are as follows:
   deci (d), 10^{-1}
   centi (c), 10^{-2}
   milli (m), 10^{-3}
   micro (μ), 10^{-6}
   nano (n), 10^{-9}
   pico (p), 10^{-12}

The rule of thumb is that prefixes greater than 10^3 are capitalized when abbreviating. Abbreviations do not need a period after them. A decimeter (dm) is a tenth of a meter, a deciliter (dL) is a tenth of a liter, and a decigram (dg) is a tenth of a gram. Pluralization is understood. For example, when referring to 5 mL of water, no "s" needs to be added to the abbreviation.

> **Review Video: Understanding Charts and Tables**
> Visit *mometrix.com/academy* and enter *Code:* **882112**

> **Review Video: Terminology for Tables and Graphs**
> Visit *mometrix.com/academy* and enter *Code:* **355505**

Line Graph

A line graph is a type of graph that is typically used for measuring trends over time. The graph is set up along a vertical and a horizontal axis. The variables being measured are listed along the left side and the bottom side of the axes. Points are then plotted along the graph as they correspond with their values for each variable. For instance, imagine a line graph measuring a person's income for each month of the year. If the person earned $1500 in January, there should be a point directly above January (perpendicular to the horizontal axis) and directly to the right of $1500 (perpendicular to the vertical axis). Once all of the lines are plotted, they are connected with a line from left to right. This line provides a nice visual illustration of the general trends. For instance, using the earlier example, if the line sloped up, then one would see that the person's income had increased over the course of the year.

> **Review Video: Line Graph**
> Visit *mometrix.com/academy* and enter *Code:* **480147**

Bar Graph

The bar graph is one of the most common visual representations of information. Bar graphs are used to illustrate sets of numerical data. The graph has a vertical axis (along which numbers are listed), and a horizontal axis (along which categories, words, or some other indicators are placed). One example of a bar graph is a depiction of the respective heights of famous basketball players: the vertical axis would contain numbers ranging from five to eight feet, and the horizontal axis would contain the names of the players. The length of the bar above the player's name would illustrate his height, and the top of the bar would stop perpendicular to the height listed along the left side. In this representation, one would see that Yao Ming is taller than Michael Jordan because Yao's bar would be higher.

> **Review Video: Bar Graph**
> Visit *mometrix.com/academy* and enter *Code:* **226729**

Pie Chart

A **pie chart**, also known as a circle graph, is useful for depicting how a single unit or category is divided. The standard pie chart is a circle with designated wedges. Each wedge is proportional in size to a part of the whole. For instance, consider a pie chart representing a student's budget. If the student spends half of his or her money on rent, then the pie chart will represent that amount with a line through the center of the pie. If she spends a quarter of her money on food, there will be a line extending from the edge of the circle to the center at a right angle to the line depicting rent. This illustration would make it clear that the student spends twice the amount of money on rent as she does on food.

> **Review Video: Pie Chart**
> Visit *mometrix.com/academy* and enter *Code:* **895285**

A pie chart is effective at showing how a single entity is divided into parts. They are not effective at demonstrating the relationships between parts of different wholes. For example, an unhelpful use of a pie chart would be to compare the respective amounts of state and federal spending devoted to infrastructure since these values are only meaningful in the context of the entire budget.

> **Review Video: Drawing Conclusions from Graphic Organizers**
> Visit *mometrix.com/academy* and enter *Code:* **363785**

Scientific Investigation

Lab Glassware

Graduated Cylinders and Burettes

Graduated cylinders are used for precise measurements and are considered more accurate than flasks or beakers. They are made of either polypropylene (which is shatter-resistant and resistant to chemicals but cannot be heated) or polymethylpentene (which is known for its clarity). They are lighter to ship and less fragile than glass.

To read a graduated cylinder, it should be placed on a flat surface and read at eye level. The surface of a liquid in a graduated cylinder forms a lens-shaped curve. The measurement should be taken from the bottom of the curve. A ring may be placed at the top of tall, narrow cylinders to help avoid breakage if they are tipped over.

A burette, or buret, is a piece of lab glassware used to accurately dispense liquid. It looks similar to a narrow graduated cylinder, but includes a stopcock and tip. It may be filled with a funnel or pipette.

Flasks, Beakers, and Pipettes

Two types of flasks commonly used in lab settings are Erlenmeyer flasks and volumetric flasks, which can also be used to accurately measure liquids. Erlenmeyer flasks and beakers can be used for mixing, transporting, and reacting, but are not appropriate for accurate measurements.

A pipette can be used to accurately measure small amounts of liquid. Liquid is drawn into the pipette through the bulb and a finger is then quickly placed at the top of the container. The liquid measurement is read exactly at the meniscus. Liquid can be released from the pipette by lifting the finger. There are also plastic disposal pipettes. A repipette is a hand-operated pump that dispenses solutions.

Balances

Unlike laboratory glassware that measures volume, balances such as triple-beam balances, spring balances, and electronic balances measure mass and force. An electronic balance is the most accurate, followed by a triple-beam balance and then a spring balance.

One part of a triple-beam balance is the plate, which is where the item to be weighed is placed. There are also three beams that have hatch marks indicating amounts and hold the weights that rest in the notches. The front beam measures weights between 0 and 10 grams, the middle beam measures weights in 100 gram increments, and the far beam measures weights in 10 gram increments.

The sum of the weight of each beam is the total weight of the object. A triple beam balance also includes a set screw to calibrate the equipment and a mark indicating the object and counterweights are in balance. Analytical balances are accurate to within 0.0001 g.

Scientific Inquiry

Scientific Method
The scientific method of inquiry is a general method by which ideas are tested and either confirmed or refuted by experimentation. The first step in the scientific method is formulating the problem that is to be addressed. It is essential to define clearly the limits of what is to be observed, since that allows for a more focused analysis.

Once the problem has been defined, it is necessary to form a hypothesis. This educated guess should be a possible solution to the problem that was formulated in the first step.

The next step is to test that hypothesis by experimentation. This often requires the scientist to design a complete experiment. The key to making the best possible use of an experiment is observation. Observations may be quantitative, that is, when a numeric measurement is taken, or they may be qualitative, that is, when something is evaluated based on feeling or preference. This measurement data will then be examined to find trends or patterns that are present.

> ➤ **Review Video: Experimental Science Project**
> Visit *mometrix.com/academy* and enter *Code:* **584444**

> ➤ **Review Video: Observations**
> Visit *mometrix.com/academy* and enter *Code:* **295845**

From these trends, the scientist will draw conclusions or make generalizations about the results, intended to predict future results. If these conclusions support the original hypothesis, the experiment is complete and the scientist will publish his conclusions to allow others to test them by repeating the experiment. If they do not support the hypothesis, the results should then be used to develop a new hypothesis, which can then be verified by a new or redesigned experiment.

> ➤ **Review Video: Hypothesis and Null Hypothesis**
> Visit *mometrix.com/academy* and enter *Code:* **113239**

Experimental Design

Designing relevant experiments that allow for meaningful results is not a simple task. Every stage of the experiment must be carefully planned to ensure that the right data can be safely and accurately taken.

Ideally, an experiment should be controlled so that all of the conditions except the ones being manipulated are held constant. This helps to ensure that the results are not skewed by unintended consequences of shifting conditions. A good example of this is a placebo group in a drug trial. All other conditions are the same, but that group is not given the medication.

In addition to proper control, it is important that the experiment be designed with data collection in mind. For instance, if the quantity to be measured is temperature, there must be a temperature device such as a thermocouple integrated into the experimental setup. While the data are being collected, they should periodically be checked for obvious errors. If there are data points that are orders of magnitude from the expected value, then it might be a good idea to make sure that no experimental errors are being made, either in data collection or condition control.

Once all the data have been gathered, they must be analyzed. The way in which this should be done depends on the type of data and the type of trends observed. It may be useful to fit curves to the data to determine if the trends follow a common mathematical form. It may also be necessary to perform a statistical analysis of the results to determine what effects are significant. Data should be clearly presented.

> **Review Video: <u>Identification of Experimental Problem and Design</u>**
> *Visit **mometrix.com/academy** and enter **Code: 653245***

> **Review Video: <u>Analysis of Results and Assessment of Flaws</u>**
> *Visit **mometrix.com/academy** and enter **Code: 406674***

> **Review Video: <u>Looking for Changes</u>**
> *Visit **mometrix.com/academy** and enter **Code: 385199***

Controls

A valid experiment must be carefully controlled. All variables except the one being tested must be carefully maintained. This means that all conditions must be kept exactly the same except for the independent variable.

Additionally, a set of data is usually needed for a control group. The control group represents the "normal" state or condition of the variable being manipulated. Controls can be negative or positive. Positive controls are the variables that the researcher expects to have an effect on the outcome of the experiment. A positive control group can be used to verify that an experiment is set up properly. Negative control groups are typically thought of as placebos. A negative control group should verify that a variable has no effect on the outcome of the experiment.

The better an experiment is controlled, the more valid the conclusions from that experiment will be. A researcher is more likely to draw a valid conclusion if all variables other than the one being manipulated are being controlled.

> ➤ **Review Video:** <u>Identifying Controls in a Research Summary</u>
> *Visit **mometrix.com/academy** and enter **Code: 911077***

Variables

Every experiment has several variables; however, only one variable should be purposely changed and tested. This variable is the manipulated or independent variable. As this variable is manipulated or changed, another variable, called the responding or dependent variable, is observed and recorded.

> ➤ **Review Video:** <u>Identifying Variables</u>
> *Visit **mometrix.com/academy** and enter **Code: 627181***

All other variables in the experiment must be carefully controlled and are usually referred to as constants. For example, when testing the effect of temperature on solubility of a solute, the independent variable is the temperature, and the dependent variable is the solubility.

All other factors in the experiment such as pressure, amount of stirring, type of solvent, type of solute, and particle size of the solute are the constants.

> ➤ **Review Video:** <u>Variables in an Experiment</u>
> *Visit **mometrix.com/academy** and enter **Code: 648641***

> ➤ **Review Video:** <u>Percent Yield</u>
> *Visit **mometrix.com/academy** and enter **Code: 565738***

Events and Objects

<u>Events</u>
A cause is an act or event that makes something happen, and an effect is the thing that happens as a result of the cause. A cause-and-effect relationship is not always explicit, but there are some terms in English that signal causes, such as *since*, *because*, and *due to*. Terms that signal effects include *consequently, therefore, this lead(s) to*.

A single cause can have multiple effects (e.g., *Single cause*: Because you left your homework on the table, your dog engulfs the assignment. *Multiple effects*: As a result, you receive a failing grade; your parents do not allow you to visit your friends; you miss out on the new movie and holding the hand of a potential significant other).

A single effect can have multiple causes (e.g.. *Single effect*: Alan has a fever. *Multiple causes*: An unexpected cold front came through the area, and Alan forgot to take his multi-vitamin to avoid being sick.)

An effect can in turn be the cause of another effect, in what is known as a cause-and-effect chain. (e.g., As a result of her disdain for procrastination, Lynn prepared for her exam. This led to her passing her test with high marks. Hence, her resume was accepted and her application was approved.)

<u>Scale</u>

From the largest objects in outer space to the smallest pieces of the human body, there are objects that can come in many different sizes and shapes. Many of those objects need to be measured in different ways. So, it is important to know which unit of measurement is needed to record the length or width and the weight of an object.

An example is taking the measurements of a patient. When measuring the total height of a patient or finding the length of an extremity, the accepted measure is given in meters. However, when one is asked for the diameter of a vein, the accepted measure is given in millimeters. Another example would be measuring the weight of a patient which would be given in kilograms, while the measurement of a human heart would be given in grams. The same idea for scale holds true with time as well. When measuring the lifespan of a patient, the accepted measure is given in days, months, or years. However, when measuring the number of breaths that a patient takes, the accepted measure is given in terms of minutes (e.g., breaths per minute).

> **Review Video: <u>Making Summaries</u>**
> *Visit **mometrix.com/academy** and enter **Code: 837767***

Evaluation of Models

Review a Scientific Explanation with Logic and Evidence

<u>Data Collection</u>

A valid experiment must be measurable. Data tables should be formed, and meticulous, detailed data should be collected for every trial. First, the researcher must determine exactly what data are needed and why those data are needed. The researcher should know in advance what will be done with those data at the end of the experimental research. The data should be repeatable, reproducible, and accurate. The researcher should be sure that the procedure for data collection will be reliable and consistent. The researcher should validate the measurement system by performing practice tests and making sure that all of the equipment is correctly calibrated and periodically retesting the procedure and equipment to ensure that all data being collected are still valid.

> ➢ **Review Video: <u>Tables</u>**
> *Visit **mometrix.com/academy** and enter **Code: 769453***

> ➢ **Review Video: <u>Identifying Units and Trends in a Chart</u>**
> *Visit **mometrix.com/academy** and enter **Code: 638347***

<u>Scientific Process Skills</u>

Perhaps the most important skill in science is that of observation. Scientists must be able to take accurate data from their experimental setup or from nature without allowing bias to alter the results. Another important skill is hypothesizing. Scientists must be able to combine their knowledge of theory and of other experimental results to logically determine what should occur in their own tests.

The data-analysis process requires the twin skills of ordering and categorizing. Gathered data must be arranged in such a way that it is readable and readily shows the key results. A skill that may be integrated with the previous two is comparing. Scientists should be able to compare their own results with other published results. They must also be able to infer, or draw logical conclusions, from their results. They must be able to apply their knowledge of theory and results to create logical experimental designs and determine cases of special behavior.

Lastly, scientists must be able to communicate their results and their conclusions. The greatest scientific progress is made when scientists are able to review and test one another's work and offer advice or suggestions.

> ➢ **Review Video: <u>Scientific Process Skills</u>**
> *Visit **mometrix.com/academy** and enter **Code: 601624***

<u>Scientific Statements</u>

Hypotheses are educated guesses about what is likely to occur, and are made to provide a starting point from which to begin design of the experiment. They may be based on results of previously observed experiments or knowledge of theory, and follow logically forth from these.

Assumptions are statements that are taken to be fact without proof for the purpose of performing a given experiment. They may be entirely true, or they may be true only for a given set of conditions under which the experiment will be conducted. Assumptions are necessary to simplify experiments; indeed, many experiments would be impossible without them.

Scientific models are mathematical statements that describe a physical behavior. Models are only as good as our knowledge of the actual system. Often models will be discarded when new discoveries are made that show the model to be inaccurate. While a model can never perfectly represent an actual system, they are useful for simplifying a system to allow for better understanding of its behavior.

> **Review Video: <u>Basic Problem and Disagreement</u>**
> *Visit **mometrix.com/academy** and enter **Code: 843079***

> **Review Video: <u>Opposing Arguments and Supporting Evidence</u>**
> *Visit **mometrix.com/academy** and enter **Code: 355002***

Scientific laws are statements of natural behavior that have stood the test of time and have been found to produce accurate and repeatable results in all testing. A theory is a statement of behavior that consolidates all current observations. Theories are similar to laws in that they describe natural behavior, but are more recently developed and are more susceptible to being proved wrong. Theories may eventually become laws if they stand up to scrutiny and testing.

> **Review Video: <u>Fact, Conclusion, Cause and Effect, Model, and Scientific Law</u>**
> *Visit **mometrix.com/academy** and enter **Code: 534217***

The Writing Test

Overview of Writing

Brainstorm

Spend the first three to five minutes brainstorming for ideas. Write down any ideas that you might have on the topic. The purpose is to pull any helpful information from the depths of your memory. In this stage, anything goes down in a margin for notes regardless of how good or bad the idea may seem at first glance.

Strength through Different Viewpoints

The best papers will contain several examples and mature reasoning. As you brainstorm, you should consider different perspectives. There are more than two sides to every topic. In an argument, there are countless perspectives that can be considered. On any topic, different groups are impacted and many reach the same conclusion or position. Yet, they reach the same conclusion through different paths. Before writing your essay, try to *see* the topic through as many different *eyes* as you can.

In addition, you don't have to use information on how the topic impacts others. You can draw from your own experience as you wish. If you prefer to use a personal narrative, then explain the experience and your emotions from that moment. Anything that you've seen in your community can be expanded upon to round out your position on the topic.

Once you have finished with your creative flow, you need to stop and review what you brainstormed. *Which idea allowed you to come up with the most supporting information?* Be sure to pick an angle that will allow you to have a thorough coverage of the prompt.

Every garden of ideas has weeds. The ideas that you brainstormed are going to be random pieces of information of different values. Go through the pieces carefully and pick out the ones that are the best. The best ideas are strong points that will be easy to write a paragraph in response.

Now, you have your main ideas that you will focus on. So, align them in a sequence that will flow in a smooth, sensible path from point to point. With this approach, readers will go smoothly from one idea to the next in a reasonable order. Readers want an essay that has a sense of continuity (i.e., Point 1 to Point 2 to Point 3 and so on).

Start Your Engines

Now, you have a logical flow of the main ideas for the start of your essay. Begin by expanding on the first point, then move to your second point. Pace yourself. Don't spend too much time on any one of the ideas that you are expanding on. You want to have time for all of them. Make sure that you watch your time. If you have twenty minutes left to write out your ideas and you have four ideas, then you can only use five minutes per idea. Writing so much information in so little time can be an intimidating task. Yet, when you pace yourself, you can get through all of your points. If you find that you are falling behind, then you can remove one of your weaker arguments. This will allow you to give enough support to your remaining paragraphs.

Once you finish expanding on an idea, go back to your brainstorming session where you wrote out your ideas. You can scratch through the ideas as you write about them. This will let you see what you need to write about next and what you have left to cover.

Your introductory paragraph should have several easily identifiable features.
- First, the paragraph should have a quick description or paraphrasing of the topic. Use your own words to briefly explain what the topic is about.
- Second, you should list your writing points. What are the main ideas that you came up with earlier? If someone was to read only your introduction, they should be able to get a good summary of the entire paper.
- Third, you should explain your opinion of the topic and give an explanation for why you feel that way. What is your decision or conclusion on the topic?

Each of your following paragraphs should develop one of the points listed in the main paragraph. Use your personal experience and knowledge to support each of your points. Examples should back up everything.

Once you have finished expanding on each of your main points, you need to conclude your essay. Summarize what you written in a conclusion paragraph. Explain once more your argument on the prompt and review why you feel that way in a few sentences. At this stage, you have already backed up your statements. So, there is no need to do that again. You just need to refresh your readers on the main points that you made in your essay.

Don't Panic

Whatever you do during essay, do not panic. When you panic, you will put fewer words on the page and your ideas will be weak. Therefore, panicking is not helpful. If your mind goes blank when you see the prompt, then you need to take a deep breath. Force yourself to go through the steps listed above: brainstorm and put anything on scratch paper that comes to mind.

Also, don't get clock fever. You may be overwhelmed when you're looking at a page that has is mostly blank. Your mind is full of random thoughts and feeling confused, and the clock is ticking down faster. You have already brainstormed for ideas. Therefore, you don't have to keep coming up with ideas. If you're running out of time and you have a lot of ideas that you haven't written down, then don't be afraid to make some cuts. Start picking the best ideas that you have left and expand on them. Don't feel like you have to write on all of your ideas.

A short paper that is well written and well organized is better than a long paper that is poorly written and poorly organized. Don't keep writing about a subject just to add sentences and avoid repeating a statement or idea that you have explained already. The goal is 1 to 2 pages of quality writing. That is your target, but you should not mess up your paper by trying to get there. You want to have a natural end to your work without having to cut something short. If your essay is a little long, then that isn't a problem as long as your ideas are clear and flow well from paragraph to paragraph. Remember to expand on the ideas that you identified in the brainstorming session.

Leave time at the end (at least three minutes) to go back and check over your work. Reread and make sure that everything you've written makes sense and flows well. Clean up any spelling or grammar mistakes. Also, go ahead and erase any brainstorming ideas that you weren't able to include. Then, clean up any extra information that you might have written that doesn't fit into your paper.

As you proofread, make sure that there aren't any fragments or run-ons. Check for sentences that are too short or too long. If the sentence is too short, then look to see if you have a specific subject and an active verb. If it is too long, then break up the long sentence into two sentences. Watch out for any "big words" that you may have used. Be sure that you are using difficult words correctly. Don't misunderstand; you should try to increase your vocabulary and use difficult words in your essay. However, your focus should be on developing and expressing ideas in a clear and precise way.

The Short Overview

Depending on your preferences and personality, the essay may be your hardest or your easiest section. You are required to go through the entire process of writing a paper in a limited amount of time which is very challenging.

Stay focused on each of the steps for brainstorming. Go through the process of creative flow first. You can start by generating ideas about the prompt. Next, organize those ideas into a smooth flow. Then, pick out the ideas that are the best from your list.

Create a recognizable essay structure in your paper. Start with an introduction that explains what you have decided to argue. Then, choose your main points. Use the body paragraphs to touch on those main points and have a conclusion that wraps up the topic.

Save a few moments to go back and review what you have written. Clean up any minor mistakes that you might have made and make those last few critical touches that can make a huge difference. Finally, be proud and confident of what you have written!

Practice Test

English

United States Coast Guard

The United States Coast Guard (1) <u>was founded in 1790</u> as the branch of military service responsible for safeguarding the country's sea-related interests. (2)

(3) <u>It was originally created</u> to protect the U.S. (4) <u>from smugglers, and to enforce</u> tariff and trade laws. It may seem like this would be a job for the Navy, but the purpose of the Navy is very different from that of the Coast Guard. The Navy's job is (5) <u>to engage in combat and defend the seas</u> from threats to the U.S. and its interests worldwide.

(6) The United States Coast Guard is actually a part of the Department of Homeland Security and is considered a federal law enforcement agency.
The mission of the department is to protect and to enforce laws on our coastlines and in our ports and to safeguard other interests within American waters.

In addition to enforcing maritime (7) <u>law, we need to recognize that the United States Coast Guard also serves</u> as a guardian of the environment.
(8) This includes stopping waste and other types of pollution from being dumped into the ocean, preventing and helping to clean up oil spills, and even ensuring that species of marine life that could threaten the balance of existing environments are prevented from being introduced.

(9) <u>This is a real important</u> job for the Coast Guard because there would not be much of a coastline to protect if our seas were too polluted to entertain or to sustain us. (10)
On the whole, the United States Coast Guard personnel (11) <u>perform the following in a single day:</u> save 12 lives; respond to 64 search and rescue cases; keep 842 pounds of cocaine off the streets; service 116 buoys and fix 24 discrepancies; screen 720 commercial vessels and 183,000 crew and passengers; issue 173 credentials to merchant mariners; investigate 13 marine accidents; inspect 68 containers and 29 vessels for compliance with air emissions standards; perform 28 safety and environmental examinations of foreign vessels; board 13 fishing boats to ensure compliance with fisheries laws; and (12) <u>explore and investigate 10 pollution incidents</u>.

The United States Coast Guard (1) was founded in 1790 as the branch of military service responsible for safeguarding the country's sea-related interests.

1. A. NO CHANGE
   B. was founded in 1790,
   C. were founded in 1790
   D. will have been founded in 1790

---

2. The author wants to add the following statement:
   While this branch of military service has seen several changes in its tasks, the mission of the branch has not changed since its founding.

Should the author make the addition here?
   F. Yes, this sentence offers a smooth transition to the following sentence and informs readers of what they can expect for the remainder of the passage.
   G. No, this sentence is vague and distracting for readers.
   H. Yes, the purpose of the passage is to address the many responsibilities of the U.S. Coast Guard.
   J. No, the dependent phrase of this sentence is already addressed in the next sentence, and the independent clause is addressed in the following paragraphs.

---

(3) It was originally created to protect the U.S. from smugglers, and to enforce tariff and trade laws.

3. A. NO CHANGE
   B. It was originally established
   C. The branch was originally created
   D. Originally, it was created

It was originally created to protect the U.S. (4) from smugglers, and to enforce tariff and trade laws.

4. F. NO CHANGE
   G. from smugglers, and enforce
   H. from smugglers, and to promote
   J. from smugglers and to enforce

The Navy's job is (5) to engage in combat and defend the seas from threats to the U.S. and its interests worldwide.

5. A. NO CHANGE
   B. to engage in combats and defend the seas
   C. to engage in combat, and defend the seas
   D. to engage in combat and to defend the seas

---

6. How can the following sentence be revised for conciseness?

(6) The United States Coast Guard is actually a part of the Department of Homeland Security and is considered a federal law enforcement agency.

    F. NO CHANGE
    G. As part of the Department of Homeland Security, the United States Coast Guard is considered a federal law enforcement agency.
    H. As part of the Department of Homeland Security, we know the United States Coast Guard to be a federal law enforcement agency.
    J. The Department of Homeland Security considers the United States Coast Guard to be actually a part a federal law enforcement agency.

In addition to enforcing maritime (7) <u>law, we need to recognize that the United States Coast Guard also serves</u> as a guardian of the environment.

7. A. NO CHANGE
    B. law, also serving the United States Coast Guard
    C. law we need to recognize that the United States Coast Guard serves
    D. law, the United States Coast Guard also serves

---

8. Which of the following sentences, if placed before sentence 10, would create a better transition from the second paragraph to the third paragraph?
    F. The "Coastie" life is one that just about anyone would want to choose.
    G. The life of a Coast Guard member (or "Coastie") can be routine and boring, depending on what type of job the "Coastie" has.
    H. There are many things that the Coast Guard can do to enforce laws while at sea or patrolling our waterways.
    J. Enforcement of laws and protection of the environment are just two of the many responsibilities that a member of the Coast Guard (or "Coastie") can expect to have in the line of duty.

---

(9) <u>This is a real important</u> job for the Coast Guard because there would not be much of a coastline to protect if our seas were too polluted to entertain or to sustain us.

9. A. NO CHANGE
    B. This is not a real important
    C. This is a real, important
    D. This is a really important

This is a real important job for the Coast Guard because there would not be much of a coastline to protect if our seas were too polluted to entertain or to sustain us. (10)

On the whole, the United States Coast Guard personnel perform the following in a single day...

10. The author wants to add the following statement:
If we do our part to maintain clean coastlines, then this will allow the Coast Guard to focus more on performing routine inspections or search and rescue missions.

Should the author make the addition here?
    F. Yes, this comes as helpful information to readers who are not familiar with the responsibilities of the Coast Guard.
    G. No, this sentence would distract from author's original purpose of the passage which is to inform, not persuade.
    H. Yes, this leads in well to the next paragraph on the responsibilities of Coast Guard members.
    J. No, this sentence suggests that readers are responsible for cleaning coastlines.

On the whole, the United States Coast Guard personnel (11) <u>perform the following in a single day:</u> save 12 lives...

11. A. NO CHANGE
    B. complete the following in a single day:
    C. accomplish the following in one day:
    D. perform the following in a day:

... board 13 fishing boats to ensure compliance with fisheries laws; and (12) <u>respond to and investigate 10 pollution incidents</u>.

12. F. NO CHANGE
    G. investigate 10 pollution incidents
    H. explore, and investigate 10 pollution incidents
    J. explore to investigate 10 pollution incidents

---

13. Adding which of the following sentences to paragraph 3 would make it more credible?
    A. This information comes from the official Coast Guard Web site.
    B. The average age of Coast Guard members is 28.
    C. The Coast Guard has a long history of service.
    D. There are 33,200 enlisted Coast Guard members.

---

14. If the writer's main goal were to explain the requirements for becoming a member of the United States Coast Guard, then would this passage achieve that goal?

    F. Yes, the author lists the daily objectives of Coast Guard members and notes how they are "a guardian of the environment."

    G. No, the author only provides a general listing of the things that Coast Guard members are expected to accomplish a day.

    H. Yes, the author notes the difference between the U.S. Navy and the Coast Guard in the second paragraph

    J. No, the author gives clarity on some of the differences between the U.S. Navy and the Coast Guard and mentions none of the necessary pieces to becoming a member of the U.S. Coast Guard.

15. Which of the following would be the best conclusion for this essay?

    A. There is much more that we can learn about the Coast Guard. To list all of the great things about this organization would take all day. The opportunities available to members of the Coast Guard are endless, and we should all consider becoming a "Coastie."

    B. Being a "Coastie" would be the fulfillment of anyone's dreams. Who wouldn't want a career that is full of adventure and honor? There is no better job that a person could pursue as their life's work.

    C. The Coast Guard is a very diverse and exciting branch of the U.S. military. Though many may not believe it is as important as the Navy, the Army, the Marines, or the Air Force, it's plain to see that the Coast Guard plays a vital role in ensuring our nation's security and prosperity.

    D. The Coast Guard provides little support toward defending our nation from threats, as its members are always so close to home. Greater purpose can be found in a different branch of service. The threats that the Coast Guard faces are insignificant when compared to those faced by the Army, the Navy, the Marines, or the Air Force.

New Zealand Inhabitants

[1]

(16) <u>The islands of New Zealand are among the most remote</u> of all the Pacific islands.

(17) New Zealand is an archipelago, with two large (18) <u>islands, and a number of smaller</u> ones. Its climate is far cooler than the rest of Polynesia.

(19) Nevertheless, according to Maori legends, it was colonized in the early fifteenth century by a wave of Polynesian voyagers who traveled southward in their canoes and settled on North Island. (20) <u>At this time, New Zealand has been known already to the Polynesians, who had probably first landed there some 400 years earlier.</u>
At this time the Polynesians knew their surroundings in New Zealand after landing there probably some 400 years earlier.

[2]

The Polynesian (21) <u>southward migration was limited by</u> the availability of food. Traditional Polynesian tropical crops such as taro and yams will grow on North Island, but the climate of South Island is too cold for them. (22)
(23) <u>The first settlers were forced</u> to rely on hunting and gathering, and, (24) <u>of course, fishing. Especially on South Island,</u> most settlements remained close to the sea. At the time of the Polynesian incursion, enormous flocks of moa birds had their rookeries on the island shores. These flightless birds were easy prey for the settlers, and within a few centuries had been hunted to extinction. (25) <u>Fish, shellfish and the roots of the fern</u> were other important sources of food, but even these began to diminish in quantity as the human population increased. The Maori had few other choices (26) <u>of meat among: dogs, smaller birds, and rats.</u> Archaeological evidence shows that human flesh was also eaten, and (27) <u>that tribal warfare increased after the moa disappeared markedly.</u>

[3]

By far the most important farmed crop in prehistoric New Zealand was the sweet potato. This tuber is hearty enough to grow throughout the islands and could be stored to provide food during the winter months when other food-gathering activities were difficult. (28) The availability of the (29) <u>sweet potato made possible a significant increase in the human population.</u> (30)

(16) <u>The islands of New Zealand are among the most remote</u> of all the Pacific islands.

16. F. NO CHANGE
    G. The island of New Zealand is among the most remote
    H. The islands of New Zealand are between the most remote
    J. The islands of New Zealand are among the more remote

---

(17) New Zealand is an archipelago, with two large islands, and a number of smaller ones. Its climate is far cooler than the rest of Polynesia.

17. What is the BEST way to revise and combine sentence 2 and sentence 3?
    A. Its climate is far cooler than the rest of Polynesia because New Zealand is an archipelago, with two large islands and a number of smaller ones.
    B. New Zealand is an archipelago, with two large islands and a number of smaller ones, and its climate is far cooler than the rest of Polynesia.
    C. Its climate is far cooler than the rest of Polynesia; however, New Zealand is an archipelago, with two large islands and a number of smaller ones.
    D. New Zealand is an archipelago, with two large islands and a number of smaller ones; thus, its climate is far cooler than the rest of Polynesia.

New Zealand is an archipelago, with two large (18) <u>islands, and a number of smaller</u> ones.

18. F. NO CHANGE
    G. islands and the amount of smaller
    H. islands and a number of smaller
    J. islands and an amount of smaller

---

19. How can the following sentence be revised for precision and conciseness?

Nevertheless, according to Maori legends, it was colonized in the early fifteenth century by a wave of Polynesian voyagers who traveled southward in their canoes and settled on North Island.

    A. NO CHANGE
    B. According to Maori legends, New Zealand was colonized in the early fifteenth century by Polynesian voyagers who traveled in their canoes to settle on North Island.
    C. Nevertheless, it was colonized according to Maori legends, by a wave of Polynesian voyagers who traveled southward in their canoes and settled on North Island.
    D. Those who traveled southward in their canoes settled on North Island because it was colonized in the early fifteenth century by a wave of Polynesian voyagers according to Maori legends.

---

(20) At this time, New Zealand has been known already to the Polynesians, who had probably first landed there some 400 years earlier.

20. F. NO CHANGE
    G. New Zealand will have been known already to the Polynesians who had probably first landed there some 400 years earlier.
    H. The Polynesians, who had probably first landed there some 400 years earlier, at this time have known New Zealand.
    J. At this time, the Polynesians knew their surroundings in New Zealand after landing there probably some 400 years earlier.

The Polynesian (21) southward migration was limited by the availability of food.

21. A. NO CHANGE
    B. Southward migration is limited by
    C. southward migration had been limited by
    D. Southward migration has been limited by

Traditional Polynesian tropical crops such as taro and yams will grow on North Island, but the climate of South Island is too cold for them. (22) The first settlers were forced to rely on hunting and gathering, and, of course, fishing. Especially on South Island, most settlements remained close to the sea.

22. The author is thinking about adding this sentence to the passage.

Coconuts will not grow on either island.

Should the author add this sentence at this point in the paragraph?
    F. Yes. This information is evidence that will help readers understand the predicament of Polynesian people.
    G. No. While the statement is true, the sentence does not transition well in the paragraph.
    H. Yes. This statement transitions well from the previous sentence to the next on the struggle to find and maintain food for Polynesians.
    J. No. This statement does include an explanation of the purpose of coconuts to the Polynesian people.

(23) The first settlers were forced to rely on hunting and gathering, and, of course, fishing.

23. A. NO CHANGE
    B. The first settlers forced themselves
    C. The first settlers will have been forced
    D. This harsh environment forced the first settlers

The first settlers were forced to rely on hunting and gathering, and, of course, fishing. Especially on South Island, most settlements remained close to the sea.

24. Which choice most effectively transitions from sentence 9 to sentence 10 (reproduced above) at the underlined portion?

    F. of course, fishing, but especially on South Island
    G. of course, fishing; however, on South Island
    H. of course, fishing: especially on South Island
    J. of course, fishing; therefore, on South Island

---

(25) Fish, shellfish and the roots of the fern were other important sources of food, but even these began to diminish in quantity as the human population increased.

25. A. NO CHANGE
    B. Fish, shellfish, and the roots of the fern
    C. Fish, Shellfish, and the roots of the fern
    D. Fish, shellfish and the root of the fern

The Maori had few other choices (26) of meat among: dogs, smaller birds, and rats.

26. F. NO CHANGE
    G. of meat among: dogs, smaller birds and rats
    H. with: dogs, smaller birds, and rats
    J. of meat: dogs, smaller birds, and rats

Archaeological evidence shows that human flesh was also eaten, and that tribal warfare (27) increased after the moa disappeared markedly.

27. A. NO CHANGE
    B. increased markedly after the moa disappeared.
    C. increased after the moa disappeared.
    D. increased markedly after their disappearance.

---

28. Which is the best placement for sentence 18 in this passage?
    F. Before sentence 16
    G. After sentence 16
    H. After sentence 19
    J. In its current place

The availability of the sweet potato made possible a (29) <u>significant increase in the human population</u>.

29. A. NO CHANGE
   B. increase in the human population.
   C. significant increase in the Maori population.
   D. significant increase in the population.

_____

30. The author wants to add the following statement at the end of the passage:

Thus, Maori tribes often were located near the best sweet potato farmlands in encampments called pa, which were fortified with earthen embankments.

Should the author make the addition at the end of this passage?
   F. Yes, this information is evidence that supports the topic of the third paragraph.
   G. No, this sentence is unnecessary and does not support the topic of the third paragraph.
   H. Yes, this sentence is further proof that the Maori tribe was the most advanced of New Zealand inhabitants.
   J. No. While this information supports the topic, the author should reconsider the placement of the sentence in this passage.

The Wright Brothers

After Orville and (31) <u>Wilbur Wright will have flown their</u> first airplane in 1903, the age of flying slowly began. Many new pilots (32) <u>learned how to fly in World War I, which</u> the United States joined in 1917. During the war, the American public loved hearing stories about the daring pilots and their air fights. But after the war ended, many Americans thought that men and women belonged on the ground and not in the air.

(33) In the years after the war and through the Roaring Twenties, America's pilots found themselves without jobs. Some of them gave up flying altogether. **A**

Pilot Eddie (34) <u>Rickenbacker, who used to be called America's Ace of Aces, became</u> a car salesman. But other (35) <u>pilots found new and creative things</u> to do with their airplanes.

B The (36) <u>airplane was used by pilot Casey Jones</u> to help get news across the country. (37) <u>When a big news story broke, Jones</u> flew news photos to newspapers in different cities. (38) <u>Another pilot, Roscoe Turner, traveled</u> around the country with a lion cub in his plane. The cub was the mascot of an oil company, and Turner convinced the company that flying the cub around would be a good advertisement. The Humane Society wasn't very happy (39) <u>about this idea, and they convinced Turner</u> to make sure the lion cub always wore a parachute. **C**

(40) Other pilots took people for short airplane rides, often charging five dollars for a five-minute ride (by comparison, you could buy a loaf of bread for about ten cents in 1920).

These pilots, called barnstormers, often used dangerous tricks to get customers: two barnstormers once stood on a plane's wings and played tennis while the plane flew at 70 miles per hour! Many barnstormers advertised their shows as a 'flying circus.' **D**

During the 1920s, the U.S. Post Office developed airmail. Before airmail, the post traveled on trains and (42) <u>can take weeks to reach a destination.</u>

(43) Flying for the post office was dangerous work. Early pilots didn't have sophisticated instruments and safety equipment on their planes.

Many of them had to bail out and use their parachutes when their planes iced up in the cold air or had other trouble.

After Orville and (31) <u>Wilbur Wright will have flown their</u> first airplane in 1903, the age of flying slowly began.

31. A. NO CHANGE
    B. Wilbur Wright, have flew their
    C. Wilbur Wright flew their
    D. Wilbur Wright will have flied their

Many new pilots (32) <u>learned how to fly in World War I, which</u> the United States joined in 1917.

32. F. NO CHANGE
    G. trained for flight in World War I, which
    H. studied flying during World War I, which
    J. learned how to fly in World War I which

In the years after the war and through the Roaring Twenties, America's pilots found themselves without jobs. Some of them gave up flying altogether.

33. What is the best way to combine sentences 5 and 6?
    A. Some of America's pilots in the years after the war and through the Roaring Twenties found themselves without jobs because they gave up flying altogether.
    B. In the years after the war and through the Roaring Twenties, America's pilots found themselves without jobs; thus some of them gave up flying altogether.
    C. Some of America's pilots gave up flying altogether in the years after the war and through the Roaring Twenties, and they found themselves without jobs.
    D. In the years after the war and through the Roaring Twenties, America's pilots found themselves without jobs because some of them gave up flying altogether.

Pilot Eddie (34) <u>Rickenbacker, who used to be called America's Ace of Aces, became</u> a car salesman.

34. F. NO CHANGE
    G. Rickenbacker, who will have been known as America's Ace of Aces, became
    H. Rickenbacker who used to be called America's Ace of Aces became
    J. Rickenbacker, who used to be called America's ace of aces, became

---

But other (35) <u>pilots found new and creative things</u> to do with their airplanes.

35. A. NO CHANGE
    B. pilots found creative things
    C. pilots attempted new and creative things
    D. pilots found new, creative tricks

The (36) airplane was used by pilot Casey Jones to help get news across the country.

36. F. NO CHANGE
   G. The airplane was used by Casey Jones, a pilot,
   H. Pilot Casey Jones used his airplane
   J. The airplane was flown by pilot Casey Jones

---

(37) When a big news story broke, Jones flew news photos to newspapers in different cities.

37. A. NO CHANGE
   B. When a big, news story broke, Jones
   C. When an important story broke, Jones
   D. When a big news story arrived, Jones

---

(38) Another pilot, Roscoe Turner, traveled around the country with a lion cub in his plane.

38. F. NO CHANGE
   G. Another pilot, Roscoe Turner, flew
   H. A pilot, Roscoe Turner, traveled
   J. Roscoe Turner, another pilot, traveled

The Humane Society wasn't very happy (39) about this idea, and they convinced Turner to make sure the lion cub always wore a parachute.

39. A. NO CHANGE
   B. about this idea: they convinced Turner
   C. about this idea; Turner was convinced
   D. about this idea and they convinced Turner

---

40. What is the best revision to the following sentence?

Other pilots took people for short airplane rides, often charging five dollars for a five-minute ride (by comparison, you could buy a loaf of bread for about ten cents in 1920).

   F. NO CHANGE
   G. In the same time period that you could buy a loaf of bread for about ten cents, there were pilots who took people for short airplane rides by charging five dollars for a five-minute ride.
   H. Pilots took people for short airplane rides by charging five dollars for a five-minute ride, or you could buy a loaf of bread for about ten cents in 1920.
   J. Often charging five dollars for a five-minute ride, pilots took people for short airplane rides, however; you could buy a loaf of bread for about ten cents in 1920 by comparison.

These pilots, called barnstormers, often used dangerous tricks <u>to get customers: two barnstormers once stood</u> on a plane's wings and played tennis while the plane flew at 70 miles per hour!

41. A. NO CHANGE
    B. customers, two barnstormers once stood
    C. customers: two "barnstormers" once stood
    D. customers: two barnstormers stood

---

(42) Before airmail, the post traveled on trains and <u>can take weeks to reach a destination.</u>

42. F. NO CHANGE
    G. can take weeks to finally reach a destination.
    H. could take weeks to reach a destination.
    J. could take weeks to reach it's destination.

Flying for the post office was dangerous work. Early pilots didn't have sophisticated instruments and safety equipment on their planes.

43. What is the best way to combine sentences 15 and 16?
    A. Flying for the post office was dangerous work, but early pilots didn't have sophisticated instruments and safety equipment on their planes.
    B. Early pilots didn't have sophisticated instruments and safety equipment on their planes which made flying for the post office dangerous work.
    C. Flying for the post office was dangerous work; however, early pilots didn't have sophisticated instruments and safety equipment on their planes.
    D. Early pilots didn't have sophisticated instruments and safety equipment on their planes, nor was flying for the post office dangerous work.

---

44. The author wants to add the following statement:

The most famous pilot of the 1920s, Charles A. Lindbergh, participated in an air race to fly across the Atlantic Ocean in May 1927.

Where is the best place for this sentence to be added in the passage?
    F. Point A in Paragraph 1
    G. Point B in Paragraph 2
    H. Point C in Paragraph 2
    J. Point D in Paragraph 3

---

45. If the author wanted to argue that the purpose of the passage was to explain the reasons for men and women needing to remain on the ground after the war, would the author be able to maintain this claim?

A. Yes, the first paragraph reviews the contribution that pilots made during WWI.

B. No, the passage does not focus enough on the practical aspects of the airplane compared to entertainment.

C. Yes, the author gives context to the privileges of flight and the early achievements of flight.

D. No, the author does not provide reasons for why the American public thought that the pilots should remain on the ground instead of pursuing more opportunities with flight.

Buddhism, Western Society, and the Self

[1]

(46) In Western society, the American individual self is generally prioritized over the collective self. This is evidenced in such things as the privatization of medicine and conceptions of ownership. In recent decades, however, there has been an increased tension (47) beside Western societies with institutions and ideologies that prioritize the individual and those that prioritize the collective. This is evidenced in the struggles that Western Buddhists face.

[2]

Central to Buddhist belief is the idea of "egolessness." While this term may seem to imply the absence of the individual ego or selfhood, this is (49) not the case; consequently, "egolessness" is a prioritization of the relationships between and among people over selfish concerns. "Egolessness" may also be thought of as an antonym of "ego-toxicity," that condition where an individual (50) places his or her concerns before any other person or group's concerns. (51) In Western societies, ego-toxicity is the reigning condition. Buddhists who live in such societies often find themselves caught between their ideology of egolessness and environmental ego-toxicity.

[3]

While a Western perspective might find it difficult to (53) understand how a Buddhist can keep egolessness; in Western society, Buddhists are able to maintain such a perspective as a natural consequent of their beliefs. The Western perspective expects moral actions to be quid pro quo; to put it another way, (54) a Westerner assumes that if he or she does something considered "good," then he or she should and will be rewarded. Buddhists, on the other hand, believe that good should be done out of compassion for all (55) beings, and to do good is to do good for all beings, including the self. Approaching society and social action in an egoless manner has begun to become more prevalent in secular institutions and movements (56) as can be seen in the healthcare field. The struggle between the ego and the collective continues, however.

[4]

Buddhist practitioners show through their actions that it is possible to do good in the world without giving up one's personhood. (57) When ego-toxicity is abandoned, it is possible to care for one's self and the rest of the world through compassionate, egoless behavior.

(46) In Western society, the American individual self is generally prioritized over the collective self.

46. F. NO CHANGE
    G. In Western society, the self
    H. In western society, the American self
    J. In Western society, the individual self

In recent decades, however, there has been an increased tension (47) beside Western societies with institutions and ideologies that prioritize the individual and those that prioritize the collective.

47. A. NO CHANGE
    B. among Western societies
    C. between Western societies
    D. underneath western societies

---

48. What is the purpose of the first paragraph?
    F. To criticize Buddhist notions of the self.
    G. To criticize contemporary Western notions of the self.
    H. To introduce the tension between individuality and collectivity in Western society.
    J. To introduce the idea of "egolessness."

While this term may seem to imply the absence of the individual ego or selfhood, this is (49) not the case; consequently, "egolessness" is a prioritization of the relationships between and among people over selfish concerns.

49. A. NO CHANGE
    B. not the case; rather, "egolessness" is a prioritization
    C. not the case; therefore", egolessness" is a prioritization
    D. not the case; accordingly ",egolessness" is a priority

---

"Egolessness" may also be thought of as an antonym of "ego-toxicity," that condition where an individual (50) places his or her concerns before any other person or group's concerns.

50. F. NO CHANGE
    G. places their concerns before any other person's concerns.
    H. places his or her concerns before any other person's or group's concerns.
    J. places their concerns before any other person or group's concerns.

---

51. This sentence appears in the second paragraph: "In Western societies, ego-toxicity is the reigning condition." Which of the following would be the most logical organization?
    A. NO CHANGE
    B. Move it to the end of the paragraph
    C. Move it to the paragraph's beginning
    D. Move it out of the paragraph entirely

52. Which of the following best describes the purpose of the second paragraph?
    F. It introduces the distinction between "egolessness" and "ego-toxicity."
    G. It makes light of the conflicts that Buddhists in Western societies experience.
    H. It praises egolessness as the only moral way of living.
    J. It harshly denounces ego-toxicity.

While a Western perspective might find it difficult to (53) <u>understand how a Buddhist can keep egolessness;</u> in Western society, Buddhists are able to maintain such a perspective as a natural consequent of their beliefs.

53. A. NO CHANGE
    B. understand how a Buddhist could maintain egolessness,
    C. understand how a Buddhist could stay egolessness
    D. believe what a Buddhist could maintain egolessness

The Western perspective expects moral actions to be quid pro quo; to put it another way, a Westerner assumes that if he or she does something considered "good," (54) <u>then he or she should and will be rewarded.</u>

54. F. NO CHANGE
    G. then he or she will be rewarded.
    H. then they should be rewarded.
    J. then they will be rewarded.

Buddhists, on the other hand, believe that good should be done out of compassion for all (55) <u>beings, and to do good is to do good for all beings, including</u> the self.

55. A. NO CHANGE
    B. beings, and to do good is good for all beings, including
    C. beings and to do good is to do good for all beings including
    D. beings, and this is done for all beings including

56. Which of the following choices gives the most specific information about how social action in an egoless manner has become more prevalent in secular institutions and movements?

Approaching society and social action in an egoless manner has begun to become more prevalent in secular institutions and movements (56) <u>as can be seen in the healthcare field</u>.

    F. NO CHANGE
    G. like the restoration of generosity among those in healthcare.
    H. such as the transition to a more socialized form of medical treatment in some Western
       countries
    J. as was seen with the members of the medical field in Europe.

---

(57) When ego-toxicity is abandoned, it is possible to care for one's self and the rest of the world through compassionate, egoless behavior.

57. A. NO CHANGE
    B. When ego-toxicity can be abandoned it is possible for one's self to care for the rest of the
       world through compassionate, egoless behavior.
    C. When ego-toxicity is abandoned it could be possible to care for one's self and the rest of the
       world through compassionate, egoless behavior.
    D. When ego-toxicity is abandoned, it is possible to care for one's self and the rest of the world
       through compassionate, egoless behavior.

---

58. In this passage, which sentence in the first paragraph states a main idea that is developed in subsequent paragraphs?
    F. The second sentence
    G. The fourth sentence
    H. The third sentence
    J. The first sentence

---

59. The style, mode, or type of text in this passage is best characterized as which of these?
    A. Description
    B. Persuasion
    C. Exposition
    D. Narration

---

60. Which of these accurately describes a pattern in the first and/or last sentences of all the paragraphs in this passage?

  F. The last sentence of each paragraph identifies half a main conflict; the final sentence completes it.
  G. The first sentence of each paragraph identifies a main conflict, with the final sentence reiterating.
  H. The first sentence of each paragraph identifies a main conflict, with the final sentence resolving it.
  J. The last sentence of each paragraph identifies a main conflict, with the final sentence resolving it

The Beginnings of Basketball

[1]

(61) Basketball is, arguably, one of the most popular and most exciting sports of our time. (62) Behind this fast-paced sport, however, is a rich history. **A** There have been many changes made to the game over the years, but the essence remains the same. From its humble beginnings in 1891, (63) basketball has grown to have worldwide appeal.

[2]

In 1891, Dr. James Naismith, a teacher and (64) Presbyterian minister, needed an indoor game to keep college students busy during long winter days in Springfield, (65) Massachusetts at the Springfield YMCA Training School. This need prompted the creation of basketball, which was originally played by tossing a soccer ball into an empty peach basket nailed to the gym wall. **B**(67) Additionally, there was two teams but only one basket in the original game.

[3]

Because of the simplicity of (68) basketball, the game spread across the nation within 30 years of its invention in Massachusetts. **C** As more teams formed, the need for a league became apparent. The smaller National Basketball League (NBL) formed soon after. On (69) June 6, 1946 the Basketball Association of America (BAA) was formed. In 1948, the BAA absconded the NBL, and the National Basketball Association (NBA) was born. The NBA played its first full season in 1948-49 and is still going strong today.

[4]

Though much has changed in our world since 1891, the (72) popularity of the sport of basketball has remained strong. From (72) it's humble start in a YMCA gym to the multi-million-dollar empire it is (74) today, the simple fun of the sport has endured. Although many changes have been made over the years, the essence of basketball has remained constant. **D** Its rich history and simplicity ensure that basketball will always be a popular sport around the world.

(61) Arguably the sport of highest popularity and greatest excitement <u>of our time, is basketball.</u>

61. A. NO CHANGE
     B. of our time is basketball.
     C. among our time, is basketball.
     D. of our day and age, is basketball.

Behind this fast-paced sport, however, is a rich history. There have been many changes made to the game over the years, but the essence remains the same.

62. What is the BEST way to revise and combine sentence 2 and sentence 3?
     F. Behind this fast-paced sport is a rich history; however, there have been many changes made to the game over the years.
     G. Over the years the essence remains the same for this fast-paced sport with its rich history.
     H. Behind this fast-paced sport is a rich history, but the essence remains the same.
     J. The essence remains the same for this fast-paced sport with its rich history even though there have been many changes made to the game over the years.

From its humble beginnings in 1891, (63) <u>basketball has grown to have worldwide appeal.</u>

63. A. NO CHANGE
     B. basketball has grown to have world-wide appeal.
     C. basketball grew to have worldwide appeal.
     D. basketball has grown due to its worldwide appeal.

In 1891, Dr. James Naismith, a teacher and (64) <u>Presbyterian minister, needed</u> an indoor game to keep college students busy during long winter days in Springfield, Massachusetts at the Springfield YMCA Training School.

64. F. NO CHANGE
     G. Presbyterian Minister needed
     H. presbyterian minister, needed
     J. a Presbyterian Minister, founded

In 1891, Dr. James Naismith, a teacher and Presbyterian Minister, needed an indoor game to keep college students busy during long winter days in Springfield, (65) <u>Massachusetts at the Springfield YMCA Training School.</u>

65. A. NO CHANGE
     B. Massachusetts, at the Springfield YMCA training school.
     C. Massachusetts, at the Springfield YMCA Training School.
     D. Massachusetts at the Springfield YMCA training school.

What is the BEST placement for this sentence in the passage?

One thing that sets the history of basketball apart from other major sports is the fact that it was created with the intent to be played indoors.

66. F. Point A in Paragraph 1
    G. Point B in Paragraph 2
    H. Point C in Paragraph 3
    J. Point D in Paragraph 4

---

(67) Additionally, <u>there was two teams but only one</u> basket in the original game.

67. A. NO CHANGE
    B. there were two teams; but only one
    C. there was two teams, but only one
    D. there were two teams but only one

Because of the simplicity of (68) <u>basketball, the game spread</u> across the nation within 30 years of its invention in Massachusetts.

68. F. NO CHANGE
    G. basketball, the sport had spread
    H. basketball the game spread
    J. basketball, the game had spread

---

69. The style, mode, or type of text in this passage is best characterized as which of these?
    A. Description
    B. Persuasion
    C. Exposition
    D. Narration

On (70) <u>June 6, 1946 the Basketball Association of America (BAA)</u> was formed.

70. F. NO CHANGE
    G. June 6, 1946, the Basketball Association of America (BAA)
    H. June 6, 1946 the basketball association of America (BAA)
    J. June 6, 1946; the Basketball Association of America (BAA)

Though much has changed in our world since 1891, the (71) popularity of the sport of basketball has remained strong.

71. A. NO CHANGE
    B. popularity of basketball has remained strong.
    C. popularity of the sport of basketball has been constant.
    D. attention of the sport of basketball has been constant.

From (72) it's humble start in a YMCA gym to the multi-million-dollar empire it is today, the simple fun of the sport has endured.

72. F. NO CHANGE
    G. it's humble start in a YMCA gymnasium to the multi-million-dollar
    H. it's humble start in a YMCA gym to the multi-million dollar
    J. its humble start in a YMCA gym to the multi-million-dollar

---

From it's humble start in a YMCA gym to the multi-million-dollar empire it is (73) today, the simple fun of the sport has endured.

73. A. NO CHANGE
    B. today, the fun of the sport has
    C. today: the simple fun of the sport has
    D. today, the simple fun of the sport had

---

[3]
(9) Because of the simplicity of basketball, the game had spread across the nation within 30 years of its invention in Massachusetts. (10) As more teams formed, the need for a league became apparent. (11) The smaller National Basketball League (NBL) formed soon after. (12) On June 6, 1946 the Basketball Association of America (BAA) was formed. (13) In 1948, the BAA absconded the NBL, and the National Basketball Association (NBA) was born. (14) The NBA played its first full season in 1948-49 and is still going strong today.

74. Which of the following changes would most improve the organization and clarity of paragraph 3 of this essay?
    F. The paragraph is correct as it is written
    G. Move sentence 10 to the beginning of the paragraph
    H. Switch sentences 11 and 12
    J. Switch sentences 13 and 14

---

75. If the author wanted to argue that the purpose of the passage was to explain the influence of the YMCA on sports, would the author be able to maintain this claim?

A. Yes, the author demonstrated that James Naismith invented a sport.
B. No, the thirty years after its invention was influential than the YMCA.
C. Yes, some of the most respected athletes in America were members at a YMCA.
D. No, the author would need to show how the YMCA influenced more than just basketball.

Mathematics

1. Determine the number of diagonals of a dodecagon.
    A. 12
    B. 24
    C. 54
    D. 72
    E. 108

2. The expression $-2i \times 7i$ is equal to
    F. -14
    G. 14
    H. $14\sqrt{-1}$
    J. $-14\sqrt{-1}$
    K. None of the above.

3. On a road map, $\frac{1}{4}$ inch represents 8 miles of actual road distance. The towns of Dinuba and Clovis are measured to be $2\frac{1}{8}$ inches apart on the map. What is the actual distance, in miles, between the two towns?
    A. 32
    B. 40
    C. 60
    D. 64
    E. 68

4. Put the following numbers in order from the least to greatest 2^3, 4^2, 6^0, 9, 10^1.
    F. 2^3, 4^2, 6^0, 9, 10^1
    G. 6^0, 9, 10^1, 2^3, 4^2
    H. 10^1, 2^3, 6^0, 9, 4^2
    J. 6^0, 2^3, 9, 10^1, 4^2
    K. 10^1, 2^3, 9, 10^1, 4^2, 6^0

5. In the figure below, ΔJKL is dilated to the image ΔJ'K'L'.

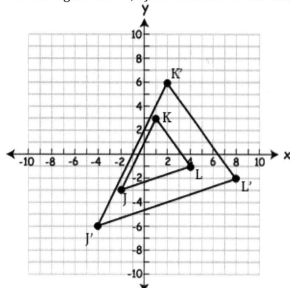

What is the scale factor of the dilation?

A. $\frac{1}{3}$

B. $\frac{1}{2}$

C. 2

D. 3

E. None of the above.

6. Which of the following expressions is equivalent to $(x - 3)^2$?

F. $x^2 - 3x + 9$

G. $x^2 - 6x - 9$

H. $x^2 - 6x + 9$

J. $x^2 + 3x - 9$

K. $x^2 + 3x + 9$

7. Given the double bar graph shown below, which of the following statements is true?

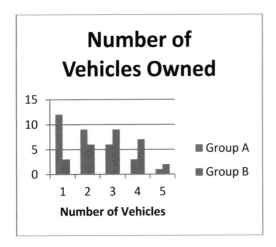

A. Group A is negatively skewed, while Group B is approximately normal.
B. Group A is positively skewed, while Group B is approximately normal.
C. Group A is positively skewed, while Group B is neutral.
D. Group A is approximately normal, while Group B is negatively skewed.
E. Group A is approximately normal, while Group B is positively skewed.

8. Which of the following is true about the relationship between the two triangles shown below?

F. The triangles are similar.
G. The triangles are congruent.
H. The triangles are equilateral.
J. Both Answer G and Answer H are true.
K. Both Answer F and Answer G are true.

9. The volume of a rectangular box is found by multiplying its length, width, and height. If the dimensions of a box are $\sqrt{3}$, $2\sqrt{5}$, and 4, what is its volume?

A. $2\sqrt{60}$
B. $4\sqrt{15}$
C. $8\sqrt{15}$
D. $24\sqrt{5}$
E. $2\sqrt{15}$

10. Abe averages 3 miles per hour running and Beatriz averages 4 miles per hour running. How much further can Beatriz go in $\frac{1}{2}$ hour than Abe can?

F. 2 miles

G. 1 mile

H. $\frac{1}{2}$ mile

J. $\frac{1}{4}$ mile

K. $\frac{1}{8}$ mile

11. Elijah spends $30 for a state fair ticket and $3.50 per ride. Which of the following expressions could be used to find the total amount spent, if riding x rides?

A. $3.50 + 30x$

B. $33.50x$

C. $30 + 3.50x$

D. $33.50 + 3.50x$

E. $33.50 - 3.50x$

12. The matrix represents the number of students in the class periods of each teacher. Which of the following statements can be made from the information in the matrix?

$$
\begin{array}{c}
 & \text{Smith} \quad \text{Tan} \\
\begin{array}{c} \text{1st} \\ \text{2nd} \\ \text{3rd} \end{array}
& \begin{bmatrix} 31 & 25 \\ 29 & 27 \\ 34 & 30 \end{bmatrix}
\end{array}
$$

F. Smith has 12 more students than Tan.

G. Smith is more popular with students than Tan.

H. Tan has smaller class sizes because she teaches harder classes.

J. Smith wants 3 students from 1st period to transfer into Tan's class.

K. None of the above.

13. If rectangle $ABCD$ is dilated by a scale factor of $\frac{1}{2}$ to create its image $A'B'C'D'$, how does the slope of $\overleftrightarrow{AC}$ compare to the slope of $\overleftrightarrow{A'C'}$?

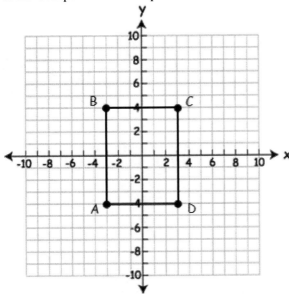

A. The slope of $\overleftrightarrow{A'C'}$ is half the slope of $\overleftrightarrow{AC}$.
B. The slope of $\overleftrightarrow{A'C'}$ is double the slope of $\overleftrightarrow{AC}$.
C. The slope of $\overleftrightarrow{A'C'}$ is the same as the slope of $\overleftrightarrow{AC}$.
D. The slope of $\overleftrightarrow{A'C'}$ is the reciprocal of the slope of $\overleftrightarrow{AC}$.
E. The slope of $\overleftrightarrow{A'C'}$ is not comparable to the slope of $\overleftrightarrow{AC}$.

14. A dress is marked down by 20% and placed on a clearance rack, on which is posted a sign reading, "Take an extra 25% off already reduced merchandise." What fraction of the original price is the final sales price of the dress?

F. $\frac{2}{5}$

G. $\frac{9}{20}$

H. $\frac{11}{20}$

J. $\frac{3}{5}$

K. $\frac{1}{4}$

15. Given the equation, $ax + b = c$, what is the value of x?

   A. $\dfrac{c+b}{a}$

   B. $\dfrac{ca}{b}$

   C. $c - ba$

   D. $\dfrac{c-b}{a}$

   E. $c + ba$

16. Anna walks from her house to school each day. If she walks 8 blocks east of her house, then turns and walks 6 blocks south to arrive at school, how far is her school in a direct line from her house?

   F. 10 blocks
   G. 12 blocks
   H. 14 blocks
   J. 16 blocks
   K. 18 blocks

17. In Figure 1 (pictured below), the distance from A to D is 48. The distance from A to B is equal to the distance from B to C. If the distance from C to D is twice the distance of A to B, how far apart are B and D?

   A. 12
   B. 16
   C. 19
   D. 24
   E. 36

Figure 1

Question 18 is based upon the following diagram:

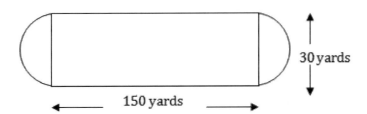

30 yards

150 yards

18. A company is building a track for a local high school. There are two straight sections and two semi-circular turns. Given the dimensions, which of the following most closely measures the perimeter of the entire track?
    F. 300 yards
    G. 180 yards
    H. 360 yards
    J. 395 yards
    K. 120 yards

19. Solve: $\begin{bmatrix} 4 & 2 \\ 7 & 12 \end{bmatrix} + \begin{bmatrix} -1 & 15 \\ 3 & -5 \end{bmatrix}$.
    A. $\begin{bmatrix} 3 & 17 \\ 10 & 7 \end{bmatrix}$
    B. $\begin{bmatrix} 3 & 1 \\ 10 & 15 \end{bmatrix}$
    C. $\begin{bmatrix} 19 & 17 \\ 2 & 7 \end{bmatrix}$
    D. $\begin{bmatrix} 19 & 1 \\ 2 & 15 \end{bmatrix}$
    E. $\begin{bmatrix} 3 & 17 \\ 2 & 15 \end{bmatrix}$

20. Approximately what percent of 81 is 36?
    F. 34
    G. 44
    H. 54
    J. 64
    K. 74

21. Which of the following represents the solution of the following system of linear equations:
$5x + 9y = -7$,
$2x - 4y = 20$?
    A. x = 3, y = 2
    B. x = 4, y = 3
    C. x = 4, y = -3
    D. x = 3, y = -2
    E. x = 3, y = -3

Question 22 refers to the following information:

    Raul, Eli, Henry and Lex all bought the same shirt from different stores for different prices. They spent $18.00, $18.50, $15.39 and $19.99 respectively.

22. What is the average price the four men spent for the shirt?
    F. $15.97
    G. $16.97
    H. $17.97
    J. $18.97
    K. $19.97

23. Simplify: $(3 - 6i)(5 + 4i)$
    A. 39 - 18i
    B. 15 - 24i
    C. -9 - 18i
    D. $-18i^2$
    E. 8 - 2i

24. A farmer installed a new grain silo on his property for the fall harvest. The silo is in the shape of a cylinder with a diameter of 8 m and a height of 24 m. How much grain will the farmer be able to store in the silo?
    F. 402.1 m³
    G. 1,206.4 m³
    H. 1,608.5 m³
    J. 2, 450.5 m³
    K. 4,825.5 m³

25. John puts his money into a bank account that pays monthly interest. His monthly balance (in dollars) after t months is given by the exponential function $b(t) = 315(1.05)^t$. How much money did John initially put into the account?
    A. $5
    B. $105
    C. $300
    D. $315
    E. $350

26. A building is installing a new ramp at their front entrance.

Based on the figure above, what is the length of the ramp, shown by *x*?
- F. 11.6 ft
- G. 16.9 ft
- H. 20.8 ft
- J. 25.0 ft
- K. None of the above.

27. If Fahrenheit and Celsius are related by the formula $F = \left(\frac{9}{5}\right)C + 32$, what is the temperature in degrees Fahrenheit of a location with an average temperature of 20 degrees Celsius?
- A. 58
- B. 63
- C. 68
- D. 73
- E. 78

28. A rectangle with a perimeter of 92 inches has a length of 14 inches longer than its width. What is its width in inches?
- F. 8
- G. 16
- H. 32
- J. 40
- K. 44

29. Given the table below, which of the following best represents the probability that a student is enrolled at TAMU or prefers lattes?

	Latte	Cappuccino	Frappuccino	Total
TAMU	350	225	175	750
NMSU	325	300	275	900
Total	675	525	450	1650

- A. 55%
- B. 60%
- C. 65%
- D. 70%
- E. 75%

30. A librarian makes time-and-a-half for each hour that he works over 40 hours per week. The linear function $s(h) = 27h + 720$ represents his weekly salary (in dollars) if he works h hours more than 40 hours that week. For example, his weekly salary is $s(10) = 990$ dollars if he works 50 hours in one week (because 10 + 40 = 50). What is his hourly salary after he has already worked the initial 40 hours in one week?

F. $7.20 per hour
G. $18.00 per hour
H. $27.00 per hour
J. $48.00 per hour
K. $72.00 per hour

31. Edward draws a card from a deck of cards, does not replace it, and then draws another card. What is the probability that he draws a heart and then a spade?

A. $\frac{1}{16}$
B. $\frac{1}{2}$
C. $\frac{1}{17}$
D. $\frac{13}{204}$
E. $\frac{1}{3}$

32. There are 100 bacteria in a Petri dish. The number of bacteria doubles every day, so that on the first day, there are 100 bacteria; on the second, there are 200; on the third, there are 400; and so on. Write a formula for the number of bacteria on the nth day.

F. $b(n) = 100 \cdot 2^{n-1}$
G. $b(n) = 100n$
H. $b(n) = 100n^2$
J. $b(n) = 200(n-1)$
K. $b(n) = 200n^2$

Questions 33 - 34 refer to the following information:

The 180 campers in Group A got to choose which kind of sandwich they wanted on the picnic. The results of the choice are given in the table below.

Sandwich	# of Campers
PB & J	60
Turkey	45
Egg salad	15
Veggie	60

33. Approximately what percentage of the campers chose either turkey or egg salad?
    A. 66
    B. 45
    C. 33
    D. 15
    E. 7

34. Which expression correctly provides the ratio of campers who chose veggie sandwiches to those who chose turkey?
    A. 1:4
    B. 2:3
    C. 1:3
    D. 4:3
    E. 3:2

35. In the figure below, circle O is a unit circle, and the measure of $\angle AOB$ is $\frac{\pi}{3}$.

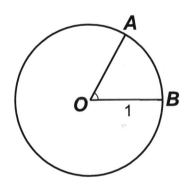

What is the length of $\widehat{AB}$?

    F. $\frac{\pi}{6}$

    G. $\frac{\pi}{3}$

    H. $\frac{2\pi}{3}$

    J. π

    K. 2π

36. Evaluate the quotient and express in standard form: $\frac{15-5i}{4-2i}$.

    F. $\frac{25+5i}{6}$

    G. $\frac{7+5i}{2}$

    H. $\frac{5+i}{2}$

    J. $\frac{7+i}{2}$

    K. $\frac{7+5i}{6}$

37. Donald rolls a die. If the die lands on a 1 or 2, he wins $5.00. If the die lands on a 3, he loses $1.00. If the die lands on a 4, 5 or 6, he loses $2.50. Which of the following statements is true?

    I. He can expect to win $0.25 after 1 roll.
    II. He can expect to lose $0.50 after 1 roll.
    III. His expected winnings for 50 rolls sum to $12.50.
    IV. His expected losses for 50 rolls sum to $25.00.

    A. I only
    B. I and III only
    C. II only
    D. II and IV only
    E. IV only

38. If $A = \begin{bmatrix} 1 & -3 \\ -4 & 2 \end{bmatrix}$ and $B = \begin{bmatrix} 1 & -3 \\ -4 & -2 \end{bmatrix}$, then $A - B = ?$

    F. $\begin{bmatrix} 2 & -6 \\ -8 & 0 \end{bmatrix}$

    G. $\begin{bmatrix} 0 & 0 \\ 0 & 0 \end{bmatrix}$

    H. $\begin{bmatrix} 0 & 0 \\ 0 & 4 \end{bmatrix}$

    J. $\begin{bmatrix} 0 & 3 \\ 4 & 2 \end{bmatrix}$

    K. $\begin{bmatrix} 0 & -6 \\ -8 & 4 \end{bmatrix}$

39. The table below displays the value of the linear function $g(x)$ for five different values of x.

x	−2	−1	0	1	2
$g(x)$	10	7	4	1	−2

Write an explicit formula for $g(x)$.
    A. $g(x) = -4x + 3$
    B. $g(x) = -4x + 4$
    C. $g(x) = -3x + 3$
    D. $g(x) = -3x + 4$
    E. $g(x) = -2x + 4$

Question 40 is based on the following diagram:

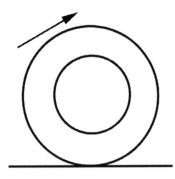

40. A tire on a car rotates at 500 RPM (revolutions per minute) when the car is traveling at 50 km/hr (kilometers per hour). What is the circumference of the tire? Give your answer in meters.
    F. $\dfrac{50,000}{2\pi}$

    G. $\dfrac{50,000}{60 \times 2\pi}$

    H. $\dfrac{50,000}{60}$

    J. $\dfrac{10}{6}$

    K. $\dfrac{10}{60 \times 2\pi}$

41. Given the equation, $\dfrac{2}{x-8} = \dfrac{3}{x}$, what is the value of x?
    A. 16
    B. 20
    C. 24
    D. 28
    E. 32

42. Sophie is painting a wall in her living room red. She can cover 36 square feet with one gallon of paint. If the wall is 8 feet high and 15 feet long, how many gallons, to the nearest gallon, does she need?

    F. 2
    G. 3
    H. 4
    J. 5
    K. 6

43. If $g(x) = 3x + x + 5$, evaluate $g(2)$.

    A. $g(2) = 8$
    B. $g(2) = 9$
    C. $g(2) = 13$
    D. $g(2) = 17$
    E. $g(2) = 19$

44. $\overline{AB}$ is tangent to Circle O. Find the length of $\overline{OB}$.

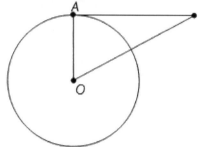

    F. 13
    G. 16
    H. 17
    J. 23
    K. 64

45. The table below shows the average amount of rainfall Houston receives during the summer and autumn months.

Month	Amount of Rainfall (in inches)
June	5.35
July	3.18
August	3.83
September	4.33
October	4.5
November	4.19

What percentage of rainfall received during this timeframe, is received during the month of October?

    A. 13.5%
    B. 15.1%
    C. 16.9%
    D. 17.7%
    E. 18.38%

46. Use factoring to identify the zeroes of the function $f(x) = x^2 + 5x - 24$.

    F. −24
    G. −8 and 3
    H. −6 and 4
    J. 6 and -4
    K. 24

47. Which function has the same x-intercept as the function graphed below?

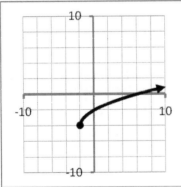

    A. $g(x) = -4x - 12$
    B. $g(x) = x^2 - 12x + 36$
    C. $g(x) = x^3 + 6x^2 - 2x - 2$
    D. $g(x) = \frac{6}{x-3}$
    E. $g(x) = x^2 - 12x - 36$

48. What is the constant of proportionality represented by the table below?

x	y
2	−8
5	−20
7	−28
10	−40
11	−44

F. −12
G. −8
H. −6
J. −4
K. 4

49. The possible combinations of candy bars and packages of suckers that Amanda may purchase are represented by the graph shown below.

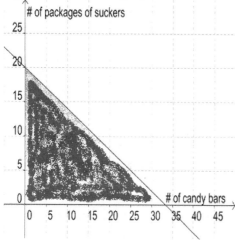

Which of the following inequalities represents the possible combinations of candy bars and packages of suckers that she may purchase?
A. $0.75x + 1.5y \leq 20$
B. $0.5x + 1.25y \leq 25$
C. $0.75x + 1.25y \leq 25$
D. $1.25x + 0.75y \leq 20$
E. $0.5x + .75y \leq 20$

50. A local craft store specializes in selling marbles. To display their most popular sized marble, the store created a 3 ft × 2 ft × 6 in glass box and completely filled the box with 5,184 marbles. What is the density of marbles per cubic foot in the glass box?
F. 144 marbles/cubic foot
G. 864 marbles/cubic foot
H. 1,728 marbles/cubic foot
J. 15,522 marbles/cubic foot
K. None of the above.

51. Calculate the average rate of change of the function $f(x) = -3x + 1$, over the range from $x = 1$ to $x = 5$.

    A. −4
    B. −3
    C. 3
    D. 4
    E. -4

52. Portia tosses a coin 1,000 times. Which of the following best represents the number of times she can expect to get tails?

    F. 350
    G. 400
    H. 450
    J. 500
    K. 1000

53. The sides of quadrilateral *PQRS* are tangent to the circle. What is the perimeter of quadrilateral *PQRS*?

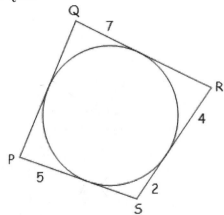

    A. 36
    B. 30
    C. 24
    D. 20
    E. 18

54. James won a cash raffle prize. He paid taxes of 30% on the prize and had $14,000 remaining. How much was the original prize?

    F. $42,000
    G. $40,000
    H. $30,000
    J. $20,000
    K. $18,000

55. In $\triangle ABC$, $\cos A =$

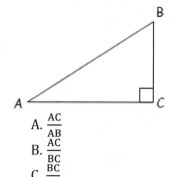

   A. $\dfrac{AC}{AB}$

   B. $\dfrac{AC}{BC}$

   C. $\dfrac{BC}{AC}$

   D. $\dfrac{BC}{AB}$

   E. None of the above.

56. The city of Minneapolis, Minnesota covers 54.9 square miles of land and has a population of 382,578. What is the population density of Minneapolis?

   F. 126.9 persons/square mile

   G. 6,968.6 persons/square mile

   H. 4,533,532.2 persons/square mile

   J. 248,890,917.9 persons/square mile

   K. None of the above.

57. On Peter's homework assignment of a state map, $\frac{1}{2}$ inch represents 12 miles. If a distance is 84 miles, how many inches long will it be in Peter's map?

   A. 3

   B. 3.5

   C. 5

   D. 5.5

   E. 6

58. Which of the following numbers has the digit 3 in the hundredths place?

   F. 315

   G. 3.15

   H. 0.0315

   J. 0.00315

   K. 0.000315

59. A pump fills a cylindrical tank with water at a constant rate. The function $L(g) = 0.3g$ represents the water level of the tank (in feet) after g gallons are pumped into the tank. The function $w(t) = 1.2t$ represents the number of gallons that can be pumped into the tank in t minutes. Write a function $L(t)$ for the water level of the tank after t minutes.

A. $L(t) = 0.25t$
B. $L(t) = 0.36t$
C. $L(t) = 0.9t$
D. $L(t) = 3.6t$
E. $L(t) = 4t$

60. As shown below, four congruent isosceles trapezoids are positioned such that they form an arch. Find x for the indicated angle.

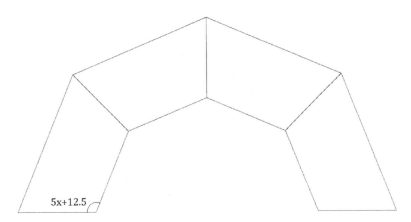

5x+12.5

F. $x = 11$
G. $x = 20$
H. $x = 24.5$
J. $x = 135$
K. The value of x cannot be determined from the information given.

Reading

Passage 1: Humanities: This passage is adapted from President Franklin D. Roosevelt's *State of the Union Address* in January of 1941.

Many subjects connected with our social economy call for immediate improvement. As examples:

We should bring more citizens under the coverage of old-age pensions and unemployment insurance. We should widen the opportunities for adequate medical
5   care. We should plan a better system by which persons deserving or needing gainful employment may obtain it.

I have called for personal sacrifice. And I am assured of the willingness of almost all Americans to respond to that call. A part of the sacrifice means the payment of more money in taxes. In my Budget Message I will recommend that a greater portion of this
10   great defense program be paid for from taxation than we are paying for today. No person should try, or be allowed, to get rich out of the program; and the principle of tax payments in accordance with ability to pay should be constantly before our eyes to guide our legislation. If the Congress maintains these principles, the voters, putting patriotism ahead of pocketbooks, will give you their applause.

15   In the future days, which we seek to make secure, we look forward to a world founded upon four essential human freedoms. The first is freedom of speech and expression—everywhere in the world. The second is freedom of every person to worship God in his own way—everywhere in the world. The third is freedom from want—which, translated into world terms, means economic understandings which will
20   secure to every nation a healthy peacetime life for its inhabitants—everywhere in the world. The fourth is freedom from fear—which, translated into world terms, means a world-wide reduction of armaments to such a point and in such a thorough fashion that no nation will be in a position to commit an act of physical aggression against any neighbor—anywhere in the world.

25   That is no vision of a distant millennium. It is a definite basis for a kind of world attainable in our own time and generation. That kind of world is the very antithesis of the so-called new order of tyranny which the dictators seek to create with the crash of a bomb. To that new order we oppose the greater conception—the moral order. A good society is able to face schemes of world domination and foreign revolutions alike
30   without fear.

Since the beginning of our American history, we have been engaged in change—in a perpetual peaceful revolution—a revolution which goes on steadily, quietly adjusting itself to changing conditions—without the concentration camp or the quick-lime in the ditch. The world order which we seek is the cooperation of free countries, working
35   together in a friendly, civilized society.

This nation has placed its destiny in the hands and heads and hearts of its millions of free men and women; and its faith in freedom under the guidance of God. Freedom means the supremacy of human rights everywhere. Our support goes to those who struggle to gain those rights and keep them. Our strength is our unity of purpose. To that high concept there can be no end save victory.

40

1. Which statement best supports the idea that FDR believed that America is constantly evolving toward a better situation?
   A. Since the beginning of our American history, we have been engaged in change—in a perpetual peaceful revolution—a revolution which goes on steadily, quietly adjusting itself to changing conditions—without the concentration camp or the quick-lime in the ditch.
   B. This nation has placed its destiny in the hands and heads and hearts of its millions of free men and women; and its faith in freedom under the guidance of God.
   C. To that new order we oppose the greater conception—the moral order. A good society is able to face schemes of world domination and foreign revolutions alike without fear.
   D. The fourth is freedom from fear—which, translated into world terms, means a world-wide reduction of armaments to such a point and in such a thorough fashion that no nation will be in a position to commit an act of physical aggression against any neighbor—anywhere in the world.

2. In this text, FDR claims that raising taxes will result in a patriotic populace that will happily support the government. What might be one argument against this idea?
   F. Americans are uninterested in pursuing freedom of any kind, and the four freedoms listed here are not considered important.
   G. The average citizen already feels overburdened by taxes and feels the money is not being well-spent by the government.
   H. Individuals will easily assent to the idea of a greater tax burden since it will naturally lead to a more prosperous state.
   J. Patriots of all kinds are part of the natural makeup of America, and some will feel that the support of government is something that should be contemplated and debated.

3. What is a major theme that Roosevelt articulates in his speech?
   A. It is important for all people to have access to the benefits of an old-age system that supports citizens when they can no longer work.
   B. Patriotic people will feel the need to pay more taxes to the government in order to obtain certain benefits they would not be able to afford.
   C. People who want to work should be able to find work without bias and without undue hardship.
   D. There are four basic freedoms that are vital to the health of people: speech, worship, freedom from want, and freedom from fear.

4. The last sentence in this passage is, "To that high concept there can be no end save victory." In the context of the preceding text, which of the following is the most precise meaning of the word "**end**"?
   F. Death
   G. Purpose
   H. Outcome
   J. Conclusion

5. FDR spoke of "the so-called new order of tyranny which the dictators seek to create with the crash of a bomb." In the context of this passage, which is the most accurate meaning of the word "**order**"?
    A. A command given by a military leader
    B. An authoritative decision or direction
    C. An arrangement of items in sequence
    D. A system of societal and world politics

6. When FDR spoke of "personal sacrifice", which of these did he explicitly give as an example of it?
    F. Higher taxation
    G. Military service
    H. Arms reduction
    J. Four freedoms

7. FDR described America's constant engagement in change as "a perpetual peaceful revolution...without the concentration camp or the quick-lime in the ditch." In this description, we can infer his implicit reference to which war(s)?
    A. Revolutionary
    B. World War I
    C. World War II
    D. To all of them

8. FDR identified aspects of the social economy needing to be improved immediately. As evidence of this need, which example did he NOT cite in this passage?
    F. Expanding retirement benefits
    G. Expanding healthcare benefits
    H. Expanding draft by the military
    J. Expanding labor opportunities

9. As represented in this passage, the power and tone of FDR's speech are enhanced by which?
    A. Short, simple sentences
    B. Long, complex sentences
    C. Long compound sentences
    D. (b), (c), complex-compound

10. What can readers infer from lines 15 - 24 of President Roosevelt's message?
    F. The President attempted to name every right in the 1st Amendment but failed.
    G. Roosevelt is more concerned about the people of other nations than American citizens.
    H. The President is uncertain on whether he can deliver on such a large promise.
    J. President Roosevelt is deeply concerned with individual rights and liberties.

Passage II: Literary Narrative: The following passage is adapted from Jack London's *The Call of the Wild* (1903).

Buck did not read the newspapers, or he would have known that trouble was brewing, not alone for himself, but for every tide-water dog, strong of muscle and with warm, long hair, from Puget Sound to San Diego. Because men, groping in the Arctic darkness, had found a yellow metal, and because steamship and transportation

5   companies were booming the find, thousands of men were rushing into the Northland. These men wanted dogs, and the dogs they wanted were heavy dogs, with strong muscles by which to toil, and furry coats to protect them from the frost.

Buck lived at a big house in the sun-kissed Santa Clara Valley. Judge Miller's place, it was called. It stood back from the road, half hidden among the trees, through which

10   glimpses could be caught of the wide cool veranda that ran around its four sides. The house was approached by gravelled driveways which wound about through wide-spreading lawns and under the interlacing boughs of tall poplars. At the rear things were on even a more spacious scale than at the front. There were great stables, where a dozen grooms and boys held forth, rows of vine-clad servants' cottages, an endless and

15   orderly array of outhouses, long grape arbors, green pastures, orchards, and berry patches. Then there was the pumping plant for the artesian well, and the big cement tank where Judge Miller's boys took their morning plunge and kept cool in the hot afternoon.

And over this great demesne Buck ruled. Here he was born, and here he had lived

20   the four years of his life. It was true, there were other dogs, There could not but be other dogs on so vast a place, but they did not count. They came and went, resided in the populous kennels, or lived obscurely in the recesses of the house after the fashion of Toots, the Japanese pug, or Ysabel, the Mexican hairless,—strange creatures that rarely put nose out of doors or set foot to ground. On the other hand, there were the fox

25   terriers, a score of them at least, who yelped fearful promises at Toots and Ysabel looking out of the windows at them and protected by a legion of housemaids armed with brooms and mops.

But Buck was neither house-dog nor kennel-dog. The whole realm was his. He plunged into the swimming tank or went hunting with the Judge's sons; he escorted

30   Mollie and Alice, the Judge's daughters, on long twilight or early morning rambles; on wintry nights he lay at the Judge's feet before the roaring library fire; he carried the Judge's grandsons on his back, or rolled them in the grass, and guarded their footsteps through wild adventures down to the fountain in the stable yard, and even beyond, where the paddocks were, and the berry patches. Among the terriers he stalked

35   imperiously, and Toots and Ysabel he utterly ignored, for he was king,—king over all creeping, crawling, flying things of Judge Miller's place, humans included.

His father, Elmo, a huge St. Bernard, had been the Judge's inseparable companion, and Buck bid fair to follow in the way of his father. He was not so large,—he weighed only one hundred and forty pounds,—for his mother, Shep, had been a Scotch shepherd

40   dog. Nevertheless, one hundred and forty pounds, to which was added the dignity that comes of good living and universal respect, enabled him to carry himself in right royal fashion. During the four years since his puppyhood he had lived the life of a sated aristocrat; he had a fine pride in himself, was even a trifle egotistical, as country

gentlemen sometimes become because of their insular situation. But he had saved
45   himself by not becoming a mere pampered house-dog. Hunting and kindred outdoor
delights had kept down the fat and hardened his muscles; and to him, as to the cold-
tubbing races, the love of water had been a tonic and a health preserver.

And this was the manner of dog Buck was in the fall of 1897, when the Klondike
strike dragged men from all the world into the frozen North. But Buck did not read the
50   newspapers, and he did not know that Manuel, one of the gardener's helpers, was an
undesirable acquaintance. Manuel had one besetting sin. He loved to play Chinese
lottery. Also, in his gambling, he had one besetting weakness—faith in a system; and this
made his damnation certain. For to play a system requires money, while the wages of a
gardener's helper do not lap over the needs of a wife and numerous progeny.

55   The Judge was at a meeting of the Raisin Growers' Association, and the boys were
busy organizing an athletic club, on the memorable night of Manuel's treachery. No one
saw him and Buck go off through the orchard on what Buck imagined was merely a
stroll. And with the exception of a solitary man, no one saw them arrive at the little flag
station known as College Park. This man talked with Manuel, and money chinked
60   between them.

11. What is the purpose of paragraphs 2-5?
    A. To introduce all of the story's characters
    B. To show Buck's personality
    C. To introduce Buck
    D. To show Buck's affection for Toots and Ysabel

12. Which sentence or phrase shows Buck's attitude about Judge Miller's place?
    F. They came and went, resided in the populous kennels, or lived obscurely in the recesses of
       the house
    G. The whole realm was his
    H. He had a fine pride in himself
    J. And to him, as to the cold-tubbing races, the love of water had been a tonic and a health
       preserver

13. The author uses the detail in paragraph 1 to
    A. Describe Buck's life
    B. Foreshadow Buck's story
    C. Describe the story's setting
    D. Introduce the story's villain

14. What is the significance of the Klondike strike in 1897?
    F. It will lead to changes in Buck's life
    G. It will cause more dogs to move to Judge Miller's place
    H. It changed Elmo's life
    J. It caused the Raisin Growers' Association to meet more frequently

15. The author organizes this selection mainly by
    A. Describing Buck's life in the order in which it happened
    B. Outlining Buck's history
    C. Showing Buck's life and then showing a moment of change
    D. Comparing Buck's life at Judge Miller's place to what came afterwards

16. Which answer choice best describes the purpose of the selection?
    F. To set up a story by providing background information
    G. To show Buck in a moment of heroism
    H. To give details about the Klondike strike
    J. To introduce all the dogs that live at Judge Miller's

17. This selection is part of a longer work. Based on the selection, what might be a theme of the larger work?
    A. Change
    B. Family
    C. Hard work
    D. Relationships

18. Which sentence from the passage foreshadows the rest of the story?
    F. And over this great demesne Buck ruled
    G. These men wanted dogs, and the dogs they wanted were heavy dogs, with strong muscles by which to toil, and furry coats to protect them from the frost
    H. His father, Elmo, a huge St. Bernard, had been the Judge's inseparable companion and Buck bid fair to follow in the way of his father
    J. But he had saved himself by not becoming a mere pampered house-dog

19. What is the most logical explanation for Manuel taking Buck away from Judge Miller's place?
    A. Manuel is taking the dog in order to find gold in the "frozen North."
    B. Buck will be trained to be a service dog for the Judge's daughters.
    C. Manuel needs the protection as he meets with the man at College Park.
    D. The dog will be used for hunting events.

20. Who is the narrator of this passage?
    F. Buck
    G. Mollie and Alice
    H. Judge Miller
    J. A non-participant narrator

Passage III: Natural Science: The following passage is adapted from Albert Einstein's paper on *Relativity: The Special and General Theory* (1916, revised 1924).

In order to attain the greatest possible clearness, let us return to our example of the railway carriage supposed to be travelling uniformly. We call its motion a uniform translation ("uniform" because it is of constant velocity and direction, "translation" because although the carriage changes its position relative to the embankment yet it
5 does not rotate in so doing). Let us imagine a raven flying through the air in such a manner that its motion, as observed from the embankment, is uniform and in a straight line. If we were to observe the flying raven from the moving railway carriage, we should find that the motion of the raven would be one of different velocity and direction, but that it would still be uniform and in a straight line. Expressed in an abstract manner we
10 may say : If a mass m is moving uniformly in a straight line with respect to a co-ordinate system K, then it will also be moving uniformly and in a straight line relative to a second co-ordinate system K1 provided that the latter is executing a uniform translatory motion with respect to K. In accordance with the discussion contained in the preceding section, it follows that:

15 If K is a Galilean co-ordinate system, then every other co-ordinate system K' is a Galilean one, when, in relation to K, it is in a condition of uniform motion of translation. Relative to K1 the mechanical laws of Galilei-Newton hold good exactly as they do with respect to K.

We advance a step farther in our generalization when we express the tenet thus: If,
20 relative to K, K1 is a uniformly moving co-ordinate system devoid of rotation, then natural phenomena run their course with respect to K1 according to exactly the same general laws as with respect to K. This statement is called the principle of relativity (in the restricted sense).

As long as one was convinced that all natural phenomena were capable of
25 representation with the help of classical mechanics, there was no need to doubt the validity of this principle of relativity...

Nevertheless, there are two general facts which at the outset speak very much in favor of the validity of the principle of relativity. Even though classical mechanics does not supply us with a sufficiently broad basis for the theoretical presentation of all
30 physical phenomena, still we must grant it a considerable measure of "truth," since it supplies us with the actual motions of the heavenly bodies with a delicacy of detail little short of wonderful. The principle of relativity must therefore apply with great accuracy in the domain of mechanics. But that a principle of such broad generality should hold with such exactness in one domain of phenomena, and yet should be
35 invalid for another, is a priori not very probable.

We now proceed to the second argument, to which, moreover, we shall return later. If the principle of relativity (in the restricted sense) does not hold, then the Galilean co-ordinate systems K, K1, K2, etc., which are moving uniformly relative to each other, will not be equivalent for the description of natural phenomena. In this case we should be constrained to believe that natural laws are capable of being formulated in a particularly simple manner, and of course only on condition that, from amongst all possible Galilean co-ordinate systems, we should have chosen one (K[0]) of a particular state of motion as our body of reference. We should then be justified (because of its merits for the description of natural phenomena) in calling this system "absolutely at rest," and all other Galilean systems K "in motion." If, for instance, our embankment were the system K[0] then our railway carriage would be a system K, relative to which less simple laws would hold than with respect to K[0]. This diminished simplicity would be due to the fact that the carriage K would be in motion (i.e. "really") with respect to K[0]. In the general laws of nature which have been formulated with reference to K, the magnitude and direction of the velocity of the carriage would necessarily play a part. We should expect, for instance, that the note emitted by an organ pipe placed with its axis parallel to the direction of travel would be different from that emitted if the axis of the pipe were placed perpendicular to this direction.

Now in virtue of its motion in an orbit round the sun, our earth is comparable with a railway carriage travelling with a velocity of about 30 kilometers per second. If the principle of relativity were not valid we should therefore expect that the direction of motion of the earth at any moment would enter into the laws of nature, and also that physical systems in their behavior would be dependent on the orientation in space with respect to the earth. For owing to the alteration in direction of the velocity of revolution of the earth in the course of a year, the earth cannot be at rest relative to the hypothetical system K[0] throughout the whole year. However, the most careful observations have never revealed such anisotropic properties in terrestrial physical space, i.e. a physical non-equivalence of different directions. This is very powerful argument in favor of the principle of relativity.

21. Which of the following choices best supports the claim of Einstein's theory of special relativity as accurate?
    A. the movement of the Earth around the sun
    B. Galilean co-ordinate systems and their application in classical mechanics
    C. the idea of chance in quantum mechanics
    D. the two different parts of relativity

22. What might be one question to ask to begin an argument against Einstein's theory of relativity?
    F. If relativity holds true, what does that say about the classical rules of motion?
    G. If relativity is valid, then why can it not explain all parts of the natural world, including the rules of quantum mechanics?
    H. If the natural laws concerning quantum mechanics are true, then shouldn't the classical rules of motion be suspect?
    J. If the natural laws formulated with reference to K are measurable, then wouldn't the magnitude and direction of the velocity of the carriage be important?

23. Which of the following choices provides the best meaning for the truth?

Even though classical mechanics does not supply us with a sufficiently broad basis for the theoretical presentation of all physical phenomena, still we must grant it a considerable measure of "truth," since it supplies us with the actual motions of the heavenly bodies with a delicacy of detail little short of wonderful.

  A. correctness regarding the abstract meaning of classical mechanics
  B. honesty regarding the movement of objects according to the rules of relativity
  C. validity regarding an understanding of the classical rules of motion
  D. exactness regarding the movement of small bodies on a coordinate plane

24. In lines 31-32, Einstein writes that classical mechanics describes astronomical movements with "a delicacy of detail little short of wonderful." In this context, what is the best synonym for the meaning of "delicacy"?
  F. A fragility
  G. A sensitivity
  H. A rare delight
  J. A soft texture

25. If a reader did not know the meaning of the phrase *a priori*, s/he could ascertain it from the sentence: "But that a principle of such broad generality should hold with such exactness in one domain of phenomena, and yet should be invalid for another, is a priori not very probable." Based on this context, to which of these is its meaning closest?
  A. Existing in the first place
  B. Having the highest priority
  C. Something happening after the fact
  D. General to specific/independently true

26. Einstein describes the detail with which classical mechanics describes celestial motions as "little short of wonderful." Rhetorically, this is most an example of which of these?
  F. Understatement
  G. Overstatement
  H. Amplification
  J. Metabasis

27. Within this passage, which of the following conclusions proposed by Einstein is predicated upon the condition that the principle of relativity is valid?
  A. "...then the Galilean co-ordinate systems K, K1, K2, etc., which are moving uniformly relative to each other, will not be equivalent for the description of natural phenomena."
  B. "...natural laws are capable of being formulated in a particularly simple manner, and...only on condition that...we...have chosen one...of a particular state of motion as our body of reference."
  C. "If, relative to K, K1 is a uniformly moving co-ordinate system devoid of rotation...then natural phenomena run their course with respect to K1 according to exactly the same general laws as with respect to K."
  D. "...we should therefore expect that the direction of motion of the earth at any moment would enter into the laws of nature, and also that physical systems in their behavior would be dependent on the orientation in space with respect to the earth."

28. What might Einstein mean when he writes that "we must grant it a considerable measure of "'truth,'" in paragraph five?
    F. correctness regarding the abstract meaning of classical mechanics
    G. honesty regarding the movement of objects according to the rules of relativity
    H. validity regarding an understanding of the classical rules of motion
    J. exactness regarding the movement of small bodies on a coordinate plane

29. Which of the following most accurately represents Einstein's use of claims and counterclaims in this passage?
    A. From one paragraph to the next, statements of claims and statements of counterclaims are presented alternately; the last two sentences summarize how these contrast.
    B. The first three paragraphs present a series of counterclaims; the following four present arguments that logically refute those counterclaims and then support his claims.
    C. The first five paragraphs mainly explain his claims; the last two state counterclaims, explaining results to expect if they were true; the last two sentences reassert his claims.
    D. Every paragraph begins by presenting a claim, then a counterclaim, then refutation of the counterclaim; and ends with repeating the original claim for emphasis.

30. Among the following, which sentence introduces evidence supporting Einstein's assertions?
    F. "This is very powerful argument in favor of the principle of relativity."
    G. "We now proceed to the second argument, to which, moreover, we shall return later."
    H. "Nevertheless, there are two general facts...in favor of the validity of the principle of relativity."
    J. "In order to attain the greatest possible clearness, let us return to our example of the railway carriage..."

` Science

Black History Month is unnecessary. In a place and time in which we overwhelmingly elected an African American president, we can and should move to a post-racial approach to education. As *Detroit Free Press* columnist Rochelle Riley wrote in a February 1 column calling for an end to Black History Month, "I propose that, for the first time in American history, this country has reached a point where we can stop celebrating separately, stop learning separately, stop being American separately."

5

In addition to being unnecessary, the idea that African American history should be focused on in a given month suggests that it belongs in that month alone. It is important to instead incorporate African American history into what is taught every day as American history. It needs to be recreated as part of mainstream thought and not as an optional, often irrelevant, side note. We should focus efforts on pushing schools to diversify and broaden their curricula.

10

There are a number of other reasons to abolish it: first, it has become a shallow commercial ritual that does not even succeed in its (limited and misguided) goal of focusing for one month on a sophisticated, intelligent appraisal of the contributions and experiences of African Americans throughout history. Second, there is a paternalistic flavor to the mandated bestowing of a month in which to study African American history that is overcome if we instead assert the need for a comprehensive curriculum. Third, the idea of Black History Month suggests that the knowledge imparted in that month is for African Americans only, rather than for all people.

15

20

<u>Passage B</u>

Black History Month is still an important observance. Despite the important achievement of the election of our first African American president, the need for knowledge and education about African American history is still unmet to a substantial degree. Black History Month is a powerful tool in working towards meeting that need. There is no reason to give up that tool now, and it can easily coexist with an effort to develop a more comprehensive and inclusive yearly curriculum.

25

Having a month set aside for the study of African American history doesn't limit its study and celebration to that month; it merely focuses complete attention on it for that month. There is absolutely no contradiction between having a set-aside month and having it be present in the curriculum the rest of the year.

30

Equally important is that the debate *itself* about the usefulness of Black History Month can, and should, remind parents that they can't necessarily count on schools to teach African American history as thoroughly as many parents would want.

Although Black History Month has, to an extent, become a shallow ritual, it doesn't have to be. Good teachers and good materials could make the February curriculum deeply informative, thought-provoking, and inspiring. The range of material that can be covered is rich, varied, and full of limitless possibilities.

35

Science

Blood consists of a liquid called *plasma*, in which many different types of blood cells are suspended. The plasma also contains many dissolved proteins. These proteins may be studied by subjecting the plasma to *electrophoresis,* in which it is subjected to an electric field, which pulls the proteins through a porous gel. Proteins typically have a negative charge on their surface, so they move toward the anode (positive electrode) in an electric field. The gel acts as a molecular sieve: it interferes with the movement, or *migration*, of the larger proteins more than the small ones, allowing the proteins to be separated on the basis of size. The further the proteins move during the experiment, the smaller they must be.

The experiment results in an *electropherogram*, such as the one shown in the figure below. This is a plot, or graph, of protein concentration versus migration, and corresponds to a graph of concentration versus size. Concentration is measured by passing light of a certain wavelength through the gel: proteins absorb the light, and the resulting *absorbance* measurement is proportional to protein concentration. Many major blood component proteins, such as albumin and several identified by Greek letters, have been discovered in this way. When disease is present, some component proteins may break down into smaller fragments. Others may aggregate, or clump together, to form larger fragments. This results in a change in the electropherogram: new species, corresponding to the aggregates or breakdown products, may be present, and the sizes of the normal peaks may be changed as the concentration of normal products is altered.

The Figure shows an electropherogram from a sick patient with an abnormal component in her blood (arrow). Peaks corresponding to some normal plasma proteins have been labeled.

Please examine the electropherogram and answer the following questions.

1. Which blood component protein is present in the greatest amounts in the plasma?
   A. Albumin
   B. $\alpha 1$
   C. $\alpha 2$
   D. β

2. Which of the following is the fastest-moving component in the electropherogram?
   F. Albumin
   G. $\alpha 1$
   H. $\alpha 2$
   J. γ

3. Which of the following statements is true about component $\alpha 1$?
   A. The molecules move through the gel faster than those of component $\alpha 2$, but slower than Albumin.
   B. The molecules are larger than albumin, but smaller than all the other components.
   C. The molecules are smaller than albumin, but larger than all the other components.
   D. It is not a protein.

4. Which of the components identified on the electropherogram is the smallest molecule?
   F. Albumin
   G. $\alpha 1$
   H. $\alpha 2$
   J. γ

5. Which of the following is true of the unknown component identified by the arrow?
   A. The molecules are larger than the β component, but smaller than albumin
   B. The molecules are larger than the β component, but smaller than the γ component.
   C. The molecules move more slowly in the gel than all the other components except one.
   D. The molecules move more rapidly in the gel than all the other components except one.

6. Which of the following may be true of the unknown component identified by the arrow?
   F. It is formed of albumin molecules that have aggregated.
   G. It is formed of $\alpha 1$ molecules that have aggregated.
   H. It is formed of $\alpha 2$ molecules that have aggregated.
   J. It is formed of γ molecules that have aggregated.

7. Which of the following may not be true of the unknown component identified by the arrow?
   A. It is formed of albumin molecules that have broken down into fragments.
   B. It is formed of $\alpha 1$ molecules that have broken down into fragments.
   C. It is formed of $\alpha 2$ molecules that have broken down into fragments.
   D. It is formed of γ molecules that have broken down into fragments.

8. The blood of healthy individuals does not contain the unknown component indicated by the arrow. The experiment therefore proves
    F. The unknown component causes the patient's sickness.
    G. The unknown component results from the patient's sickness.
    H. The more of the unknown component there is, the sicker the patient will be.
    J. None of the above.

In a study performed to determine the migration patterns of fish, 34,000 juvenile sablefish of the species *Anoplopoma fimbria* were tagged and released into waters of the eastern Gulf of Alaska during a twenty-year period. The tagged fish were all juveniles (less than 2 years of age), so that the age of the recovered fish could be determined from the date on the tag. This allowed age-specific movement patterns to be studied. Tagged fish were recovered from sites in the Bering Sea, throughout the Gulf of Alaska, and off the coast of British Columbia. The fish were recovered by commercial fishermen, with the results reported to the scientists performing the study. A total of 2011 tagged fish were recovered. It was found that fish spawned in coastal waters move to deeper waters when they are older. At the same time, they migrate north and west, across the Gulf of Alaska toward the Aleutian Islands. Eventually, they return to the eastern Gulf as adults.

The figure shows tag recoveries from sablefish tagged as juveniles by age (in years) and by depth (in meters) for all the areas in the study. The size of each circle is proportional to the number of recoveries. The range for each data point is 1 to 57 recoveries. The symbol x represents the median age.

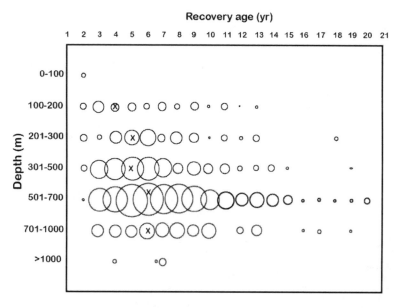

9. If a circle in the graph is twice the size (area) of another circle, this indicates that:
    A. It represents twice as many fish.
    B. The fish it represents were twice as old.
    C. Both A and B.
    D. None of the above.

10. The greatest number of tagged fish were recovered at depths of
    F. 101 – 200 m.
    G. 201 – 300 m.
    H. 301 – 500 m.
    J. 501 – 700 m.

11. What percentage of the released, tagged fish were recovered for this study?
    A. 2011
    B. 20
    C. 6
    D. Can't determine from the data given.

12. The median age of tagged fish recovered at depths between 301 and 500 meters is approximately
    F. 2 years.
    G. 5 years.
    H. 9 years.
    J. Data not shown.

13. Not all the tagged fish were recovered in this study. Which of the following reasons may be responsible for the losses?
    A. Some fish died during the study.
    B. The tags fell off some of the fish during the study.
    C. Some fish die as a result of being tagged.
    D. All of the above.

14. The largest fish are found at depths of
    F. 101 – 200 m.
    G. 201 – 300 m.
    H. 301 – 500 m.
    J. Can't determine from the data given.

15. Which of the following statements is supported by the data in the figure?
    A. Fish return to the eastern Gulf of Alaska to spawn.
    B. Sablefish move progressively deeper with age.
    C. Sablefish prefer cold waters.
    D. Younger fish swim faster than older ones.

16. The data indicate that sablefish may live as long as
    F. 10 years.
    G. 30 years.
    H. 20 years.
    J. 5 years.

Most particles studied by physicists are unstable. Given enough time, an unstable particle will break apart into two or more smaller particles or fragments. This event is called a decay. By carefully observing and logically classifying these decays according to some well-understood laws of nature, particle physicists have built a catalog of subatomic particles down to their most fundamental constituent parts.

Some particles, like the proton and electron, appear to be stable for very long times. They don't change into other particles, which is to say they don't decay. Most other particles have dominant decay modes. They decay into one combination of particles more often than into other combinations. Many particles also have rare decay modes. Someone who has the patience to watch a million or so decays, might see one of these rare combinations.

Two of the laws of nature that have been used to understand decays are *conservation of charge* and *conservation of energy*. Conservation of charge says that the net charge of all particles produced in a decay should equal the total charge of the original particle. Conservation of energy implies that the total mass of the resulting particles should not be greater than the mass of the original particle. Mass does not seem to be conserved in many decays until one accounts for the mass that is converted into the kinetic energy of the resulting particles as they move away from the original center of mass at some nonzero speed. Mass and energy can be measured with the same units: particle physicists use MeV (1.000 mega-electron volt = 1.602 x 10^{-13} joule = 1.783 x 10^{-30} kilogram).

At the most fundamental level, matter is thought to be made up of quarks and leptons. Quarks form the large baryons and mesons. There are six quarks named up (u), down (d), strange (s), charm (c), bottom (b), and top (t). (The last two are sometimes fancifully referred to as "beauty" and "truth.") Each comes in three "colors" and each has an antiparticle making 36 in all. The six quarks have been confirmed through indirect observations, but not isolated as individual particles.

Refer to the accompanying table of subatomic particles to answer the questions.

Table:

HADRONS - made of quarks

* BARYONS - made of three quarks or three anti-quarks
  NUCLEONS - contain no strange quarks

PARTICLE	CHARGE	MASS(MeV)
proton	1	938.27231
anti-proton	-1	938.27231
neutron	0	939.56563
anti-neutron	0	939.56563

HYPERONS - contain one or more strange quarks

PARTICLE	CHARGE	MASS(MeV)
lambda	0	1115.684
anti-lambda	0	1115.684
positive sigma	1	1189.37
anti-positive sigma	-1	1189.37
neutral sigma	0	1192.55
anti-neutral sigma	0	1192.55
negative sigma	-1	1197.436
anti-negative sigma	1	1197.436
neutral xi	0	1314.9
anti-neutral xi	0	1314.9
negative xi	-1	1321.32
anti-negative xi	1	1321.32
negative omega	-1	1672.45
positive omega	1	1672.45

* MESONS - made of one quark and one anti-quark

PARTICLE	CHARGE	MASS(MeV)
positive pion	1	139.56995
negative pion	-1	139.56995
neutral pion	0	134.9764
positive kaon	1	493.677
negative kaon	-1	493.677
neutral kaon	0	497.672
anti-neutral kaon	0	497.672
eta	0	547.45

LEPTONS - elementary particles not made of quarks

PARTICLE	CHARGE	MASS(MeV)
positron	1	0.51099907
electron	-1	0.51099907
electron neutrino	0	0
electron anti-neutrino	0	0
positive muon	1	105.658389
negative muon	-1	105.658389
muon neutrino	0	0
muon anti-neutrino	0	0
positive tau	1	1777
negative tau	-1	1777
tau neutrino	0	0
tau anti-neutrino	0	0

17. Which of the following particles has the greatest mass?
    A. Muon
    B. Electron
    C. Proton
    D. Lambda

18. Which of the following particles are made of quarks?
    F. Neutrino
    G. Muon
    H. Proton
    J. None of these

19. When a particle decays, the total charge on the resulting particles must always
    A. be neutral.
    B. be equal to 0.
    C. satisfy the law of conservation of mass.
    D. be equal to the charge of the original particle.

20. The most massive uncharged particles are found among the
    F. Leptons.
    G. Mesons.
    H. Baryons.
    J. Hyperons.

21. A lambda particle decays and one of the products is a proton. A second particle is also formed. Which of the following is the second particle?
    A. Negative pion
    B. Positron
    C. Electron neutrino
    D. Neutron

22. A positive muon decays and one of the products is a positron. If a second particle is also formed, which of the following might it be?
    F. Proton
    G. Tau
    H. Neutrino
    J. Kaon

23. A negative omega particle decays into a lambda particle and a negative kaon. How much energy is released?
    A. 63.09 MeV
    B. 1115.68 MeV
    C. 493.68 MeV
    D. 1672.45 MeV

24. Tom weighs 60 kilograms. What is his mass in MeV?
    F. 6×10^{11}
    G. 33.65×10^{30}
    H. 60
    J. Cannot be determined

Pollutants typically enter seawater at *point sources*, such as sewage discharge pipes or factory waste outlets. Then, they may be spread over a wide area by wave action and currents. The rate of this dispersal depends upon a number of factors, including depth, temperature, and the speed of the currents. Chemical pollutants often attach themselves to small particles of sediment, so that studying the dispersal of sediment can help in understanding how pollution spreads.

In a study of this type, a team of scientists lowered screened collection vessels to various depths to collect particles of different sizes. This gave them an idea of the size distribution of particles at each depth. Figure A shows the results for six different sites (ND, NS, MD, MS, SD, and SS). The particle size is plotted in *phi* units, which is a logarithmic scale used to measure grain sizes of sand and gravel. The 0 point of the scale is a grain size of 1 millimeter, and an increase of 1 in phi number corresponds to a decrease in grain size by a factor of ½, so that 1 phi unit is a grain size of 0.5 mm, 2 phi units is 0.25 mm, and so on; in the other direction, -1 phi unit corresponds to a grain size of 2 mm and -2 phi units to 4 mm.

Grains of different size are carried at different rates by the currents in the water. The study also measured current speed and direction, pressure and temperature at different depths, and at different times of year. The results were used in a computer *modeling program* to predict the total transport of sediments both along the shore (north-south) and perpendicular to it (east-west). Figure B shows the program's calculation of the distance particles would have been transported during the study period. The abbreviation *mab* in the figure stands for *meters above bottom*.

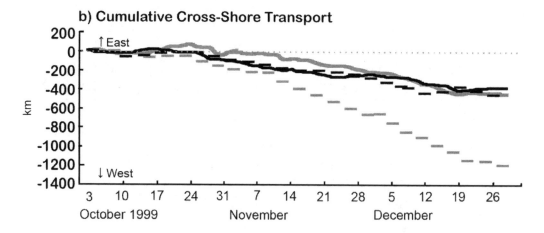

25. Which of the following sites was found to have the smallest average particle size?

    A. ND

    B. NS

    C. MD

    D. MS

26. With the exception of a few outliers, all of the phi values were in the range 1.0 to 4.0. This means that
    F. All particles studied were smaller than 0.5 mm.
    G. All particles studied were between 1.0 and 4.0 mm.
    H. No screens larger than 4.0 m were used in the study.
    J. All particles were larger than 0.5 mm.

27. For which site is it *least* true that the mean particle size represents the entire population?
    A. ND
    B. NS
    C. MD
    D. MS

28. What particle size corresponds to a phi value of -3?
    F. 2mm
    G. 0.5 mm
    H. 0.0625 mm
    J. 8 mm

29. In Figure B, the absolute value of the slope of the curves corresponds to
    A. The speed of transport.
    B. The size of the particles.
    C. The phi value.
    D. The depth.

30. The data indicates that along a NS axis
    F. Transport is faster in deeper waters.
    G. Transport is faster in shallower waters.
    H. Transport is the same at all depths.
    J. There is no correlation between transport speed and depth.

31. The data indicates that along the EW axis
    A. Transport is faster in deeper waters.
    B. Transport is faster in shallower waters.
    C. Transport is the same at all depths.
    D. There is no correlation between transport speed and depth.

32. Which of the following is closest to the overall direction of transport?
    F. N
    G. NW
    H. NE
    J. SE

Wind can provide a renewable source of energy. The energy of the wind is actually solar energy, as the sun warms the Earth's surface by varying amounts at different locations. This creates differential pressures as the warm air expands, and initiates air motions. High altitude airflows are similar to ocean currents, but near the surface, winds are affected by surface features.

Wind turbines capture this energy with a set of rotors that are set into rotation by the wind. The rotors are made of lightweight fiberglass or carbon fiber, and are held aloft on a tall tower. It is important to hold the blades high above the ground to avoid wind shear, a difference in airflow at different points along the rotor blades which can damage them. The blades rotate at about 40 rpm. Through a gearbox, they rotate a driveshaft at about 1500 rpm. The shaft, in turn, drives a generator.

The power P available from moving air is proportional to the cube of the wind velocity:

$$P = \frac{1}{2}\rho A v^3$$

where A is the cross section covered by the blades, ρ is the air density, and v is the air velocity. As the air passes through the rotor, it slows down. The turbine cannot take all the energy from the air, since then it would stop dead behind the rotor. Theoretically, the maximum efficiency that can be achieved is 59%. Figures A and B show a power curve for a 600 kilowatt (kW) wind turbine. To avoid damage from excessive winds, starting with wind speeds of 15 m/sec, the blades are adjusted to limit the power to 600 kW. For winds above 25 m/sec, the turbine is shut down.

One drawback of wind turbines has been the noise they make, but modern designs with slow-rotating blades are fairly quiet. Figure C shows the noise spectrum of a large turbine. The x-axis shows the frequency of sound in Hertz, and the y-axis shows the level of sound at each frequency. The total noise is 50 decibels (dB), which is less than the noise in a typical office.

920 kW Wind Turbine Noise Spectrum 200 m downwind from turbine
Total noise 50 dB. 1/3 Octave Bands

33. What wind velocity provides the maximum efficiency for this turbine?
    A. 5 m/s
    B. 7 m/s
    C. 10 m/s
    D. 12 m/s

34. What wind velocity provides the maximum power output from this turbine?
    F. 5 m/s
    G. 7 m/s
    H. 10 m/s
    J. 15 m/s

35. Why does the curve in Figure A flatten for wind velocities greater than 15 m/sec?
    A. The generator runs less efficiently.
    B. The rotors are being trimmed to prevent damage.
    C. Surface turbulence makes the rotors turn more slowly.
    D. None of the above.

36. For wind speeds between 5 and 10 m/sec, we expect the curve in Figure A to increase
    F. Linearly
    G. Irregularly
    H. Exponentially
    J. Sinusoidally

37. An ideal wind turbine operates at 100% efficiency and generates 200 kW of power at a wind velocity of 6 m/sec. How much power will be available at a wind velocity of 12 m/sec?
    A. 400 kW
    B. 800 kW
    C. 1200 kW
    D. 1600 kW

38. A wind turbine operating at 50% efficiency generates 100 kW of power at a wind velocity of 6 m/sec. If it also works at 50% efficiency at winds of 12 m/sec, how much power will it generate?
    F. 400 kW
    G. 800 kW
    H. 1200 kW
    J. 1600 kW

39. Figure C shows that
    A. Most of the noise is at high frequencies.
    B. Most of the noise is at low frequencies.
    C. Most of the noise is at middle frequencies.
    D. The total noise is less than 40 dB.

40. The energy captured by wind turbines is created by
    F. Surface features.
    G. Carbon fiber materials.
    H. A generator.
    J. The sun.

Answer Key and Explanations

English

Number	Answer	Number	Answer	Number	Answer
1	A	26	J	51	A
2	J	27	A	52	F
3	C	28	J	53	B
4	J	29	C	54	G
5	D	30	F	55	D
6	G	31	C	56	H
7	D	32	J	57	J
8	J	33	B	58	H
9	D	34	J	59	B
10	G	35	A	60	J
11	D	36	H	61	B
12	G	37	C	62	J
13	A	38	J	63	A
14	J	39	A	64	F
15	C	40	G	65	C
16	F	41	A	66	G
17	B	42	H	67	D
18	H	43	B	68	F
19	B	44	G	69	C
20	J	45	D	70	G
21	A	46	J	71	B
22	G	47	B	72	J
23	D	48	H	73	A
24	J	49	B	74	H
25	B	50	H	75	D

1. A: Choice B is wrong because the comma is not necessary. Choice C is incorrect because the singular subject of *United States Coast Guard* needs the singular verb *was*. Choice D is incorrect because the future perfect verb tense is incorrect as the event was completed in the past.

2. J: This sentence adds no information to the passage that is not already in the surrounding sentences, and the sentence is unnecessary as a transition.

3. C: This is the best answer choice because the vague pronoun *It* has been replaced with a specific noun.

4. J: This is the best answer choice as it removes the unnecessary comma. Choice G incorrectly removes the infinitive signifier *to* from the sentence. Choice H changes *enforce* to *promote* which alters the author's meaning of the laws being upheld to the laws being advertised.

5. D: This is the correct choice because it correctly adds parallelism to the sentence with the additional infinitive signifier. Choice B makes *combat* plural which is unnecessary. Choice C adds a comma that is not needed in the sentence.

6. G: This is the best answer because it contains the same intent as the original sentence yet it is more concise than the original. Choice H is incorrect because of the dangling modifier. Choice J is incorrect because it is not only the Department of Homeland Security that considers the Coast Guard to be a federal law enforcement agency.

7. D: The problem with this sentence is a dangling modifier.

8. J: Sentence 10 basically provides a laundry list of things that Coast Guard members do on a daily basis. The only answer choice that introduces this effectively is J.

9. D: The correct word is *really* because this sentence calls for an adverb, not an adjective.

10. G: The purpose of this passage is to provide a brief history of the Coast Guard and a brief overview of their duties. As the answer choice notes, the author should use this sentence in a persuasive passage instead of an informative one in order to maintain the focus and the purpose of the passage.

11. D: The question deals with concise word choice and eliminating unnecessary language. The article "a" signifies one or single. So, it is sufficient to write "perform the following in a day."

12. G: This question also deals with concise word choice. If the Coast Guard is investigating a pollution incident, then it is understood that they have explored the incident as well.

13. A: Paragraph 3 gives information about what the Coast Guard does in an average day, but there is no indication as to where this very specific information comes from. Adding a line saying that the information came from the official Coast Guard Web site would add credibility.

14. J: The question asks for "the requirements for becoming a member of the U.S. Coast Guard." Since the passage merely lists responsibilities of Coast Guard personnel and notes a key difference between them and the Navy, readers cannot be expected to see another purpose of the passage for the requirements of being U.S. Coast Guard personnel.

15. C: This answer choice best sums up the information in this essay, and rounds out the writer's discussion about the organization as a whole. Answers A and B talk about the Coast Guard as a career, which isn't a theme in this essay. Answer D contradicts the information and ideas in the essay.

16. F: An island is a land mass that is surrounded by water at all points. In the following sentence, readers are told that New Zealand has "two large islands and a number of smaller ones." So, Choice G cannot be correct since it changes the meaning of New Zealand to being a single island. Choice H is wrong because the preposition *between* is for comparing two things, but the islands of New Zealand are being compared to "all the Pacific islands." Choice J is incorrect because the adjective *more* is the comparative degree which is used for comparing two things. Yet, the author is comparing New Zealand to "all the Pacific islands."

17. B: Although it is a simple combination, this connection of sentence 2 and sentence 3 is the one that remains grammatically correct, maintains the author's original intent, and is logical.

18. H: The error in this sentence is the unnecessary comma after *islands*. Choice G and J change out *number* for *amount*. Since the number of islands can be counted, the word *number* is still needed for this sentence.

19. B: Choice C is incorrect because the information about the migration occurring in the 15th century was deleted unnecessarily. Choice D is incorrect because it merely rearranges material. Choice B improves the sentence by removing the pronoun "it" and the direction of their travel which is understood to be southward.

20. J: This revision to the sentence is the best choice as it uses punctuation correctly and applies the correct use of verb tense.

21. A: Choice B and D incorrectly capitalize southward. Choice C incorrectly changes the verb tense to past perfect.

22. G: Although this statement is placed in the correct paragraph, the sentence should not be added at this point without further development in the sentence and paragraph.

23. D: This statement is the best choice as the revision connects to previous sentence on the difficult climate circumstances and maintains the author's original meaning with an active voice.

24. J: This is the best choice because it transitions correctly from sentence 9 to sentence 10 and maintains the author's original meaning.

25. B: With items in a series, a comma is needed after *shellfish* to separate each item correctly, and *shellfish* should not be capitalized.

26. J: With the other choices, there are no complete statements that come before the colon.

27. A: The adverb *markedly* does not need to be removed as it was in Choice C. As for Choice B and D, the adverb does not need to be moved because it is modifying the verb *disappeared* meaning that it became quite noticeable that the moa population was dropping and causing more tribal warfare.

28. J: Sentence 18 functions best in its current place as sentence 16 functions as a topic sentence on the sweet potato, and sentence 18 logically comes after sentence 17 stating how the sweet potato could grow in many areas and survive the winter months as well.

29. C: This revision is the best choice as the population is specified instead of a general "human population" which is already understood as the passage covers the settlement of the islands of New Zealand by Polynesian voyagers.

30. F: The author has stated that "the most important farmed crop in prehistoric New Zealand was the sweet potato." In the final paragraph, the author has shared how the sweet potato was relied upon for food at almost every point of the year and improved the population of people who lived on the islands. So, the addition of how the Maori people lived alongside their sweet potato farmlands is more evidence to support the topic sentence of this paragraph.

31. C: Choice B is incorrect because the present-perfect tense needs the past participle form for the verb, and *flew* is only the past form. Choice A and Choice D are incorrect because the future perfect tense points to an action that will take place at an appointed time in the future which is not accurate for this sentence structure.

32. J: The comma can be removed as this is not an appositive or absolute phrase. The piece following World War I is an adjective clause. So the comma is not needed since it is not an introductory clause.

33. B: The other answer choices show a relationship between American pilots not having work because they gave up flying airplanes. The original sentences intend the opposite. Some American pilots returned from World War I without work to fly planes. So, they had to give up flying altogether and find other jobs.

34. J: Since the pilot has already been named in the sentence, the author does not need to capitalize *ace of aces*. Choice G is incorrect because the verb tense does not need to be changed. Choice H is not correct because the clause is non-essential to the sentence and needs to have commas to separate it from the rest of the sentence.

35. A: Choice B is not the best selection because *new* and *creative* are not exact synonyms. So, it is not redundant to say something is new and creative. Choice C is not the best choice because the verb *found* is sufficient and acceptable. Choice D is not the best choice because *things* has been exchanged for *tricks*. However, the following sentence highlights a pilot who transported news stories which is a service, not a stunt.

36. H: The issue being addressed with this sentence is a matter of a passive verb being exchanged for an active verb. Choice H is the best selection as it has a clear subject and an active voice verb.

37. C: Choice B is wrong because *big* and *news* are not coordinate adjectives in this context. Choice D is not the best choice because *broke* as a verb is being used correctly. The issue with this sentence is one of concise word choice. The previous sentence states that Jones used "his airplane to help get news across the country," and the following clause to the sentence in question states that Jones flew photos "to newspapers in different cities." Since it is understood within the larger context that Casey Jones is working with news stories, the author can write instead that "When an important story broke, Jones flew news photos to newspapers in different cities."

38. J: Choice G is not the best selection because the name of the pilot is essential information to know and should not be closed off with comma marks. Choice H is not the best selection because this sentence is starting a transition from Casey Jones to Roscoe Turner. So, a transition like "Another pilot" is needed for this sentence. Choice J is the best option because the words "another pilot" are not essential in the sentence structure and can be closed off with comma marks as readers learn that Roscoe Turner traveled "with a lion cub in his plane."

39. A: Choice B is incorrect because a colon cannot be used to separate two independent clauses unless what comes after the colon is an explanation of the preceding statement or a lengthy and formal quote. While the punctuation in Choice C is acceptable, the change from an active voice to a passive voice is not the best choice. Choice D is not correct because a comma is needed to separate the two independent clauses that are joined by a conjunction.

40. G: Choice H and Choice J are not the best revisions for this sentence because they set up an "either-or" and a contrast respectively which is not the original intent of the sentence. Choice G is the best selection as it provides context to the cost of an airplane ride without setting up a contrast.

41. A: Choice B is not correct because exchanging the colon for a comma would create a comma splice. Choice C is not correct because the quotation marks are not necessary as the word *barnstormers* is not being used in any special sense. Choice D is not correct because the author intends to convey an example that these barnstormers attempted the feat at one point, not regularly. So, it is not something that needs to be corrected.

42. H: The error in the sentence is an incorrect verb tense. Choice G is incorrect because *finally* creates a split modifier. Choice J is incorrect because the pronoun is a contraction, not the possessive pronoun.

43. B: This is the best choice because it correctly transitions from the sentence 15 to sentence 16 and maintains the original meaning of the author.

44. G: Point A is not the best choice because the previous and following sentences highlight how pilots had to resign from their flight hobby, not the accomplishments of famous pilots. Choice H and Choice J are not unacceptable places for the sentence, but Choice G is the best selection as the final sentence of the first paragraph suggests that examples will follow, and Mr. Lindbergh's feat is an example of a creative task for an airplane.

45. D: If the author wanted the purpose of the passage to focus on the American public's opinion on what the pilots should pursue after returning from WWI, then readers would need to be provided with reasons for their concerns about men and women pursuing careers in flight.

46. J: The need for revision with this sentence comes with the unnecessary adjective American. The passage understands that the American is already included since the sentence begins with "In Western society. The *individual self* should not be reduced to *individual* as it is a term used in psychology fields. In addition, Western is correct to be capitalized.

47. B: This is the best choice as there are multiple "Western societies," and the preposition among compares multiple options whereas the preposition "between" compares only two options.

48. H: In general, the first paragraph in an essay (of any length) introduces the discussion at hand or frames a particular debate. Most introductory paragraphs do not introduce extensive content. In this paragraph, there is no clear stance taken on either Buddhist or Western notions of the self, and so choices F and G are inappropriate. Choice H is a good answer because it stresses that the purpose of the first paragraph is to introduce a tension and not to make judgments one way or another. Choice J is inappropriate because "egolessness" is not discussed until the second paragraph. The best choice, then, is H.

49. B: This is the best choice as the revision selects a transition with the correct intent.

50. H: When using possessives for compounds, you need to be sure that the apostrophe works with the meaning of the sentence. This is the correct revision because the concerns of a person may be different from the concerns of a group. Choice G is incorrect because the pronoun *their* does not agree in number with the noun *individual*, and *group's* should not be deleted. Choice J is incorrect because the pronoun *their* does not agree in number with the noun *individual*.

51. A: The sentence is in the best position for the most logical organization. Moving it to the end of the paragraph (a) would be illogical because as it is now, it precedes the sentence "Buddhists who live in <u>such societies....</u>", which refers back to <u>"In Western societies..."</u> so reversing their order would make no sense. Moving it to the beginning of the paragraph (c) would interrupt the transition between the previous paragraph's last sentence, "...the struggles that Western Buddhists face" and the second paragraph's first sentence, "Central to Buddhist belief is the idea of 'egolessness.'" The latter sentence logically follows the former one. Not only would moving the quoted sentence interrupt this logical progression; it would moreover mention ego-toxicity prematurely—before it is introduced in the second paragraph's third sentence. The quoted sentence should not be removed entirely from the paragraph (d) as it further specifies ego-toxicity, introduced and defined in the previous sentence, as prevalent in Western societies; hence it provides essential information.

52. F: This question is easy to over think. In the second paragraph "egolessness" and "ego-toxicity" are defined and contrasted. The purpose of this paragraph, then, should mention this in some form. Choice F is good because it captures the fact that these terms are distinguished in the paragraph. Choice G is inappropriate because the paragraph only mentions the conflict that Buddhists feel—there is no judgment made on the conflict. Choices H and J are inappropriate because the paragraph does not praise one perspective over another.

53. B: This is the only revision of the phrase that uses proper grammar and punctuation.

54. G: This is the best choice as the pronouns agree with the introductory clause and the deletion of the first verb has made the sentence concise.

55. D: The original underlined portion has awkward phrasing that can be revised for clarity. Choice B is incorrect because the commas are not necessary. Choice C is not the best option because the awkward phrasing has not been revised.

56. H: This is the best choice because it is the most specific about how social action in an egoless manner has become more prevalent in secular institutions and movements.

57. J: Since the sentence ends with a period, it may not be phrased as a question, this is the correct revision.

58. H: In the first paragraph, the third sentence identifies increased tension in recent decades between individualism and collectivism in the West. This is developed in subsequent paragraphs by the discussion of ego-toxicity vs. egolessness reflecting individualism vs. collectivism. The second sentence (F) provides evidence supporting the first sentence, not a main idea. The fourth sentence (G) provides evidence supporting the third sentence. The first sentence (J) focuses only on Western emphasis of individualism over collectivism, not on the tension between the two that is a main idea on which the following paragraphs elaborate.

59. B: This passage is best characterized as persuasive because the author is making a point, arguing in its favor, and providing evidence to support it. Descriptive (A) text paints a vivid picture of a person, place, thing, scene, or situation by providing many specific sensory details to help readers imagine they are really experiencing it. Expository (C) prose provides factual information objectively without adding the author's opinions or seeking to convince readers of anything. Narrative (D) text tells readers a story.

60. J: The last sentence in each paragraph of this passage identifies "struggles", "caught between", "The struggle...continues"—all referring to a main conflict between individualism and collectivism—and the final sentence resolves it by stating that abandoning ego-toxicity enables compassionate caring for self and others. Hence none of these sentences identifies only half of this conflict, and the final sentence is not the only one to complete it (F). The first sentence of each paragraph does not identify this main conflict (G), (H); only the first sentence of the third paragraph does. In the first paragraph, the first sentence identifies Western emphasis of one over the other, not the conflict between them. In the second paragraph, the first sentence identifies the idea of "egolessness" central to Buddhist belief, not its conflict with ego-toxicity identified later in the paragraph. The final sentence does not simply reiterate the conflict (G) but resolves it.

61. B: The issue with this sentence is a comma that separates the subject from the verb. Choice C is not correct because the comma has not been removed and the preposition does not need to be changed. Choice D is not correct because the comma remains in the sentence, and the term *day and age* is an unnecessary change from *time*.

62. J: Choice G and Choice H are not the best options because the same piece of the original sentence is missing: "There have been many changes made to the game." Choice F is a nice revision, but is also removes an element from the sentence: "the essence remains the same." So, we are left with Choice J which does not remove a key part of the sentence or change the intent of the original. It merely revises the two original sentences to be combined.

63. A: Choice B is wrong because *worldwide* is one word and does not need to be hyphenated. Choice C is wrong because the present perfect verb tense does not need to be corrected because the worldwide appeal of basketball is something that started in the past and continues into the present. Choice D is not correct because the sport grew to become popular worldwide.

64. F: The capitalization in the sentence is correct as written.

65. C: The capitalization in this sentence is also correct as written, and the comma is needed after the name of the state.

66. G: Choice F is not the best option because the introduction is highlighting broad things that will be discussed in the body paragraphs. Choice H is not the best option because the focus of this paragraph is on the spread of the game after its invention and the development of organized basketball. Choice J is not the best option because new information should not be introduced in the new conclusion. So, Choice G is the best choice as it is a detail that follows directly after related information and is supporting information for this body paragraph.

67. D: The verb needs to agree with the subject in number. The verb in this sentence comes before the subject since the subject is two teams. Choice B is not the correct choice because what follows the semicolon is not an independent clause. Choice C is not the best choice because the comma and conjunction need an independent clause to separate the sentence.

68. F: Choice G and Choice J are not correct because the simple past is needed for this sentence, not the past perfect.

69. C: This writing is best characterized as an exposition or explanation of how basketball began.

70. G: The error with this sentence is the failure to add a comma after the year. Choice H is incorrect because the capitalization is correct in the original sentence. Choice J is not correct because a comma is needed, not a semicolon.

71. B: The correction to this sentence can be a revision of redundancy since basketball is already understood to be a sport. So, the best answer choice is Choice B which removes the redundancy.

72. J: The error in the sentence is with the contraction *it's*. The author should replace it with the possessive pronoun *its*.

73. A: Choice B is not correct because there is no error with describing the kind of fun that is characteristic of the sport. Choice C is wrong because a comma is needed in this situation, not a colon. Choice D is incorrect because the verb tense is correct as the event started in the past and continues into the present.

74. H: Switching sentences 11 and 12 improves the organization and clarity of paragraph 3.

75. D: This is the best choice because the question asks the influence of the YMCA on multiple sports, and this passage only addresses basketball and its invention at the YMCA.

Mathematics

Number	Answer	Number	Answer	Number	Answer
1	C	21	C	41	C
2	G	22	H	42	H
3	E	23	A	43	C
4	J	24	G	44	H
5	C	25	D	45	D
6	H	26	G	46	G
7	B	27	C	47	B
8	K	28	G	48	J
9	C	29	C	49	C
10	H	30	H	50	H
11	C	31	D	51	B
12	F	32	F	52	J
13	C	33	C	53	A
14	J	34	D	54	J
15	D	35	G	55	A
16	F	36	J	56	G
17	E	37	B	57	B
18	J	38	H	58	H
19	A	39	D	59	B
20	G	40	J	60	G

1. C: Because drawing a dodecagon and counting its diagonals is an arduous task, it is useful to employ a different problem-solving strategy. One such strategy is to draw polygons with fewer sides and look for a pattern in the number of the polygons' diagonals.

	3	0
	4	2
	5	5
	6	9
Heptagon	7	14
Octagon	8	20

A quadrilateral has two more diagonals than a triangle, a pentagon has three more diagonals than a quadrilateral, and a hexagon has four more diagonals than a pentagon. Continue this pattern to find that a dodecagon has 54 diagonals.

2. G: The product is equal to $-14i^2$. Since $i^2 = -1$, the product can be rewritten as $(-14)(-1)$, or 14.

3. E: If $\frac{1}{4}$ inch represents 8 miles, then 1 inch represents 4 x 8 = 32 miles. Two inches represents 2 x 32 = 64 inches. An $\frac{1}{8}$ of a mile represents 8 ÷ 2 = 4 miles. Then $2\frac{1}{8}$ inches represents 64 + 4 = 68 miles.

4. J: When a number is raised to a power, you multiply the number by itself by the number of times of the power. For example, $2^3 = 2 \times 2 \times 2 = 8$. A number raised to the power of 0 is always equal to 1. So, 6^0 is the smallest number shown. Similarly, for the other numbers: $9^1 = 9$; $10^1 = 10$; $4^2 = 4 \times 4 = 16$

5. C: To determine the scale factor of the dilation, compare the coordinates of $\Delta J'K'L'$ to the coordinates of ΔJKL. J is at (−2 −3) and J' is at (−4, −6), which means that the coordinates of J were multiplied by a scale factor of 2 to get the coordinates of J'. K is at (1, 3) and K' is at (2, 6). L is at (4, −1) and L' is at (8, −2). As can be seen, the coordinates of K and L were also multiplied by a scale factor of 2 to get to the coordinates of K' and L'. Answer B is the scale factor going from $\Delta J'K'L'$ to ΔJKL. Answer D results if 3 was incorrectly added or subtracted from the y-coordinates in points K and L to get K' and L'. Answer A is the reciprocal of answer D.

6. H: The expression can be written as $(x - 3)(x - 3)$. Distribution gives $x^2 - 3x - 3x + 9$. Combining like terms gives $x^2 - 6x + 9$.

7. B: Data is said to be positively skewed when there are a higher number of lower values, indicating data that is skewed right. An approximately normal distribution shows an increase in frequency, followed by a decrease in frequency, of approximately the same rate.

8. K: Since the two triangles have all three corresponding pairs of sides and corresponding pairs of angles marked congruent, then the two triangles are congruent. Similar triangles are the same shape but not necessarily the same size; they have congruent angles. All congruent triangles are similar triangles, so Answer K is the best choice. In Answer H, equilateral triangles are triangles that have sides with all the same measure within the same triangle, not in relation to another triangle.

9. C: The volume of the box is the product of $\sqrt{3}$, $2\sqrt{5}$, and 4. To multiply two or more square root radicals, multiply the coefficients and then multiply the radicands:
$$\sqrt{3} \times 2\sqrt{5} \times 4 = 2\sqrt{15} \times 4$$
$$= 8\sqrt{15}$$

10. H: If Abe goes 3 miles in one hour, he goes half of that or $1\frac{1}{2}$ miles in one half hour. Similarly, Beatriz can go 2 miles in one half hour. The answer therefore $= 2 - 1\frac{1}{2} = \frac{1}{2}$.

11. C: The cost of the ticket is constant and represents the value of the y-intercept. The cost per ride is variable and represents the slope. Therefore, the expression that could be used to find the total amount spent is $30 + 3.50x$, where x represents the number of rides.

12. F: Statements G, H, and J all infer non-quantitative issues that are not presented in the matrix. Smith does have more students than Tan, but since the reasons this is the case are not presented in the matrix, we cannot conclude anything about those reasons.

13. C: Since rectangle $ABCD$ is centered at the origin and $\overleftrightarrow{AC}$ passes through the origin, any dilation of rectangle $ABCD$ will leave that line unchanged. Since A has the coordinates (–3 –4) and C has the coordinates (3, 4), the slope of $\overleftrightarrow{AC} = \frac{4-(-4)}{3-(-3)} = \frac{8}{6} = \frac{4}{3}$. When rectangle $ABCD$ is dilated by a scale factor of $\frac{1}{2}$ to create image $A'B'C'D'$, A' has the coordinates (–1.5, –2) and C' has the coordinates (1.5, 2). The slope of $\overleftrightarrow{A'C'} = \frac{2-(-2)}{1.5-(-1.5)} = \frac{4}{3}$. Therefore, the slope of $\overleftrightarrow{A'C'}$ is the same as the slope of $\overleftrightarrow{AC}$.

14. J: When the dress is marked down by 20%, the cost of the dress is 80% of its original price; thus, the reduced price of the dress can be written as $\frac{80}{100}x$, or $\frac{4}{5}x$, where x is the original price. When discounted an extra 25%, the dress costs 75% of the reduced price, or $\frac{75}{100}\left(\frac{4}{5}x\right)$, or $\frac{3}{4}\left(\frac{4}{5}x\right)$, which simplifies to $\frac{3}{5}x$. So the final price of the dress is three-fifths of the original price.

15. D: The literal equation may be solved for x by first subtracting b from both sides of the equation. Doing so gives $ax = c - b$. Dividing both sides of the equation by a gives $x = \frac{c-b}{a}$.

16. F: Note that Anna's route creates a right triangle. Use the Pythagorean Theorem to calculate the answer. $8^2 + 6^2 = x^2$. $64 + 36 = x^2$. $100 = x^2$. $x = 10$.

17. E: Segment AD = 48. Because the length of CD is 2 times the length of AB, let $AB = x$ and let $CD = 2x$. Since $AB = BC$, let $BC = x$ also. The total length of $AD = AB + BC + CD = x + x + 2x = 4x = 48$. Thus, $x = 12$ and $BC + CD = x + 2x = 3x = 3 \times 12 = 36$.

18. J: First, add the two straight 150 yard portions. Also, note that the distance for the two semi-circles put together is the circumference of a circle. The radius (r) of that circle is half of the dimension given as the width of the track. In other words, it is 15 yards. Now, use the formula for the circumference of a circle: $2\pi r$. Then, add it to the length of the two straight portions of the track. So, you have:
$Length = (2\pi \times 15) + (2 \times 150) = 394.25$
Choice J is the closest to this calculated answer.

19. A: Matrices can be added or subtracted only if they have the same dimensions. Since these two matrices do, each position of the resulting matrix is the sum of the values of each matrix at the corresponding positions:

$$\begin{bmatrix} 4 & 2 \\ 7 & 12 \end{bmatrix} + \begin{bmatrix} -1 & 15 \\ 3 & -5 \end{bmatrix} = \begin{bmatrix} 4-1 & 2+15 \\ 7+3 & 12-5 \end{bmatrix} = \begin{bmatrix} 3 & 17 \\ 10 & 7 \end{bmatrix}$$

20. G: 36/81 = x/100. 81x = 3600. x = approximately 44

21. C: Using the method of elimination to solve the system of linear equations, each term in the top equation may be multiplied by –2, while each term in the bottom equation may be multiplied by 5. Doing so produces two new equations with x-terms that will add to 0. The sum of $-10x - 18y = 14$ and $10x - 20y = 100$ may be written as $-38y = 114$, where $y = -3$. Substituting the y-value of –3 into the top, original equation gives $5x + 9(-3) = -7$. Solving for x gives $x = 4$. Thus, the solution is x = 4 , y = –3.

22. H: 18.00 + 18.50 + 19.99 + 15.39 = 71.88. 71.88/ 4 = 17.97

23. A: Multiply the terms of the complex binomials using the FOIL method. To FOIL, multiply the First terms, the Outer terms, the Inner terms, and the Last terms, then add all the products together. Next, replace $i^2 = -1$. Finally, combine like terms. $15 + 12i - 30i - 24i^2 = 15 + 12i - 30i + 24 = 39 - 18i$.

24. G: The volume of the cylinder is the amount of grain that the farmer will be able to store in the silo. The formula for the volume of a cylinder is $V = \pi r^2 h$, where r is the radius and h is the height. The cylinder has a diameter of 8 m. So, the radius is half of the diameter or 4 m. The height is 24 m. So, your equation becomes $V = \pi(4\ m)^2(24\ m) = 1,206.4$ m³.

25. D: The general form of the interest exponential is $A(t) = P(1 + r)^t$, where P is the initial principal, r the interest rate (as a decimal), and t the number of interest yield periods after the initial investment. Clearly, P is $315 in this case. Furthermore, the exponential function $b(t) = 315(1.05)^t$ starts at 315 when $t = 0$ and is multiplied by 1.05 every time t increases by 1. Therefore, John initially put $315 into the bank account.

26. G: Based on the location of the 34°, the 14 ft section is the adjacent leg and the ramp length is the hypotenuse of the right triangle. Therefore, in order to solve for x, it needs to be set up as $\cos 34° = \frac{adjacent\ leg}{hypotenuse}$ or $\cos 34° = \frac{14}{x}$. The value of x is found using the calculation $x = \frac{14}{\cos 34°} = 16.9$ ft. Answer F incorrectly set up the equation as $\cos 34° = \frac{x}{14}$. Answer H incorrectly used $\tan 34° = \frac{14}{x}$. Answer J incorrectly used $\sin 34° = \frac{14}{x}$.

27. C: (9/5 x 20) + 32 = 36 + 32 = 68

28. G: 2W + 2(W + 14) = 92. 2W + 2W + 28 = 92. 4W = 64. W = 16

29. C: The probability may be written as $P(A\ or\ B) = \frac{750}{1650} + \frac{675}{1650} - \frac{350}{1650}$, which simplifies to $P(A\ or\ B) = \frac{1075}{1650}$ or approximately 65%.

30. H: The linear function $s(h) = 27h + 720$ starts at 720 when $h = 0$ and increases by 27 every time h increases by 1. Therefore, for every hour after 40, the librarian earns $27, so his salary is $27 per hour.

31. D: Since he does not replace the first card, the events are dependent. The sample space will decrease by 1 for the second draw because there will be one less card to choose. Thus, the probability may be written as $P(A\ and\ B) = \frac{13}{52} \cdot \frac{13}{51}$, or $P(A\ and\ B) = \frac{169}{2652}$ or $\frac{13}{204}$.

32. F: The number of bacteria forms a geometric sequence: 100, 200, 400, 800, 1600, etc. Notice that, if you ignore the two zeroes, these numbers are all powers of two (i.e. $2^0, 2^1, 2^2, 2^3, 2^4$, etc.). In other words, they are all 100 multiplied by a power of two, so the sequence can be written as an exponential function of the form $y = 100 \cdot 2^x$. However, since this sequence begins with an exponent of 0 on the first day, rather than 1, and an exponent of 1 on the second day rather than 2, you need to subtract 1 from n to get the correct power of 2. Thus, the function $b(n) = 100 \cdot 2^{n-1}$ represents the number of bacteria on the nth day.

33. C: The number of students who chose either turkey or egg salad is 45 + 15 = 60. 60/180 = 1/3, or approximately 33%.

34. D: The ratio indicates the number of people who chose veggie (60) to the number of people who chose turkey (45). 60:45 = 4:3

35. G: An arc is a piece of a circle. In the figure, $\widehat{AB}$ is the piece of the circle that starts at point A and ends at B. In general an arc length s is given by $s = \theta R$, where R is the radius of the circle containing the arc and θ is the angle subtended by radii drawn to the endpoints of the arc. In a unit circle, the length of an arc is simply the measure of the angle (in radians) subtended by the angle. Therefore, the arc length of $\widehat{AB}$ is equal to the measure of $\angle AOB$, so its length is $\frac{\pi}{3}$.

36. J: Standard form for complex numbers requires the denominator be completely real, that is, have no imaginary part. When dividing complex numbers, $\frac{a+bi}{c+di}$, first, multiply by "a well-chosen 1"; that is, multiply the quotient by a fraction with the value 1 written so as the product of the denominators is completely real. This is accomplished by multiplying by the conjugate of the denominator over itself: $\frac{c-di}{c-di}$. Then, FOIL both numerator and denominator, and combine like terms and simplify, remembering that $i^2 = -1$:

$$\frac{15-5i}{4-2i} \cdot \frac{4+2i}{4+2i} = \frac{60+30i-20i-10i^2}{16+8i-8i-4i^2} = \frac{60+10i+10}{16+4} = \frac{70+10i}{20} = \frac{10(7+i)}{2\cdot 10} = \frac{7+i}{2}$$

37. B: The expected value is equal to the sum of the product of the probabilities of the rolls and the amount he will win or lose. The probability of rolling a 1 or 2 is $\frac{2}{6}$. The probability of rolling a 3 is $\frac{1}{6}$. The probability of rolling any other number is $\frac{3}{6}$. Since he will win \$5.00 if he rolls a 1 or 2, lose \$1.00 if he rolls a 3, and lose \$2.50 if he rolls any other number, the expected value is $\left(5\cdot\frac{2}{6}\right) + \left(-1\cdot\frac{1}{6}\right) + \left(-2.50\cdot\frac{3}{6}\right)$, which equals 0.25. Thus, he can expect to win \$0.25 after one roll and $(50\cdot\$0.25)$, or \$12.50, after 50 rolls.

38. H: When subtracting A from B, the difference matrix can be written as
$\begin{bmatrix} 1-1 & -3-(-3) \\ -4-(-4) & 2-(-2) \end{bmatrix}$, which reduces to $\begin{bmatrix} 0 & 0 \\ 0 & 4 \end{bmatrix}$.

39. D: Linear functions can be written in the form $g(x) = ax + b$. To determine the value of a, notice that $g(x)$ decreases by 3 every time x increases by 1: when x goes from 0 to 1, the value of the function goes from 4 to 1; and when x goes from 1 to 2, the function goes from 1 to –2. Since $g(x)$ decreases by 3, the value of a is –3, so the function is $g(x) = -3x + b$.

Next calculate the value of b. From the table, you can tell that $g(0) = 4$. Use this to calculate b:
$$g(0) = 4$$
$$-3(0) + b = 4$$
$$0 + b = 4$$
$$b = 4$$
Thus, the function is $g(x) = -3x + 4$.

Alternatively, writing an explicit formula in the form $g(x) = ax + $ b means solving for two variables, a and b. Use the information given in the table to write two equations relating these two variables in terms of x and $g(x)$:
$$4 = a(0) + b$$
$$1 = a(1) + b$$
The first readily solves to $b = 4$, which you can substitute into the second to solve for a:
$$1 = a(1) + 4$$
$$-3 = a(1) = a$$
Thus, the function is $g(x) = -3x + 4$.

40. J: It is not necessary to use the circle formula to solve the problem. Note that 50 km/hr matches with 50,000 meters per hour. You have the car's revolutions per minute, and the answer must be given in meters. So, the speed must be converted to meters per minute. This matches with a speed of $\frac{50,000}{60}$ meters per minute. The reason is that there are 60 minutes in an hour. In any given minute, the car travels at $\frac{50,000}{60}$ meters/min. The tires rotate 500 times around. So, this is 500 times its circumference. This matches with $\frac{50,000}{60\times500} = \frac{10}{6}$ meters per revolution. This is the circumference of the tire.

41. C: The equation may be solved by multiplying each side of the equation by the least common denominator, or $x(x-8)$. Doing so gives $x(x-8) \cdot \frac{2}{x-8} = \frac{3}{x} \cdot x(x-8)$, which simplifies to $2x = 3x - 24$, where $x = 24$.

42. H: Sophie needs to cover an area of 8 x 15 = 120 square feet. Four gallons covers 36 x 4 = 144 square feet. She needs four gallons because the next lesser amount, 3 gallons, only covers 108 square feet.

43. C: To evaluate $g(2)$, substitute 2 for every occurrence of x in the equation $g(x) = 3x + x + 5$. Then simplify the result using order of operations:

$$g(2) = 3(2) + (2) + 5$$
$$= 6 + 2 + 5$$
$$= 13$$

44. H: Since $\overline{AB}$ is tangent to Circle O, then $\overline{AB}$ forms a right angle with radius $\overline{AO}$. $\triangle AOB$ is then a right triangle, so the Pythagorean Theorem can be used to find the measure of $\overline{OB}$. Therefore, $(OB)^2 = 8^2 + 15^2 = 64 + 225 =, 289$. After taking the square root of both sides, it becomes $17 = OB$.

45. D: The total rainfall is 25.38 inches. Thus, the ratio $\frac{4.5}{25.38}$, represents the percentage of rainfall received during October. $\frac{4.5}{25.38} \approx 0.177$ or 17.7%.

46. G: The zeroes of a function are the domain values where the function equals zero. So in this case, the zeroes are the values of x for which $f(x) = 0$. To find the zeroes of the function, set up an equation and then solve it for x. The first step is to factor the quadratic expression:

$$f(x) = 0$$
$$x^2 + 5x - 24 = 0$$
$$(x + 8)(x - 3) = 0$$

When the coefficient of x^2 is 1, factor the quadratic into a product of binomials $(x + a)(x + b)$, where a and b are chosen so their product is the constant term in the quadratic (including sign), and their sum is the coefficient of the linear term in the quadratic (the x term). Then use the zero-product rule to solve the result. Using that factorization of f, write two equations and solve them both for x:

$$x + 8 = 0 \quad \text{or} \quad x - 3 = 0$$
$$x = -8 \qquad\qquad x = 3$$

Therefore, the zeroes of the function are −8 and 3.

47. B: The x-intercept of a function is the point where the line passes through the x-axis. Since the graph passes through the x-axis at (6,0), its x-intercept is 6. To determine which function has the same x-intercept, substitute 6 for x into each function and see if the result is zero. Start with choice A, $g(x) = -4x - 12$.

$$-4(6) - 12 = -24 - 12$$
$$= -36$$

Since the result is not 6, the x-intercept is not 6. Next try choice B, $g(x) = x^2 - 12x + 36$.
$$(6)^2 - 12(6) + 36 = 36 - 72 + 36$$
$$= 0$$

Thus, the function $g(x) = x^2 - 12x + 36$ has the same x-intercept as the graphed function.

48. J: The constant of proportionality is equal to the slope. Using the points, (2, –8) and (5, –20), the slope may be written as $\frac{-20-(-8)}{5-2}$, which equals –4.

49. C: The y-intercept of the inequality is 20, and the slope is –0.6. The slope can be determined by calculating the ratio of the change in y-values per change in corresponding x-values. Using the y-intercept and the point, (25, 5), the slope can be written as $\frac{5-20}{25-0}$, which equals –0.6. Since the evaluation of the inequality for x- and y-values at the origin produces a true statement, the side of the plane containing the point, (0, 0) should be shaded. The inequality, $0.75x + 1.25y \leq 25$, solved for y, may be written as $y \leq -0.6x + 20$. Thus, Choice C is the correct answer.

50. H: To determine the density of marbles per cubic foot, the calculation takes the number of marbles in the box divided by the volume of the box. The dimensions of the box are 3 ft $\times$ 2 ft $\times$ 6 in. Since the dimensions are not all in the same unit, 6 in is converted into 0.5 ft. The volume of the box then becomes 3 ft $\times$ 2 ft $\times$ 0.5 ft = 3 ft³. The density of marbles per cubic foot is then calculated as $\frac{5,184 \, marbles}{3 \, ft^3}$ = 1,728 marbles/cubic foot. Answer F incorrectly calculated the volume of the box by not converting 6 in into feet and multiplied 3 $\times$ 2 $\times$ 6 to get 36 ft³. Answer G incorrectly divided the number of marbles only by the area of the bottom of the box (3 ft $\times$ 2 ft). Answer J incorrectly multiplied the number of marbles by the volume of the box.

51. B: The average rate of change of a function $f(x)$ from x_1 to x_2 is given by $\frac{f(x_2)-f(x_1)}{x_2-x_1}$. This formula is the same as the one for slope, rewritten in the context of functions. If $x_1 = 1$ and $x_2 = 5$, the average rate of the given function is given by expression below:
$$\frac{f(x_2)-f(x_1)}{x_2-x_1} = \frac{f(5)-f(1)}{5-1}$$
Calculate the values of $f(1)$ and $f(5)$:
$$f(1) = -3(1) + 1 = -2$$
$$f(5) = -3(5) + 1 = -14$$
Then substitute these values into the expression for the average rate of change and simplify the result:
$$\frac{f(5)-f(1)}{5-1} = \frac{(-14)-(-2)}{5-1}$$

1.
$$= \frac{-12}{4}$$

2.
$$= -3$$

52. J: The theoretical probability of getting tails is $\frac{1}{2}$. Thus, she can expect to get a total of $\frac{1}{2} \cdot 1000$ tails, or 500 tails.

53. A: For any point outside a circle, there are exactly two lines tangent to the circle passing through that point. Further, the lengths of these line segments from the point to the circle are equal. In this problem, the two segments extending from Q both have a length of 7. The two segments extending from R have a length of 4. The two segments extending from S have a length of 2. The two segments extending from P have a length of 5. Therefore, the perimeter of quadrilateral $PQRS$ can be calculated at $7 + 7 + 4 + 4 + 2 + 2 + 5 + 5 = 36$.

54. J: $30/100x = 14,000$. Thus x = 20,000

55. A: The cosine function is represented by the ratio $\frac{adjacent\ leg}{hypotenuse}$. In $\triangle ABC$, the adjacent leg to $\angle A$ is AC and the hypotenuse is AB. Therefore, $\cos A = \frac{AC}{AB}$. Answer B is cot A. Answer C is tan A. Answer D is sin A.

56. G: Population density is calculated by taking the population of a city and dividing that value by the square miles of land in the city. For Minneapolis, the population density is calculated as $\frac{382,578\ persons}{54.9\ square\ miles} = 6,968.6$ persons/square mile. Answer F incorrectly calculated the population density by dividing 382,578 by 54.9^2. Answer H incorrectly multiplied the population by the land area. Answer J incorrectly multiplied the population by the 54.9^2.

57. B: If a distance of 12 miles is represented by a half inch, a distance of 84 miles would be represented by 7 half inches since $84/12 = 7$. 7 half inches = 3.5 inches.

58. H: Remember that starting at the decimal point and going right, the place values are tenths, hundredths, thousandths and so on. Thus the decimal 0.0315 has the three in the hundredths place.

59. B: The first function $L(g)$ gives the water level after g gallons are pumped into the tank. The second function $w(t)$ gives the number of gallons pumped into the tank after t minutes, which the first function calls g. Consequently, we can have L act on w: the composition of the functions $L(w(t))$ is the water level of the tank after t minutes. Calculate $L(w(t))$.

$$L(w(t)) = 0.3 \cdot w(t)$$
$$= 0.3 \cdot 1.2t$$
$$= 0.36t$$

Thus, the function $L(t) = 0.36t$ represents the water level of the tank after t minutes.

60. G: When four congruent isosceles trapezoids are arranged in an arch, the bases of the trapezoid come together to form regular octagons, the smaller of which is shown to the right. The measure of each angle of a regular octagon is $135°$. $\left(\frac{(8-2)(180°)}{8} = 135°.\right)$ From the relationship of two of the trapezoid's base angles with one of the octagon's interior angles, write and solve an equation:

$(5x + 12.5) + (5x + 12.5) + 135 = 360$
$10x + 160 = 360$
$10x = 200$
$x = 20$

Reading

Number	Answer	Number	Answer
1	A	21	A
2	G	22	G
3	D	23	C
4	H	24	G
5	D	25	D
6	F	26	F
7	D	27	C
8	H	28	H
9	D	29	C
10	J	30	H
11	C	31	B
12	G	32	J
13	B	33	D
14	F	34	G
15	C	35	C
16	F	36	F
17	A	37	C
18	G	38	J
19	A	39	D
20	J	40	J

1. A: Lines 31-34: "Since the beginning of our American history, we have been engaged in change—in a perpetual peaceful revolution—a revolution which goes on steadily, quietly adjusting itself to changing conditions—without the concentration camp or the quick-lime in the ditch."

This is the only statement listed here that directly supports the idea that FDR thought that America is constantly moving toward a better way of life.

2. G: The average citizen already feels overburdened by taxes and feels the money is not being well-spent by the government. The argument that needs to be evaluated is that people will be happy to give more money in taxes to the government. It would be safe to raise the counterargument that the general population may already believe they are paying enough in taxes and don't think the government is spending that money wisely. Not everyone will be happy to give more to the government to spend. Choices F and J do not address the question. Choice H actually agrees with FDR's premise.

3. D: There are four basic freedoms that are vital to the health of people: speech, worship, freedom from want, and freedom from fear. This speech is typically referred to as the "Four Freedoms" speech. In it, FDR articulates the basic freedoms he believes in. These freedoms are the central focus of the speech, since it supports the other ideas that he is focusing on (i.e., social issues). Choice A is a detail in the speech, Choice B is not articulated, and Choice C is not in the speech.

4. H: FDR spoke of freedom, defining it in the previous paragraph as "the supremacy of human rights everywhere." This is the "high concept" he refers to in the following paragraph/sentence. In this context, the "end" of victory does not mean death (F). It does not precisely mean purpose (G), as in the common phrase "a means to an end" (a way of achieving a purpose): he was not saying victory was the only purpose of the concept, but rather that this concept could have no other outcome (H) or result than victory. "End" can also mean conclusion (J), i.e., the termination or finishing of something, which does not fit the meaning in this context quite as precisely as (H) because it does not imply cause and effect as "outcome" does.

5. D: After describing the four freedoms he identified, FDR said the vision of a world founded on those freedoms was "no vision of a distant millennium" but "a definite basis for a kind of world attainable in our own time and generation. That kind of world is the very antithesis of the so-called new order of tyranny..." referring to the "order" that dictators wanted to impose, to which "we oppose the greater conception—the moral order. He further described the "cooperation of free countries, working together in a friendly, civilized society" as the "world order which we seek". This context establishes that "order" more nearly means a system of societal and world politics (D) rather than a military leader's command (A); an authoritative decision or direction (B), e.g., a court order or a doctor's order; or an arrangement in sequence (C), e.g., alphabetical, numerical, or chronological order.

6. F: In lines 8 – 10 FDR said, "A part of the sacrifice means the payment of more money in taxes" for "a greater portion of this great defense program".

While he called for taxpayers to support the military, in this passage he did not equate personal sacrifice with serving in the military (G). While he described worldwide arms reduction (H), he did not equate this with personal sacrifice, but with the fourth freedom: freedom from fear. The four freedoms (J) he identified were "essential human freedoms", i.e., things all human beings had rights to, not examples of personal sacrifice.

7. D: FDR implicitly referred to the American Revolutionary War (A) by contrasting it with the process of continual change which he characterized as America's ongoing "*perpetual peaceful revolution*". He continued a pattern of implicit contrast by further characterizing this peaceful revolution as adjusting to change "without the concentration camp or the quick-lime in the ditch." Concentration camps were established by the Nazis during World War II as part of the Holocaust; quicklime was used in trenches during World War I (B), when trench warfare was widely practiced. In World War II (C), soldiers dug more individual foxholes than trenches (though there were some); but quicklime was also used by Nazis in mass graves of people they murdered and on the floors of train cattle cars transporting people to concentration camps, labor camps, and death camps.

8. H: In this passage there is no mention of expanding the draft of citizens into military service. As examples of aspects of the social economy needing "immediate improvement", FDR cited, "We should bring more citizens under the coverage of old-age pensions...." (F); "We should widen the opportunities for adequate medical care" (G); and "We should plan a better system by which persons deserving or needing gainful employment may obtain it" (J).

9. D: In this passage, FDR did include some simple sentences, but they are typically not short (A). The shortest sentences in the passage have six and seven words respectively and are the only ones that short. The structure used most frequently is the complex sentence; these are typically long (B) He also included some long compound sentences (C); and some long complex-compound sentences (D).

10. J: Choice F is incorrect because while the President does name some of the rights that come under the first amendment, he is not merely reciting or trying to paraphrase the first amendment. Although President Roosevelt uses the phrase "everywhere in the world" several times, readers should also acknowledge that "everywhere in the world" includes the United States of America and neither the world or America are emphasized as being more important than the other. In addition, the President says that he Americans are seeking to make the world more secure, and he asserts that this can be achieved when all people around the world enjoy the same freedoms as Americans. So, Choice G is not the best choice. Choice H is also not the best choice because while the task is challenging and immense, the President does not seem to be wavering or doubtful on his hope for that dream.

11. C: The correct answer choice is C because paragraphs 2-5 introduce Buck and the setting in which he lives. The paragraphs accomplish this introduction by giving many detailed facts, such as the detail in paragraph 5 about the times he escorted Mollie and Alice on walks. Choice A is incorrect because two new characters, Manuel and the stranger, are introduced in paragraphs 7 and 8. While aspects of paragraphs 2-5 show Buck's personality, choice B is incorrect because the paragraphs also give other details about Buck, such as information about his parents and appearance. Choice D is incorrect because Toots and Ysabel are only mentioned in paragraphs 3 and 4. Furthermore, paragraph 4 says that he utterly ignored Toots and Ysabel, not that he is affectionate towards them.

12. G: The correct answer is choice G because the sentence indicates that Buck felt as if he owned or ruled over Judge Miller's place. The word *realm* indicates that the sentence is referring to everything. Choice F is incorrect because it talks about other dogs that came and went but does not show Buck's attitude towards them or Judge Miller's place. Choice H is incorrect because it shows Buck's opinion of himself but not his opinion of Judge Miller's place. Choice F is incorrect because it describes something that Buck enjoys, but does not give his attitude about the house and grounds at Judge Miller's.

13. B: The correct answer is choice B because details in the passage foreshadow what might happen to Buck. Phrases like "trouble was brewing" or "these men wanted dogs" indicate that Buck might be heading for trouble. Choice A is incorrect because the paragraph does not give details about Buck's life; later paragraphs give those details. Choice C is incorrect because the paragraph does not give setting details. Setting details about Buck's current situation are given in later paragraphs. Choice D is incorrect because the paragraph does not describe any characters other than Buck; it does not indicate that Buck is the villain.

14. F: Choice F is the correct answer because the Klondike strike has caused people to look for dogs like Buck. Although paragraph 1 does not directly mention the Klondike strike, the reader can infer from paragraph 6 that the events discussed refer to the Klondike strike. Choice G is incorrect because paragraph 3 makes it clear that dogs came and went even before the Klondike strike. Choice H is incorrect because Elmo is Buck's father but not a main character in the story. Choice J is incorrect because the passage does not draw a connection between the Klondike strike and the frequency of the Raisin Growers' Association's meetings.

15. C: Choice C is correct because the first part of the passage mostly describes Buck's life, but the passage ends in a moment of change when the stranger wraps a piece of rope around Buck's neck. Choice A is incorrect because the passage does not describe a sequence of events as they happen. Instead the passage gives an overview of how Buck lived before the moment of change. Although part of the passage describes Buck's history, the passage also describes the moment in which his life changes, making choice B incorrect. Choice D is incorrect because the passage only describes life at Judge Miller's place but doesn't describe what came afterwards.

16. F: The correct answer is choice F because most of the passage provides background information about Buck's life and personality. Choice G is incorrect because the passage does not describe any moments in which Buck is acting heroic; instead, it describes Buck's regular interactions with the other people and animals at Judge Miller's place. Choice H is incorrect because the passage only briefly mentions the Klondike strike. The majority of the passage describes Buck's life. Choice J is incorrect because the other dogs are described in paragraphs 3 and 4. The rest of the passage focuses on Buck.

17. A: The best answer is choice A because the passage begins by setting up Buck's life and then showing a moment where his life is about to change drastically. Choice B is incorrect because only paragraph 5 refers to family; this is not a big enough portion of the passage to imply that the larger selection is about family. Although Buck might need to work hard in the future, choice C is incorrect because the passage does not have that many clues about upcoming hard work. Choice C is incorrect because the passage does not spend time showing that Buck strongly values relationships. The end of the passage indicates that Buck is about to experience a moment of change.

18. G: The correct answer is choice G because the sentence talks about how the men want dogs; the sentence foreshadows that Buck may be the type of dog that the men want. Choice F is incorrect because it refers to Buck's attitude around Judge Miller's place but does not hint at what might be coming next. Although part of the sentence indicates that Buck hopes to follow in Elmo's footsteps, the rest of the sentence simply describes Buck's father. Choice G better foreshadows what's going to happen in the story because it more closely relates to the events in paragraph 7 and 8. Choice J is incorrect because the sentence describes Buck's personality and interests without giving clues about what's going to happen next.

19. A: At the beginning of the passage, the author explains that "every tide-water dog, strong of muscle and with warm, long hair, from Puget Sound to San Diego" were being taken to the North to help find the "yellow metal." Since, the value of gold is so high, it is the most likely explanation that Manuel took Buck in order for Manuel to pay off his debts from gambling.

20. J: In these paragraphs, the narrator oversees all of the events and explains the situation to readers in detail. So, of the choices that you have, Choice J is the best selection.

21. A: Only this choice provides support for the idea of special relativity. Choice B is used in the explanation, but does not provide support on its own. Choice C is actually part of a counterargument to relativity. Choice D only indicates that there are two sections, and does not provide any support.

22. G: If relativity is valid, then why can it not explain all parts of the natural world, including the rules of quantum mechanics? Only this choice deals closely with an argument against relativity. The classical laws of motion are in agreement with relativity. Choice C. does not pose an argument against relativity and Choice D. focuses on asking a detailed question about the thought experiment, not the entire theory.

23. C: The word "truth" was quoted because Einstein was referring to the understanding of the laws of motion we had before relativity, which did indeed seem to provide the correct answers for a great deal of physics questions. However, according to the other sentences around this word, we can conclude that it does not refer to an absolute truth because relativity turns classical ideas on their heads.

24. B: Corresponding to the noun "delicacy", one meaning of the adjective "delicate" is fragile (a) or easily damaged. This meaning is not supported by the context. As it modifies "detail", delicacy here refers to how sensitively and specifically classical mechanics describes the movements of stars, planets, etc. Another meaning of a delicacy is an expensive and/or rare delight (c), especially regarding food; e.g., caviar is considered a delicacy. This meaning makes no sense in this context. Delicacy can also refer to soft texture (d), e.g., the delicacy of a lace fabric. This meaning does not relate to the subject matter.

25. D: *A priori* is Latin, meaning literally "from the one before". In the context of Einstein's discussion, he means that because the principle of relativity can be generalized so broadly across domains, its applying so precisely in one domain predicts it would apply with comparable accuracy in another domain; and therefore, that its being valid for one domain but not another is not very likely. It is *a priori* not very likely when considering this application of a general principle to a specific domain, and this unlikeliness is logically true/valid independent of observation or experience.

26. A: The quoted phrase is most an example of understatement. To emphasize through reversal how exquisite he found the detail provided by classical mechanics, Einstein downplayed it by describing it as less than wonderful, but only a little less. He further qualified this by not writing "*nothing* short of wonderful", but "*little* short of wonderful", making it comparative rather than absolute. An example of overstatement (b) or hyperbole in this case would be something like "the most wonderful ever seen", "too wonderful to be believed", etc. Amplification (c) is repeating a word/phrase but with added details or expanded description for emphasis; e.g., "...it supplies us with the actual motions of the heavenly bodies with a delicacy of detail—a delicacy of detail so fine that it can only be perceived as wonderful." Metabasis (d) is a transitional summary that recapitulates what was said previously and predicts what will be said next, to clarify and organize discourse.

27. C: As Einstein indicated in the sentence following this one, "This statement is called the principle of relativity (in the restricted sense)." The statements in (A), (B), and (D) are all conclusions predicated upon the condition that this principle were NOT true: (A) begins with "If the principle of relativity (in the restricted sense) does not hold," continuing with the "then" clause quoted. (B) continues from (A), saying, "In this case we should be constrained to believe that..." finishing with the clause quoted. (D) is prefaced by, "If the principle of relativity were not valid" and continues with the clause quoted.

28. H: validity regarding an understanding of the classical rules of motion. The word "truth" was quoted because Einstein was referring to the understanding of the laws of motion we had before relativity, which did indeed seem to provide the correct answers for a great deal of physics questions. However, according to the other sentences around this word, we can conclude that it does not refer to an absolute truth because relativity turns classical ideas on their heads.

29. C: Of the first five paragraphs, the first four are completely positive in Einstein's assertions and explanations of his claims; the fifth is also mainly positive, with only a hint of counterclaim in its last sentence refuted to emphasize the claim's validity ("But that [this] principle...should hold...in one domain...and yet...be invalid for another, is a priori not very probable."). The last two paragraphs present counterclaims, introduced by "If the principle of relativity does not hold..." and similar clauses, followed by "then..." conclusions illustrating the logically necessary yet improbable results of such counterclaims.

30. H: Einstein's identification of "two general facts" introduces two arguments wherein he explains reasoning to support the principle of relativity. (F) is the last sentence in the excerpted passage, summarizing rather than introducing his preceding evidence. (G) introduces the second of his two "arguments" or "general facts" rather than introducing both of them. (J) is the first sentence in the excerpted passage, but it is obvious from the clause "let us return to our example" that he is revisiting an example he introduced in a previous part of his paper not included in this excerpt; hence he was not introducing new evidence there, but rather reusing previously introduced evidence to make additional points.

31. B: The entire passage makes the argument that Black History Month should be abolished, offering various reasons why this is the best course of action.

32. J: The context of the sentence suggests that post-racial refers to an approach in which race is not a useful or positive organizing principle.

33. D: The author of Passage 1 never suggests that people do not learn about African American history during Black History Month.

34. G: Passage 2 states that W.E.B. DuBois was born in 1868; his birth was therefore the first of the identified events.

35. C: The author points out in paragraph 3 of Passage 2 that the debate about how to meet the need to teach children about African American history can remind parents that this need is not yet fully met.

36. F: In paragraph 4, the author of Passage 2 states that the material available is rich and varied.

37. C: The author of Passage 2 points out that just because there is a month focused on African American history, this doesn't mean that African American history must be ignored for the rest of the year.

38. J: Choice F is not the best choice because while the authors seem to be supportive of the President, there is not enough information in the passages to draw that conclusion. Choice G is wrong because the author of Passage A merely quotes an article, and the author of Passage B makes no mention of the media. Choice H suggests that the authors would be supportive of Black History Month if it were moved to another month. However, the author of Passage A wants to remove the recognition of Black History Month, not merely change the dates. Instead, Choice J is the best option because both authors agree that revisions to curriculum in the education system are necessary to improve the understanding of black history.

39. D: Clearly both authors think it is important for students to learn about the achievements and experience of African Americans; their debate is whether observing Black History Month is the best way to achieve this goal.

40. J: The last paragraph of Passage 2 states that Abraham Lincoln and Frederick Douglass were essential civil rights activists.

Science

Number	Answer	Number	Answer
1	A	21	A
2	J	22	H
3	C	23	A
4	J	24	G
5	D	25	C
6	J	26	J
7	D	27	A
8	J	28	J
9	A	29	A
10	J	30	G
11	C	31	B
12	G	32	G
13	D	33	C
14	J	34	J
15	B	35	B
16	H	36	H
17	D	37	D
18	H	38	G
19	D	39	C
20	J	40	J

1. A: The peak for albumin is the highest in the electropherogram, so the concentration of albumin is higher than that of any other component.

2. J: The peak for component γ is furthest from the origin along the mobility axis, indicating that it has moved the furthest during the experiment.

3. C: The peak for component $\alpha 1$ lies to the right of that for albumin, indicating greater mobility, and to the right of all the other peaks, indicating lesser mobility than the components represented by those peaks. Since small molecules move faster than large ones, $\alpha 1$ must be smaller than albumin and larger than the other components.

4. J: The peak for component γ is the fastest, indicating that γ is the smallest component seen on the electropherogram.

5. D: The peak for the unknown lies between those for γ and β, indicating an intermediate size. It has moved more rapidly than all components except for component γ.

6. J: If the unknown is an aggregate, it must be larger than the components that have clumped together to form it, not smaller.

7. D: If the unknown is a breakdown product, it must be smaller than the components that have broken down to form it, not larger.

8. J: The experiment shows only that this patient's blood contains an unknown component. It does not demonstrate that the component causes the patient's disease, or that it results from it. It may be unrelated. Further experiments are required to fully characterize the relationship between the component and the illness.

9. A: As stated in the text, the size of each circle is proportional to the number of recoveries.

10. J: The graph shows that the largest number of circles, and the largest circles as well, are at this depth. Since the size of the circles is proportional to the number of fish recovered, the greatest numbers of these fish were at these depths.

11. C: 2011 fish were recovered out of 34,000 released. The percentage is given by

$$P = 100 \times \frac{2,011}{34,000} = 6\%$$

.

12. G: The median age at each depth is shown by the X symbols on the plot. For this depth, the symbol lines up approximately with the mark corresponding to 5 years on the upper axis of the graph.

13. D: Although not specifically described in the text, all of the reasons stated may occur, reducing the recovery of tagged fish. The conclusions of the study must assume that the fraction of fish recovered (sample) are representative of the population as a whole.

14. J: The chart describes the age of the fish, but does not provide any information concerning their size.

15. B: The median age of the populations recovered at each depth is shown by the X symbol on the plot, and corresponds to progressively older fish at greater depths. Although some of the other statements are true, they are not supported by the data in the figure.

16. H: The right-most symbol on the plot shows that some 20-year old fish were recovered at depths of 501-700 meters. No older fish were recovered in this study.

17. D: The table shows that the lambda particle has a mass of over 1115 MeV

18. H: Protons and other nucleons are baryons, which are made of quarks. The other choices are all leptons, which are not.

19. D: To satisfy the law of conservation of charge, the net charge of all the particles produced in a decay must equal that of the original particle. Note that while conservation of mass applies to the decay, it does not pertain to charge.

20. J: The most massive particles of neutral charge are the Xi particles, with a mass of 1314.9 MeV.

21. A: The lambda particle has no charge. The proton has a charge of +1. To satisfy the law of conservation of charge, the other particle must have a charge of -1. The negative pion is the only choice that satisfies that condition.

22. H: The mass of the muon is 105.65 MeV. That of the positron is 0.65 MeV. To satisfy the law of conservation of mass, the mass of the positron plus that of the other resulting particles cannot add up to more than 105.65 MeV. Among the choices given, only the neutrino is small enough to satisfy that condition.

23. A: To satisfy the law of conservation of mass, the mass difference between the original particle and its decay products is released as knetic energy. Since the omega particle has a mass of 1672.45 MeV, and the kaon and lambda particles have masses of 493.68 and 1115.68 MeV, respectively, the difference is 63.09 MeV.

24. G: One MeV is equivalent to 1.783×10^{-30} kilogram, so that $60 kg = \dfrac{60}{1.783 \times 10^{-30}}$ MeV = 33.65×10^{30} MeV.

25. C: Of the sites listed, the phi value for site MD, 2.73 phi, is the largest value. The text explains how phi varies inversely with particle size, so these are the smallest particles.

26. J: According to the definition of phi supplied in the text, the range 1.0 to 4.0 phi units corresponds to particle sizes in the range 0.06 to 0.5 mm.

27. A: At all of the sites except site ND, the particle size distributions are tightly centered around a well-defined modal value. At site ND, the distribution is spread out over a broader range, and there is no well-defined central value.

28. J: Each unit of added phi value in the negative direction corresponds to a doubling of the particle size, so that -1 corresponds to 2mm, -2 to 4 mm, and -3 to 8 mm.

29. A: The curves represent the distance traveled, and they approximate a straight line. The slope of the line represents the speed of travel. Although the curve in part (b) has a negative slope, the absolute value of that slope will be a positive value, representing speed of transport towards the west.

30. G: The steepest slopes correspond to the greatest values of mab, or meters above bottom. These are the shallowest waters.

31. B: The steepest slopes correspond to the greatest values of mab, or meters above bottom. These are the shallowest waters. Although the slopes are negative in this plot, it is the magnitude of the slope that indicates the speed of transport. Here, the negative value simply indicates that the sediments drift toward the west, not the east.

32. G: The upper graph shows transport toward the north. The lower graph shows transport toward the west. If these two are combined, overall transport will be toward the NW.

33. C: The efficiency curve in part B of the figure has a clear maximum value at a wind velocity of 10 m/s.

34. J: The power curve in part A of the figure increases with increasing wind velocity, until a plateau is reached at 15 m/s and above.

35. B: The text explains that for wind velocities above 15 m/s, the rotor blades are trimmed to protect the equipment. Above 25 m/s, the turbine must be shut down.

36. H: Power increases with the cube of wind velocity. This is an exponential function.

37. D: The power increases with the cube, or third power, of wind velocity, v. If the wind velocity is doubled, the power output will be proportional to the third power of the new wind velocity v'. But if v' = 2v, then
$$v'^3 = (2v)^3 = 8v^3$$
and the new power output is 8 times greater than the original output, or 1600 kW.

38. G: See question 37. Since this generator operates at 50% efficiency, only half of the theoretical power is available.

39. C: The longest bars in the histogram correspond to the middle frequencies, from about 300 to 2000 Hz.

40. J: The text explains that winds originate from differential warming of the earth's surface by the sun. It is this energy that is captured by a wind turbine.

Appendix A: Time Statistics for the ACT

ACT Time Constraints	English	Math	Reading	Science
Passages	5	N/A	4	6
Questions	75	60	40	40
Time (in minutes)	45	60	35	35
Questions/Passage	15	N/A	10	6.67
seconds/question	36	60	52.5	52.5
min/passage	9	N/A	8.75	5.83
words/passage	260	N/A	780	350
words/question	43	N/A	43	52
Reading rate (WPM)	200	200	200	200
Time used for passages (min)	7.5	N/A	12	10.5
Time left for questions	30	N/A	34.5	24.5

Appendix B: SAT/ACT Equivalency Table

ACT Composite Score	Recentered SAT I Score Verbal+Math
36	1600
35	1580
34	1520
33	1470
32	1420
31	1380
30	1340
29	1300
28	1260
27	1220
26	1180
25	1140
24	1110
23	1070
22	1030
21	990
20	950
19	910
18	870
17	830
16	780
15	740
14	680
13	620
12	560
11	500

Appendix C: Area, Volume, Surface Area Formulas

$$A = \frac{1}{2}\,bh$$

$$A = bh$$

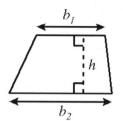

$$A = \frac{1}{2}\,h(b_1 + b_2)$$

$$p = 4s$$
$$A = s^2$$

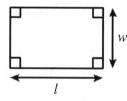

$$p = 2l + 2w$$
$$A = lw$$

$$c^2 = a^2 + b^2$$

$$C = 2\pi r$$
$$A = \pi r^2$$

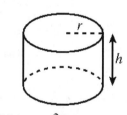

$$V = \pi r^2 h$$
$$S.A. = 2\pi rh + 2\pi r^2$$

$$V = \frac{1}{3}\,\pi r^2 h$$
$$S.A. = \pi rl + \pi r^2$$

$$V = lwh$$
$$S.A. = 2lw + 2lh + 2wh$$

$$V = \frac{1}{3}\,Bh$$
$$S.A. = \frac{1}{2}\,lp + B$$

Pi

$$\pi \approx 3.14$$

Secret Key #1 – Time Is Your Greatest Enemy

To succeed on the ACT, you must use your time wisely. Most students do not finish at least one section. For a more thorough statistical analysis of this strategy, please see the Appendix. The results are presented in the table below:

SECTION	Total amount of time allotted	Number of questions	Time to read each passage	Time to answer each question
English	45 min	75	1 min, 20 sec	30 sec
Math	60 min	60	N/A	1 min
Reading	35 min	40	3 min, 54 sec	30 sec
Science	35 min	40	2 min, 9 sec	30 sec
Writing*	40 min	1	N/A	40 min

*Writing section is optional.

As you can see, the time constraints are brutal. To succeed, you must ration your time properly.

On every section except Math, the test is separated into passages. The reason that time is so critical is that 1) every question counts the same toward your final score, and 2) the passages are not in order of difficulty. If you have to rush during the last passage, then you will miss out on answering easier questions correctly. It is natural to want to pause and figure out the hardest questions, but you must resist the temptation and move quickly.

Success Strategy #1

Wear a watch to the ACT Test. At the beginning of the test, check the time (or start a chronometer on your watch to count the minutes), and check the time after each passage to make sure you are "on schedule."

SECTION	Time	# Passages	Time per Passage
English	45 min	5	8 min
Reading	35 min	4	8 min
Science	35 min	6	5.83 min

These limits are designed with a built-in "buffer" to make sure you have time left over to make final guesses and adjustments. If you find that you are behind time during the test, work through the next passage more quickly. If you are still behind time after the next passage, skip the last question of the following passage in an attempt to catch up (unless you know it at a quick glance). Once you are caught up, maintain that pace until the end of the test.

The Math Section is the easiest to keep time on; move on if you take more than a minute on a question. Since the questions in this section are pretty much in order of difficulty, if you have time left over, come back to the earliest skipped questions, spend another minute at most, and then move on to the next skipped question. Always mark skipped questions in your workbook, *not* on the Scantron. Last minute guessing will be covered in the next chapter.

The Reading section poses the greatest challenge for time: 8 minutes for reading and answering questions about a very long passage. Unless you are an uncommonly fast reader, you should follow our advice in the Reading Section: focus on the questions, and scan for answers as necessary.

Lastly, sometimes it is beneficial to slow down if you are constantly getting ahead of time. You are always more likely to catch a careless mistake by working more slowly than quickly, and among very high-scoring students (those who are likely to have lots of time left over), careless errors affect the score more than mastery of material.

Secret Key #2 – Guessing is not Guesswork.

You probably know that guessing is a good idea on the ACT. There is no penalty for getting a wrong answer. Even if you have no idea about a question, you still have a 20-25% chance of getting it right. Unless you score above 30 or so, guessing will contribute about 3-4 points to your final score.

Monkeys Take the ACT

What most students don't realize is that to insure that 20-25% chance, you have to guess randomly. If you put 20 monkeys in a room to take the ACT, assuming they answered once per question and behaved themselves, on average they would get 20-25% of the answers right. Put 20 high school students in the room, and the average will be much lower among guessed questions. Why?

1. ACT intentionally writes deceptive answer choices that "look" right. A student has no idea about a question, so picks the "best looking" answer, which is often wrong. The monkey has no idea what looks good and what doesn't, so will consistently be lucky about 20-25% of the time.
2. Students will eliminate answer choices from the guessing pool based on a hunch or intuition. Simple but correct answers often get excluded, leaving a 0% chance of being correct. The monkey has no clue, and often gets lucky with the best choice.

This is why the process of elimination endorsed by most test courses is flawed and detrimental to your performance: students don't guess, they make an ignorant stab in the dark that is usually worse than random.

Success Strategy #2

Let me introduce one of the most valuable ideas of this course: the $5 challenge:

You only mark your "best guess" if you are willing to bet $5 on it.
You only eliminate a choice from guessing if you are willing to bet $5 on it.

Why $5? Five dollars is an amount of money that is small yet not insignificant, and can really add up fast (20 questions could cost you $100). Likewise, each answer choice on one question of the ACT will have a small impact on your overall score, but it can really add up to a lot of points in the end.

The process of elimination *is* valuable. The following shows your chance of guessing right:

If you eliminate this many choices:	0	1	2	3	4
Math (5 choices)	20%	25%	33%	50%	100%
English / Reading / Science (4 choices)	25%	33%	50%	100%	N/A

However, if you accidentally eliminate the right answer or go on a hunch with an incorrect answer, your chances drop dramatically: to 0%. By guessing among all the answer choices, you are *guaranteed* to have a shot at the right answer.

That's why the $5 test is so valuable. If you give up the advantage and safety of a pure guess, it had better be worth the risk.

What we still haven't covered is how to be sure that whatever guess you make is truly random. Here's the easiest way:

Always pick the first answer choice among those remaining.

Such a technique means that you have decided, *before you see a single test question*, exactly how you are going to guess, and since the order of choices tells you nothing about which one is correct, this guessing technique is perfectly random.

Let's try an example.

A student encounters the following problem on the math test:

What is the cosine of an angle in a right triangle that is 3 meters on the adjacent side, 5 meters on the hypotenuse, and 4 meters on the opposite side?

A. 1
B. 0.6
C. 0.8
D. 0.75
E. 1.25

The student has a small idea about this question. He is pretty sure that cosine is opposite over hypotenuse, but he wouldn't bet $5 on it. He knows that cosine is "something" over hypotenuse, and since the hypotenuse is the largest number, he is willing to bet $5 on both choices A and E not being correct. So he is down to B, C, and D. At this point, he guesses B, since B is the first choice remaining.

The student is correct by choosing B, since cosine is adjacent over hypotenuse. He only eliminated those choices he was willing to bet money on, *and* he did not let his stale memories (often things not known definitely will get mixed up in the exact opposite arrangement in one's head) about the formula for cosine influence his guess. He blindly chose the first remaining choice, and was rewarded with the fruits of a random guess.

This section is not meant to scare you away from making educated guesses or eliminating choices. You just need to define when a choice is worth eliminating. The $5 test, along with a pre-defined random guessing strategy, is the best way to make sure you reap all of the benefits of guessing.

Secret Key #3 – Practice Smarter, Not Harder

Many students delay the test preparation process because they dread the awful amounts of practice time they think necessary to succeed on the test. We have refined an effective method that will take you only a fraction of the time.

There are a number of obstacles in your way on the ACT. Among these are answering questions, finishing in time, and mastering test-taking strategies. All must be executed on the day of the test at peak performance, or your score will suffer. The ACT is a mental marathon that has a large impact on your future. Just like a marathon runner, it is important to work your way up to the full challenge. So first you just worry about questions, and then time, and finally strategy:

Success Strategy #3

1. Find a good source for ACT practice tests. The best source for these will be the current and past practice/registration packets from ACT. Your guidance counselor can provide you with the current one, and, if you're lucky, they may have a supply of old ones as well. You will need at least 3 practice tests.
2. If you are willing to make a larger time investment, consider using more than one study guide. Often the different approaches of multiple authors will help you grasp difficult concepts.
3. Take a practice test with no time constraints, with all study helps "open book." Take your time with questions and focus on applying the strategies.
4. Take another test, this time with time constraints, with all guides "open book."
5. Take a final practice test with no open material and time limits.

If you have time to take more practice tests, just repeat step 5. By gradually exposing yourself to the full rigors of the test environment, you will condition your mind to the stress of test day and maximize your success.

Secret Key #4 – Make ACT Work for You

Let me state an obvious fact: if you take the ACT three times, you will get three different scores. This is due to many factors, e.g., the way you feel on test day, the level of preparedness you have, and the fact that there are different versions of the ACT. Despite ACT's claims to the contrary, some test versions *will* be easier for you than others.

Since your qualification for scholarships will largely depend on your score, you should maximize your chances of success by taking the ACT at least twice and sending only the highest score to your colleges. We recommend taking the ACT three times to fully account for all variances in performance, preparedness, and test difficulty.

Success Strategy #4

When ACT sends out your score, it only reports the score for the date requested. This gives you enormous power.
1. Take the ACT on three occasions, never reporting your score to any college you hope to attend.
2. After receiving your highest score, send score reports for *that date only* to the college of your choice.
3. Smile and know you've not been a victim of a bad test day or a difficult test version.

Also, most colleges will accept either the SAT or ACT for admission. Take both and submit the one you do better on. A SAT/ACT equivalency table is located in the appendix.

Secret Key #5 – Test Yourself

Everyone knows that time is money. There is no need to spend too much of your time or too little of your time preparing for the test. You should only spend as much of your precious time preparing as is necessary for you to pass it.

Once you have taken a practice test under real conditions of time constraints, then you will know if you are ready for the test or not.

If you have scored extremely high the first time that you take the practice test, then there is not much point in spending countless hours studying. You are already there.

Benchmark your abilities by retaking practice tests and seeing how much you have improved. Once you score high enough to guarantee success, then you are ready.

If you have scored well below where you need to be, then knuckle down and begin studying in earnest. Check your improvement regularly through the use of practice tests under real conditions. Above all, don't worry, panic, or give up. The key is perseverance!

Then, when you go to take the test, remain confident and remember how well you did on the practice tests. If you can score high enough on a practice test, then you can do the same on the real thing.

General Strategies

The most important thing you can do is to ignore your fears and jump into the test immediately- do not be overwhelmed by any strange-sounding terms. You have to jump into the test like jumping into a pool: all at once is the easiest way.

Make Predictions

As you read and understand the question, try to guess what the answer will be. Remember that several of the answer choices are wrong, and once you begin reading them, your mind will immediately become cluttered with answer choices designed to throw you off. Your mind is typically the most focused immediately after you have read the question and digested its contents. If you can, try to predict what the correct answer will be. You may be surprised at what you can predict.

Quickly scan the choices and see if your prediction is in the listed answer choices. If it is, then you can be quite confident that you have the right answer. It still won't hurt to check the other answer choices, but most of the time, you've got it!

Answer the Question

It may seem obvious to only pick answer choices that answer the question, but the test writers can create some excellent answer choices that are wrong. Don't pick an answer just because it sounds right, or you believe it to be true. It *must* answer the question. Once you've made your selection, always go back and check it against the question and make sure that you didn't misread the question, and the answer choice does answer the question posed.

Benchmark

After you read the first answer choice, decide if you think it sounds correct or not. If it doesn't, move on to the next answer choice. If it does, mentally mark that answer choice. This doesn't mean that you've definitely selected it as your answer choice, it just means that it's the best you've seen thus far. Go ahead and read the next choice. If the next choice is worse than the one you've already selected, keep going to the next answer choice. If the next choice is better than the choice you've already selected, mentally mark the new answer choice as your best guess.

The first answer choice that you select becomes your standard. Every other answer choice must be benchmarked against that standard. That choice is correct until proven otherwise by another answer choice beating it out. Once you've decided that no other answer choice seems as good, do one final check to ensure that your answer choice answers the question posed.

Valid Information

Don't discount any of the information provided in the question. Every piece of information may be necessary to determine the correct answer. None of the information in the question is there to throw you off (while the answer choices will certainly have information to throw you off). If two seemingly unrelated topics are discussed, don't ignore either. You can be confident there is a relationship, or it wouldn't be included in the question, and you are probably going to have to determine what that relationship is to find the answer.

Avoid "Fact Traps"

Don't get distracted by a choice that is factually true, but not germane. Your search is for the choice that answers the actual question. Stay focused and don't fall for an answer that is true but incorrect. Always go back to the question and make sure you're choosing an answer that actually answers the question and is not just a true statement. An answer can be factually correct, but it *must* answer the question asked. Additionally, two answers can both be seemingly correct, so be sure to read all of the answer choices, and make sure that you get the one that *best* answers the question.

Milk the Question

Some of the questions may throw you completely off. They might deal with a subject you have not been exposed to, or one that you haven't reviewed in years. While your lack of knowledge about the subject will be a hindrance, the question itself can give you many clues that will help you find the correct answer. Read the question carefully and look for clues. Watch particularly for adjectives and nouns describing difficult terms or words that you don't recognize. Regardless of whether or not you completely understand a word, replacing it with a synonym (either provided or one you are familiar with) may help you understand what the question is asking. Rather than wracking your mind about specific, detailed information concerning a difficult term or word, mentally substitute terms that are easier to understand.

The Trap of Familiarity

Don't just choose a word because you recognize it. On difficult questions, you may not recognize a number of words in the answer choices. The test writers don't put fake, non-existent words on the test, so don't think that just because you recognize all the words in only one answer choice means that answer choice must be correct. If you recognize words in only one answer choice, then focus on that one. Is it right? Try your best to determine if it is correct. If it's not, eliminate it. Each word and answer choice you eliminate increases your chances of getting the question correct, even if you then have to guess among the unfamiliar choices.

Eliminate Answers

Eliminate choices as soon as you realize they are wrong. But be careful! Make sure you consider all of the possible answer choices. Just because one appears right, doesn't mean that the next one won't be even better! The test writers will usually put more than one good answer choice for every question, so read all of them. Don't worry if you are stuck between two that seem right. By getting down to just two remaining possible choices, your odds are now 50/50. Rather than wasting too much time, play the odds. You are guessing, but guessing wisely, because you've been able to knock out some of the answer choices that you know are wrong. If you are eliminating choices and realize that the last answer choice you are left with is also obviously wrong, don't panic. Start over and consider each choice again. There may easily be something that you missed the first time and will realize on the second pass.

Tough Questions

If you are stumped on a problem, don't waste time. Move on. Remember, though, if you can quickly check for obviously incorrect answer choices, your chances of guessing correctly are greatly improved. Before you completely give up, at least try to knock out a couple of possible answers. Eliminate what you can and then guess at the remaining answer choices before moving on.

Brainstorm

If you get stuck on a difficult question, spend a few seconds quickly brainstorming. Run through the complete list of possible answer choices. Look at each choice and ask yourself *Could this answer the question satisfactorily?* Go through each answer choice and consider it independently of the other.

By systematically going through all possibilities, you may find something that you would otherwise overlook. Remember that when you get stuck, it's important to try to keep moving.

Read Carefully

Understand the problem. Read the question and answer choices carefully. Don't miss the question because you misread the terms. You have plenty of time to read each question thoroughly and make sure you understand what is being asked. Yet a happy medium must be attained, so don't waste too much time. You must read carefully, but efficiently.

Face Value

When in doubt, use common sense. Always accept the situation in the problem at face value. Don't read too much into it. These problems will not require you to make huge leaps of logic. The test writers aren't trying to throw you off with a cheap trick. If you have to go beyond creativity and make a leap of logic in order to make an answer choice answer the question, then you should look at the other answer choices. Don't overcomplicate the problem by creating theoretical relationships or explanations that will warp time or space. These are normal problems rooted in reality. It's just that the applicable relationship or explanation may not be readily apparent and you have to figure things out. Use your common sense to interpret anything that isn't clear.

Prefixes

If you're having trouble with a word in the question or answer choices, try dissecting it. Take advantage of every clue that the word might provide. Prefixes and suffixes can be a huge help. Usually they allow you to determine a basic meaning. *Pre-* means before, *post-* means after, *pro-* is positive, and *de-* is negative. From these prefixes and suffixes, you can get an idea of the general meaning of the word and try to put it into context.

Hedge Words

Watch out for critical "hedge" words, such as *likely, may, can, often, sometimes, almost, mostly, usually, generally, rarely, sometimes,* etc.. Question writers insert these hedge words to cover every possibility. Often an answer choice will be wrong simply because it leaves no room for exception. Generally speaking, you should avoid answer choices that use all-encompassing words like *never* and *always*.

Switchback Words and Phrases

Stay alert for "switchbacks". These are the words and phrases frequently used to alert you to shifts in thought. The most common switchback term is *but*. Other common ones are *although, however, nevertheless, on the other hand, even though, while, in spite of, despite,* and *regardless of*.

New Information

Correct answer choices will rarely have completely new information included. Answer choices typically are straightforward reflections of the material in the material and will directly relate to the question. If a new piece of information is included in an answer choice that doesn't appear to relate to the topic being asked about, then that answer choice is likely incorrect. All the information needed to answer the question is usually provided for you, so you should not have to make guesses that are unsupported or choose answers that require unknown information.

Time Management

On technical questions, don't get lost on the technical terms. Don't spend too much time on any one question. If you don't know what a term means, since you don't have a dictionary, odds are you aren't going to get much further. You should immediately know if you recognize terms or not. If you don't, work with the other clues that you have, and the other answer choices and terms provided, but don't waste too much time trying to figure out a difficult term.

Contextual Clues

Look for contextual clues. An answer can be factually true but not correct. Contextual clues can often help you find the correct answer. Always keep in mind the context in which a phrase or statement is made. This will help you make important distinctions.

Don't Panic

Panicking will not answer any questions for you. Therefore, it isn't helpful. When you first see the question, if your mind goes blank, take a deep breath. Force yourself to mechanically go through the steps of solving the problem and using the strategies you've learned.

Pace Yourself

Don't get clock fever. It's easy to be overwhelmed when you're looking at a page full of questions, your mind is full of random thoughts and feeling confused, and the clock is ticking down relentlessly. Calm down and maintain the pace you've set for yourself. Monitor your pace and, as long as you are on track, you are guaranteed to have enough time for yourself.

When you get to the last few minutes of the test, it may seem like you won't have enough time left, but if you only have as many questions as you should have left at that point, then you're right on track!

Answer Selection

The best way to pick an answer choice is to eliminate all of those that are wrong, until only one is left and confirm that is the correct answer. Sometimes, though, a wrong answer choice may initially look right. Be careful, and don't make a hasty mistake. Take a second to make sure that the other choices are not equally obvious. There are only two times that you should stop before checking other answers. First is when you are absolutely positive that your answer choice is correct. Second is when time is almost out and you have to make a quick guess.

Check Your Work

Since it's extremely unlikely that you'll know the answer to every question, it's important that you get credit for the ones that you do know. Don't miss any questions through careless mistakes. If at all possible, try to take a second to look back over your answer selection and make sure you've selected the correct answer choice and haven't made a costly careless mistake (such as marking an answer choice that you didn't mean to mark). The mistakes you catch with this quick double check should more than make up for the time it takes.

Beware of Directly Quoted Answers

Sometimes an answer choice will repeat word for word a portion of the question or reference section. However, beware of such exact duplication – it may be a trap. More than likely, the correct choice will paraphrase or summarize a point, rather than having exactly the same wording.

Informal Language

Answers using formal or scientific language are better than ones that are informal. An answer choice that begins *To compare the outcomes…* is much more likely to be correct than one that begins *Because some people insisted…*

Extreme Statements

Avoid answers that throw out highly controversial ideas that are proclaimed as established fact. An answer choice that states *the process should be used in certain situations, if…* is much more likely to be correct than one that states *the process should be discontinued completely*. The first is a calm rational statement and doesn't take a definitive, one size fits all stance, but uses the word *if* to limit the times the process should be used. The second choice is an all-encompassing, uncompromising idea and far more extreme.

Answer Choice Families

When you have two or more answer choices that are direct opposites or parallels, one of them is usually the correct answer. For instance, if one answer choice states *x increases* and another answer choice states *x decreases* or *y increases,* then those two or three answer choices are very similar in construction and fall into the same family of answer choices. A family of answer choices exists when two or three answer choices are very similar in construction, and yet often have a directly opposite meaning. Usually the correct answer choice will be in that family of answer choices. The "odd man out" or answer choice that doesn't seem to fit the parallel construction of the other answer choices is more likely to be incorrect.

Additional Bonus Material

Due to our efforts to try to keep this book to a manageable length, we've created a link that will give you access to all of your additional bonus material.

Please visit http://www.mometrix.com/bonus948/act to access the information.